Praise for *ADHD Without Drugs*

If I had one book to read about ADHD, this is it. It is well-written, practical and filled with the uncommonly good common sense of an experienced and compassionate clinician with fair-minded and rigorous reviews of the state of the science.

> — **Kathi Kemper, MD, MPH**; Director, Center for Integrative Medicine; Professor of Pediatrics, Social Science Health Policy, and Family and Community Medicine, Wake Forest University Baptist Medical Center

Dr. Newmark's groundbreaking book is a practical and thought-provoking guide to the integrative approach to ADHD, one of our greatest challenges in children's health. I am delighted to offer this book as a resource to both patients and colleagues.

> — **Larry Rosen, MD**, Chief of Pediatric Integrative Medicine, Hackensack Medical Center; medical advisor to the Deirdre Imus Environmental Center; Vice-Chair of the American Academy of Pediatrics Section on Complementary and Integrative Medicine

A pioneer in pediatric integrative medicine, Dr. Newmark has written an incredibly useful guide on ADHD. It should be considered essential reading for parents, teachers, doctors and all others seeking solutions beyond medications for children with ADHD.

> — **Victoria Maizes, MD**, Executive Director of the Arizona Center for Integrative Medicine at the University of Arizona; Associate Professor of Medicine, Family and Community Medicine and Public Health

Parents are keenly interested in finding non-drug, holistic strategies that support their child's natural healing systems and that help build healthy brains. This excellent new book artfully blends the best of conventional and complementary options for kids with ADHD. Over years of clinical practice and scientific study, Dr. Newmark has developed a balanced, safe, natural approach that I will wholeheartedly recommend for all of my patients with ADHD.

> — **Timothy Culbert, MD, FAAP**, Developmental/Behavioral Pediatrician; Medical Director of Integrative Medicine Program at Children's Hospitals and Clinics of Minnesota

So many children with an abundance of life force and intensity are being diagnosed as ADHD and prescribed medications that all too often backfire and complicate the life of the child and family. This book offers an alternative: optimal health and balance — in ways that support a child's body, mind, and spirit and in ways that ultimately pave the way to greater family well-being. Dr. Newmark is an amazing physician with an amazing message.

> — **Howard Glasser, MA**, Executive Director of the Children's Success Foundation; author of *Transforming the Difficult Child – The Nurtured Heart Approach* and *All Children Flourishing – Igniting the Fires of Greatness*

'*ADHD Without Drugs*' unravels the complexities and mysteries of ADHD and presents healthy alternatives to the current mainstream of drugging our children. Dr. Newmark gives excellent insight into the problems of diagnosing ADHD and explains the rationale for a non-drug treatment. Every psychologist, doctor, and family with children needs this book.

— **Steven Gurgevich, PhD,** Clinical Assistant Professor of Medicine at the University of Arizona College of Medicine; Director of The Mind-Body Clinic at the Arizona Center of Integrative Medicine; consultant and faculty, American Society of Clinical Hypnosis

A true leader in the field of integrative pediatrics, Dr. Newmark has written a highly informative, practical, and inspirational guide for parents navigating the world of conventional and complementary medicine in their quest for optimizing the health of their children. I cannot recommend it more highly.

— **Tierona Low Dog, MD,** Chair of the United States Pharmacopeia Dietary Supplements and Botanicals Expert Committee; Advisory Council for the National Institutes of Health National Center for Complementary and Alternative Medicine

The information presented by Dr. Newmark is critically important for educators and parents who have been led to believe that the only way to respond to a high intensity child is medication. The quick remedy of medicating for the sake of 'behavior management' has robbed children of the life force that drives their creativity, enthusiasm, literally their "joie de vivre." We MUST be determined to find another way to support the growth and development of these youngsters.

— **Angela R. Smith, CAS, NCC,** elementary school counselor in Hampton, VA; Virginia Elementary School Counselor of the Year 2008

Dr. Newmark's book is *the* definitive publication on the use of integrative medicine for children with ADHD. I will recommend it unreservedly to patients and colleagues alike.

— **Kevin Barrows, MD,** Director of Clinical Programs, Osher Center for Integrative Medicine, and Associate Professor, Department of Family and Community Medicine, UCSF School of Medicine

Dr. Newmark's immense breadth of knowledge and experience in treating children with attention problems is conveyed in clear, pragmatic language. And he never loses sight of the whole child amidst the confusion of diagnosis and treatment options that typically accompanies this disorder.

— **David K. Becker, MD, MPH,** Director, Pediatric Integrative Pain Clinic and Associate Clinical Professor, UCSF Department of Pediatrics

ADHD
Without Drugs
A Guide to the
Natural Care of
Children with ADHD

ADHD
Without Drugs
A Guide to the
Natural Care of
Children with ADHD

by one of America's Leading
Integrative Pediatricians

Sanford
Newmark, MD

with a foreword by
Andrew Weil, MD

N U R T U R E D   H E A R T
P U B L I C A T I O N S

ADHD
Without Drugs
A Guide to the Natural Care of Children with ADHD

For information contact: Nurtured Heart Publications
4165 West Ironwood Hill Drive
Tucson, Arizona 85745
E-mail: adhddoc@theriver.com

For information about bulk purchasing discounts of this book or other Nurtured Heart Publications books, videos, CDs or DVDs, please contact Fulfillment Services at 800-311-3132.

For orders within the book industry, please contact Brigham Distributing at 435-723-6611.

Book design by Richard Diffenderfer
First edits by Melissa Block
Copy editing by Chris Howell
Printed by Pollock Printing, Nashville, TN.

Library of Congress Card Catalogue Number: Pending

ISBN 978-0-9826714-1-2

Printed in the United States

First Printing: April 2010

To my wife Linda Ishi:
for a lifetime of love and support. Without
her, this book could not have happened.

To my children Jesse and Safia:
for being the wonderful people they are.

And to Andrew Weil:
for leading the way.

About the Author

Sanford Newmark, MD, is a physician with 23 years of experience in pediatrics. He received his medical degree in 1984 from the University of Arizona College of Medicine and three years later completed his pediatrics residency there. For the next 14 years, Dr. Newmark practiced general pediatrics but took special interest in behavioral problems such as ADHD and autism.

In 2000, he graduated from the two-year fellowship program in integrative medicine at the Program in Integrative Medicine at the University of Arizona, which was founded by and continues to be led by Dr. Andrew Weil. Dr. Newmark was the first graduate from this program to practice general pediatrics and is now part of the program faculty.

For five years, he was Director of the Center for Pediatric Integrative Medicine, a Tucson, AZ, clinic for children with a wide variety of medical issues. In 2009 he relocated to California to join Whole Child Wellness, an integrative pediatrics practice near San Francisco.

Dr. Newmark lectures frequently on ADHD, autism, and integrative medicine, and has contributed three chapters to academic integrative medicine textbooks.

Dr. Newmark has been married to his wife, Linda, a psychologist, for 36 years. They have two children.

Acknowledgements

I would like to thank my wife Linda Ishi for her unending love, support, and encouragement, even when it meant spending long weekends watching me labor at the computer. She was also my best editor and gentle critic. All of my family and friends were unfailing in their support as well.

I also want to thank my publisher, Howard Glasser, for his faith in the project, tremendous optimism, and energy.

I thank my editor Melissa Block for her helpful suggestions, as well as Chris Howell for her careful copy editing, and Richard Diffenderfer for his talent in getting the book ready for printing.

Finally I'd like to thank Andrew Weil, Victoria Maizes, Tierona Low Dog, Randy Horwitz, David Kiefer, Anastasia Rowland-Seymour, and the rest of my friends and colleagues at the Arizona Center for Integrative Medicine. Andy led the way and took the hits when it was really hard, making it that much it easier for the rest of us to practice integrative medicine. My friends there are my true healing community, and their teaching and constant support have enabled me to be steady on the path.

— *S. Newmark*

Table of Contents

Foreword

by **Andrew Weil, M.D.**

For many years I have been very concerned about the rapidly increasing frequency of diagnosing psychiatric diseases in our children. Foremost among these is attention deficit hyperactivity disorder (ADHD). Once confined to a small percentage of children, ADHD has become epidemic over the past 25 years to the point where 6 to 8% of all children and over 10% of boys in this country are labeled as having a serious neurodevelopmental disease. Worse yet, 2.5 million children are taking psychostimulant medication on a long-term basis — medication that may have significant side-effects and unknown long-term health consequences.

We need to take a step back and find out what all this means. While I don't deny the reality of ADHD and the need for drug treatment in some children, I have serious questions about the epidemic rise in diagnosis and the rate of dispensing the drugs. Were we just failing to recognize all these impaired children 30 years ago? Are we making the diagnosis too casually? Or are factors in the environment to blame for the prevalence of symptoms of ADHD?

I do not believe that all of these children need to be treated with powerful drugs. My 30 years of experience in integrative medicine have taught me that more basic and natural interventions, aimed at improving general health rather than targeting symptoms, can have dramatic effects on behavior and learning.

I cannot think of a more qualified person to address this problem than Dr. Sanford (Sandy) Newmark. Sandy and I have been friends for many years, since he was a graduate student in anthropology and I first settled in the desert outside of Tucson, Arizona. In my book *Spontaneous Healing*, first published in 1995, I told the story of how Sandy introduced me to Dr. Robert Fulford, one of the great osteopathic physicians of our time, who became my mentor. Later, when my daughter was born, Sandy was her first pediatrician. I was delighted when he became a residential fellow in integrative medicine at the University of Arizona under my supervision and more so when he continued as a faculty member and primary pediatric consultant at the Arizona Center for Integrative Medicine.

In this book, Dr. Newmark addresses my questions about the ADHD epidemic thoroughly and masterfully. He explains in clear language what we really know about the disorder and gives logical reasons for the increasing frequency of its diagnosis. Most importantly, he outlines specific and effective steps to address the problem without immediately resorting to pharmaceutical medication.

This book represents a truly integrative approach to ADHD, covering all aspects of a child's life, both as an individual and in the context of school, family, and community. Dr. Newmark begins, as I always do, with nutrition, emphasizing the fundamental importance of right food choices for growing children, especially those with ADHD. Food sensitivities, minerals, omega-3 fatty acids, herbal treatments, and other useful alternative therapies are all covered with clarity and insight.

I especially like Dr. Newmark's emphasis throughout the book on the many positive and valuable aspects of children with ADHD. Their creativity, spontaneity, artistic, and interpersonal skills should not be sacrificed on the altar of academic success.

I strongly recommend this book to all parents, relatives, and friends of children with ADHD, as well as the teachers, doctors, and other professionals who work with them. Before going to the pharmacy, we can use an integrative approach to help these children succeed and fulfill their true potential. Dr. Newmark tells us just how to do that.

Tucson, Arizona
January 2010

Dr. Andrew Weil *is a Harvard-trained physician who is a pioneer in the field of integrative medicine, a best-selling author, and the founder and director of The Arizona Center for Integrative Medicine in Tucson. In 2005 he was named by 'Time' magazine as one of the world's 100 most influential people.*

Introduction

Attention Deficit Hyperactivity Disorder is more commonly called ADHD, and in the space of a couple of decades, has gone from a relatively uncommon syndrome to a household word. Overall, 6 to 8% of the children in the United States are being diagnosed with this disease, and 2.5 million are being treated with long-term medication. This is a 1,600% increase since the 1970s! Almost one in every 10 boys is currently diagnosed with this disease, and the medical establishment is constantly pushing for more diagnoses and treatment. It sometimes seems that every time we turn around, another child has been diagnosed with this disorder and placed on pharmaceutical medication, which the child is expected to take throughout childhood and even for life. Worse yet, there is very little solid research concerning the long-term benefits or side-effects of these medicines. [All ADHD statistics are from the Center for Disease Control web site, cdc.gov/ncbddd/adhd/data.html.]

Many of us are skeptical, alarmed, or uncertain about all of this. It just doesn't seem right that millions of our children have suddenly developed a need to take chronic medication in order to succeed in life. Some suspect that the medical establishment is creating a disease where there is none; many people believe parental discipline has become too lax or that schools are asking too much of children; others worry that we are just not "letting kids be kids." The enormous increase in the number of children being treated for ADHD is often seen as a combination of parental failure, incompetent schools and teachers, overzealous doctors, and avaricious drug companies. Critics see a society trying to solve common childhood difficulties by handing out a pill and medicating millions of children rather than taking the time to implement effective parenting and teaching approaches.

On the other side of the issue are parents whose children are having real problems. They may be falling behind and behaving poorly at school, having a hard time making or keeping friends, and being extremely difficult to manage at home. These problems persist despite the fact that these parents are providing the best care and discipline they can manage. Often, they have other children with no such difficulties and are raising all their children with the same love and caring discipline. They simply do not know what to do when their child cannot learn at school or is completely unmanageable at home or in public.

Teachers are also in a bind. How can they teach children who won't sit in their seats, who cannot seem to focus for more than two minutes at a time on their work, who distract other kids, and who fall further and further behind academically?

The pediatrician or family practice physician is asked to evaluate and fix these problems as quickly as possible so everyone can get back to their busy and overstressed lives. Often, the physician is supposed to do this in a 10- or 15-minute visit, in the quickest and easiest way possible for everyone involved. Is it any wonder that the prescription pad is pulled out so often?

Where is the truth in all this? Is ADHD just a diagnosis made up for convenience to medicate our kids instead of parenting, teaching, and doctoring them well? Or is ADHD a real and disabling condition, requiring timely intervention to prevent serious educational, social, and family problems?

I believe the truth lies somewhere in the middle. I am convinced that the condition is significantly over-diagnosed and that too many children are medicated. However, I also believe that there are children out there who need help — who have real and serious problems with their ability to regulate their own behavior and concentrate well enough to succeed academically.

Children today are exposed to a vast array of chemical toxins from the time they are conceived and throughout childhood. They are often raised with food that is not only nutritionally inadequate but actually harmful to their developing brains. They are then subjected to several hours per day of electronic media that conditions their attention span to bursts of a few seconds. In addition, the economic realities of modern life force many parents to spend less time helping their children cope within our very stressful society. Is it any wonder that our children are having more problems?

Fortunately, medications are not the only way to help these children. In my years of practice as an integrative pediatrician, many families have come to me for help to avoid placing their son or daughter on long-term medication, despite significant pressure from schools, teachers, and the medical establishment to do so. We have been able to work together to help their children succeed and indeed flourish, supporting them in their areas of difficulty and encouraging the great skills and talents that most of them have.

An integrative approach means looking at the child in his or her entirety, as a whole person, not just at a collection of symptoms that need to be fixed. It is a path that is much more complex than a simple pill, but whose rewards are so much greater.

In this book we will begin with the basics, making sure that the diagnosis of ADHD has been made correctly and not substituted for another underlying problem. We will explore the complex neurobiology of ADHD, explaining what we actually know about how the brain operates in the ADHD child.

We will show you how to evaluate for nutritional deficiencies, making sure that the nutrients vital for normal functioning are present in adequate amounts. We will look closely at dietary intake and discuss how to determine if food allergies or sensitivities are adversely affecting your child's body and nervous system. Next we will explore some important nutritional supplements, foremost among them the omega-3 fatty acids, and some common and safe herbs that may be helpful.

In addition to nutritional issues, we will present proven and effective methods to manage your child's behavior at home and to work with teachers and schools to provide a superior learning environment.

And based on my belief that there are indeed some children who need ADHD medication, I devote a chapter to discussing how to use these medications optimally and combine them with an integrative treatment program for maximum effectiveness.

Finally, we will explore some exciting alternative therapies for treating ADHD, ranging from the newer techniques of EEG neurofeedback to the ancient wisdom of traditional Chinese medicine.

If you are reading this book, you are obviously deeply committed to the well-being of children, whether as a parent, teacher, counselor, or concerned friend, and are reluctant to "solve" the complex problem of ADHD via medication only. I have written this book to help give you the tools to develop a truly integrative approach to ADHD, thereby helping your child achieve his or her maximum potential. I wish you great blessings and success on your journey.

Chapter 1
What Is ADHD – and Why Is There So Much of It?

The term Attention Deficit Hyperactivity Disorder (ADHD) refers to a syndrome in which some combination of hyperactivity, impulsivity, and difficulty with concentration or attention is severe enough to cause significant difficulties in a child or in an adult's life. If the problems with attention and concentration occur in the absence of hyperactivity, it is officially referred to as ADHD-Inattention Subtype, but is known by many as simply ADD. Whatever we call it, the diagnosis of this syndrome has reached what I would term epidemic proportions over the last 20 years.

In 1970, about 150,000 American children were taking medication for ADHD. This represented 0.2% of children (or 2 in 1,000). By 2003, the last year for which we have reliable statistics, approximately 4.5 million children were diagnosed with the disorder, and 2.5 million, or 3.4% (34 in 1,000), were taking ADHD medication for it. This represents a 16-fold increase in both the actual number of children taking medication and the percentage of medication use — a surge of 1,600 percent! Here's what it looks like in graphic form:

FIGURE 1: **Ritalin Use in the U.S.** *(estimated)*

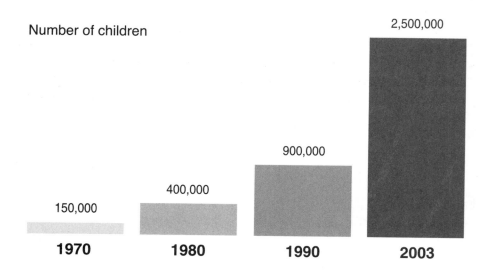

Number of children

2,500,000

900,000

400,000

150,000

1970　　**1980**　　**1990**　　**2003**

If this can't be called an epidemic, I don't know what can. Worse yet, this may be just the beginning. In some states, the percentage of boys taking medication reaches 10%; and the 'experts' continue to tell us that the condition is under-diagnosed!

What in the world has happened? How did such a significant proportion of our children develop a serious and chronic syndrome in such a short amount of time? How can we explain these numbers in a way that makes sense? Let's examine some possible explanations.

ADHD is known to be a syndrome caused by a combination of genetics and environment. (A syndrome is a collection of symptoms that tend to occur together in a predictable pattern.) That is, the tendency to develop ADHD runs in families, but other factors — not all of which are known — influence whether a child will develop ADHD and how severe the child's symptoms will be.

One thing we can say with assurance is that this epidemic is not caused by a recent change in our genetic code. Since it takes many, many generations for genetic adaptations to occur, genetic changes cannot be blamed for this sudden increase in ADHD prevalence.

So how *can* we account for this epidemic? I see four reasonable possibilities, all of which may make a substantial contribution.

■ **We are better able to recognize and diagnose children who have ADHD.** In other words, six to 10 percent of children have always experienced ADHD but we were not able to diagnose them all. Most of them slipped beneath the radar of parents, teachers, and doctors.

This is the explanation that many current ADHD experts would choose because it offers the easiest justification for putting such an enormous number of children on medication. This position asserts that these cases of ADHD were always there — we just didn't diagnose them properly. If so, what happened to these undiagnosed children? Probably many of them failed at school or dropped out early. Some may have become behavioral problems, labeled as bad kids or 'juvenile delinquents.' Or perhaps they just struggled through school, barely getting by and never fulfilling their academic or vocational potential.

There is some validity to this explanation. I think it accounts for some — but by no means all — of the huge increase in the number of children diagnosed with ADHD. It is probably true that, in the past, kids who really had ADHD and did poorly at school were instantly and erroneously labeled as slow, stupid or lazy. Many of those children probably gave up on school; they would act out, cut school, and generally find some other way of being acknowledged or at least noticed.

The fact that our society, and in particular the medical and educational communities, eventually recognized that these children needed help, rather than being left to sink or swim, is a very good thing.

■ **An expansion of the definition of ADHD has caused more children to fall within the diagnostic description.** Pediatricians who have been in practice for many years will tell you that the children diagnosed with ADHD 20 or 30 years ago were the children who were *completely* uncontrollable, *never* sat still, and tore their office to shreds in about five minutes. Today we are diagnosing children with significantly milder symptoms: kids who likely can sit perfectly comfortably in the doctor's office and play quietly at Legos for hours, but who display symptoms of poor attention, impulsivity, or hyperactivity only in school or when doing academic work. We also have added the inattentive child who has no symptoms of hyperactivity or impulsivity, but who has an impaired ability to concentrate on schoolwork.

Today, even if Johnny is able to concentrate perfectly well on what interests him, he can still be diagnosed with ADHD — as long as he does not concentrate sufficiently to do schoolwork or similar tasks he doesn't like. Some experts refer to ADHD as a disorder of *selective* attention, meaning that these children need a higher degree of motivation than other children to focus on what we want them to attend to, usually schoolwork. Including children such as these certainly represents a significant broadening of the definition of ADHD syndrome. It also opens up the possibility of applying this diagnosis to any child not doing well in school, regardless of his or her ability to control impulsivity and concentrate adequately during many other activities.

■ **There really are more children with true ADHD.** This explanation assumes that there is a true change in the neurological make-up of our children — that something has affected their neurological development, resulting in more children whose brains are 'wired' differently than was the case in previous generations.

Unfortunately, I believe this is true. It seems to me that there are more children today whose nervous systems are less naturally balanced than when I began my career as a pediatrician. They seem to be more sensitive, less resilient, and have a harder time staying focused. They tend to melt down more easily. They have a harder time adapting to simple social norms.

Change in neurological development is a very difficult thing to prove because the changes are not always dramatic or easily measurable, but it is something that I and other professionals whose opinions I respect have observed in our work with children and something that we believe represents a very real problem.

What could cause these changes? If it's not genetics — which as I stated earlier it can't be because genes don't change in the space of 30 years — it would have to be environmental.

Clearly, our environment has changed dramatically over the last 40 years in ways that could easily have damaging and very toxic effects on our children's neurological development. Let's take a closer look at these environmental factors and how they may be related to the epidemic upsurge in ADHD diagnoses.

- *Exposure to Environmental Toxins*

From the moment of conception, today's children are exposed to a very different world than they were just one or two generations ago — exposure that begins before babies are even born. It is a truly sad fact that pregnant mothers live in a highly toxic environment. The air they breathe, the water they drink, and the food they eat is contaminated with substances that did not exist a century ago and have been steadily increasing in concentration in both our environment and our bodies.

A 2005 study by the Environmental Working Group analyzed umbilical cord blood — the blood that circulates through the bloodstreams of both mother and baby before the newborn takes its first breath. In the 10 cases studied, 200 industrial chemicals on average were found in the umbilical cord blood. **Of the total 287 different chemicals found, 217 are known to be toxic to the brain and nervous system; 208 are known to cause birth defects or abnormal development in animals; and 180 are known to cause cancer in humans or animals.**[1] Coupled with the fact that the developing brain of the fetus is extremely sensitive to any environmental toxins, this finding is frightening indeed. And of course these toxins don't disappear after birth; the sensitive brain of the developing infant is also exposed to this same chemical soup along with a similar risk of adverse effects.

These risks are not just theoretical. There have been a number of studies implicating substances like lead, PCBs, organic pollutants, and mercury to an increased risk of ADHD and other behavioral problems. Thousands of other industrial chemicals have not been studied but may produce similar results. (For those who are interested, I encourage you to read Appendix A, which gives more detailed information about the relationship between environmental toxins and ADHD.)

- *Poor Nutrition*

Nutritional factors are another environmental influence likely to play a role in ADHD. Over the last 30 years, children's nutritional status has shifted drastically, and not in a good way.

Many children are growing up on a diet of industrially produced substances that barely qualify as food. These food items are not only nutritionally bereft, but include synthetic colorings and preservatives that were never meant to be ingested by humans. Sound research has demonstrated that some of these chemicals can cause hyperactivity in normal children and can worsen the behavior of hyperactive kids. It is easy to see how a child who might have some mild but manageable attention or impulsivity issues would find it harder to control these behaviors when hampered by poor nutrition and artificial chemicals.

Fortunately, we have a lot more control over what our children eat than we do over their exposure to toxins. The influence of nutrition will be explored in greater detail in later chapters.

- *The Electronic Barrage*

Another contributing factor in the increase of ADHD diagnoses is the electronic onslaught to which our children are exposed, often from birth.

In 2005, a survey[2] of young people ages 8 to 18 showed their daily activities were accounted for as follows:

Watching television – 3 hours and 51 minutes

Using the computer – 1 hour and 2 minutes

Video games – 49 minutes

Reading – 43 minutes

Several studies have examined the relationship of television watching to the incidence of ADHD. Every study has shown that **the more hours of television a child watches, the more likely he or she is to have ADHD.** However, these studies tend to only show *correlations* — they don't tell us whether the increased television watching caused the ADHD, or if ADHD children just watch more television for some reason. The studies that did try to determine whether or not television watching was actually a cause of ADHD (rather than a result) generally have indicated that it is, indeed, a cause. At this point, we can say that television watching *probably* increases the risk of developing ADHD, although the research is not definitive.

Here is another interesting fact about television: the average length of each camera shot has decreased dramatically since television was first invented. (The same is true for movies.) In other words, these media now jump from image to image at a much faster pace. This technique was popularized by *Sesame Street*, an otherwise wonderful children's program, and has progressed to the point where children are exposed to an absolute barrage of fast-moving, ever changing, highly engaging electronic images, often for several hours each day. These techniques are designed to be maximally engaging; they are, in actuality, addicting. Should it be surprising, then, that children's attention spans could be getting shorter and shorter?

Such images no doubt have an effect on the way our children's brains develop, the way in which neural connections are formed, and the way in which children learn to recognize and respond to stimuli. I cannot cite a research paper proving this, but it cannot logically be otherwise. A child's brain is in a constant state of development from birth through adolescence, with new brain cells and connections between those cells in a constant state of growth and reorganization. How could we imagine that exposure to five or more hours of electronic media every day would *not* affect their brains?

Are These Changes Part of Human Evolution?

One could make the argument — as many people do — that the kind of changes our electronic environment may be making in children's brains are just part of our evolution as a species. From this point of view, children will live in a world where computers, cell phones, Twitter, and other electronic media will dominate our environment, and the fast-moving multitasking brain will be what is required for success. Video games would then be seen as good training for the jobs of the future, and being able to focus on reading a book or listening to a lecture will be as useful as knowing how to shoe a horse.

There may be some truth in that argument, whether we like the coming changes or not. Personally, I wonder what we will lose as a species when we begin to think and function like players in a video game. For now, schools and most jobs continue to demand that people have the ability to focus on what they are doing without constant electronic stimulation. Teachers continue to assign books. Tests rely on the written word only, without a multimedia component. We need to make sure our children have the flexibility to focus — even when whatever they're focusing on isn't moving a mile a minute.

Just imagine how difficult it is for a teacher speaking in front of the class to retain a child's interest when the child spends most of his or her time in front of the fast-moving media barrage of television and video. It's no contest. That child's brain, accustomed to much more vivid stimulation, is far more likely to wander. While the emphasis on electronic media might be part of human evolution, children still need the ability to focus at a reasonable level.

■ **We are over-diagnosing ADHD — that is, labeling children with ADHD who do not really have the disorder.** In my opinion, this could well be one of the major factors behind the epidemic increase in ADHD cases. In all too many cases, the evaluation for ADHD is done in a completely inadequate manner, without according the time and effort warranted for such a diagnosis. (The third chapter discusses the ADHD evaluation process in more depth.)

It is crucial to remember here that all of the 'symptoms' of ADHD simply represent one end of the spectrum of normal behavior. Consider hyperactivity, for example. Some kids are naturally on the quiet side, and others are naturally highly active. Where is that mythical line that separates a normally highly active child from one who is "hyperactive?"

FIGURE 2: **Who is Hyperactive?**

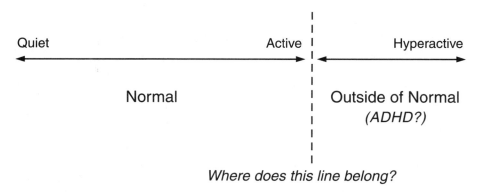

Where does this line belong?

Quantitatively, where is that line — the one that separates an active boy or girl from one with hyperactivity? How do we make that measurement? To a large extent, it's simply where each individual diagnostician decides to draw it. There is no objective standard for what separates a normally active from a hyperactive child.

The same is true for the other major traits of ADHD, including difficulty concentrating and impulsivity. Some children naturally concentrate really well and others have a harder time concentrating. Where, exactly, does this difficulty become abnormal? As for impulsivity, where is the dividing line between that enthusiastic, spontaneous child and the one whose impulsivity is abnormal or pathological? In this light, the diagnosis of a significant psychological disorder becomes far more subjective than one might hope it to be.

To the credit of diagnosticians, the ADHD diagnosis is a bit more complex than simply offering objective answers to questions such as "Is the child hyperactive? Is he impulsive? Does she have a problem with focus or attention?" Generally, standardized questionnaires that examine a wider range of behaviors are used in the diagnosis of ADHD, and they are filled out by parents, teachers, and evaluators to assess the severity of the child's symptoms. For instance, the well-known Vanderbilt Questionnaire uses measures such as the following to evaluate impulsivity issues, with 0 being never, 1 is sometimes, 2 is often and 3 very often:

Talks too much	0 1 2 3
Blurts out answers before questions have been completed	0 1 2 3
Has difficulty waiting his/her turn	0 1 2 3
Interrupts or intrudes on others (e.g., butts into conversations or games)	0 1 2 3

If your child often interrupts, blurts out answers, and talks a lot, she would be positive for the impulsivity aspect of ADHD. But really: how many kids don't interrupt? And what is "talking too much?" It all depends on your perspective, values, culture, tolerance, and many other conscious or subconscious values and prejudices. The same child could be rated quite differently depending on who is doing the evaluation.

Ah, but the experts say that, for the diagnosis to be definitive, "Some impairment from the symptoms must be present in at least two settings." In real life, this usually means the existence of significant difficulty in more than one major area of life, typically home and school. This criterion decreases the chances of false diagnoses based solely on particular characteristics. In actuality, there are kids who may exhibit the traits of ADHD but are not having any real problems in their lives (and hopefully are not diagnosed with ADHD).

However: the evaluation of what constitutes "some impairment" can get pretty subjective, too. It all depends on the perspective of whoever is making that judgment.

Here is an example of a possible problem with inattention in the home environment...or is it? Diana, who is in first grade, takes 45 minutes to get a 20-minute assignment done. She tends to hop up and down, is easily distracted, and needs Mom to remind her several times to get back to work. However, when she is done, the work is correct.

Imagine two different mothers in this situation. Mom #1 just laughs and says, "Yes, I was like that, too; I still get distracted easily but it's not a big deal!" Mom #2 is different. She is a high-achieving and focused person who is annoyed and disturbed by the need to regularly redirect Diana. She feels critical of her daughter's behavior and is worried that it will have a negative impact on Diana's success in life.

So: *does* Diana have a significant impairment resulting from inattention? It depends on which Mom, #1 or #2, she happens to have. To make it more complicated, what if Diana lives with her single-parent mom or dad who manages to arrive home about 6:30 pm with Diana and her two brothers in tow and then has to make dinner while the children are supposed to do their homework? Would that change the likelihood that Diana's behavior will constitute a significant impairment?

In terms of Diana's inattention at school, you might wonder if the teacher's evaluations would be more objective. After all, they are professionals who have experience with lots of children and should be able to judge whether a child's behaviors and abilities are really outside normal limits. I believe that is true to a certain extent, but teachers are only human, and many are operating under a great deal of pressure. Their classrooms are too full, their administrators demand higher results on standardized tests, and they are contending with more children with unbalanced nervous systems. If Diana had the same type of attention issues in class, one teacher might find it to be a major problem; another might consider it only a minor issue.

Studies Reveal Poor Agreement Between Teachers and Parents on Whether Children Have ADHD

Several studies have found that the use of standardized forms produces only poor to moderate agreement between teachers and parents on whether or not children have ADHD. In one Japanese study, 31 percent of children were rated by parents as having ADHD, while the teachers rated only seven percent of those same children as having the disorder![3] In a study in Belgium, there was no agreement between parent and teacher ratings of either inattention or hyperactivity and impulsivity.[4]

Not surprisingly, these studies aren't discussed much by those responsible for evaluating children for ADHD, but they indicate there may be a real problem in the accuracy of the diagnostic process.

The Gray Area of Over-Diagnosis

As I raise these issues about the objectivity of the ADHD diagnostic process, let me be clear about one thing: *I am not trying to say that ADHD does not exist*, nor that it cannot be correctly diagnosed. With some children, activity level is so high and degree of concentration so low that the diagnosis is obvious and essential. The seven-year-old who cannot sit still for three minutes at home or at school, and who cannot focus long enough to learn to read, obviously has a significant problem. He or she needs help of some kind.

What I *am* saying is that a large number of children truly fit in a gray area where it is hard to discern what traits represent normal behavior and what constitutes a disease or disorder. How we decide which children receive this diagnosis — a diagnosis that may result in an entire childhood of prescription medication — is both subjective and somewhat arbitrary. In other words: *we are, in fact, misidentifying far too many normal kids as having ADHD and needing medication.*

ADHD is also over-diagnosed in kids who are simply intense or oppositional. I see many children in my practice who are very difficult because, for whatever reason, their desire to please parents and teachers is far outweighed by their desire to do whatever it is they want to be doing. A typical example is Justin, a six-year-old kindergartener. Since the toddler years, he always has been an intense and difficult child. "No" was his favorite word from the time he began to speak, and he had frequent and severe temper tantrums when he didn't get his way. He can play with Legos for hours and is not particularly hyperactive, but watch out if he doesn't get what he wants. When he began school, similar difficulties arose. His teacher noted that he did well as long as he was interested, but wandered around and refused to obey instructions when he was not. He is academically ahead of most of the other children, and can sit and read wonderfully if he likes the book.

Medically speaking, Justin does not have ADHD, but I have seen many children like him who are given that diagnosis. **It makes no sense at all to say that children who are perfectly able to focus and concentrate have ADHD solely because they won't concentrate *when and where you want them to*.** They do have a problem that needs to be addressed, but ADHD is not the accurate diagnosis. (Later in this book, I will tell you how to help children like Justin; for now, recognize that there's a difference between the intense child and the child with ADHD — although there may be a significant overlap between the two.)

FIGURE 3: **ADHD and Intensity**

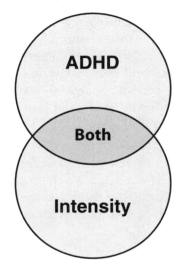

ADHD
Hyperactive, impulsive
Poor attention span
May or may not be oppositional

Intensity
Difficult, oppositional
Senstive
Often good attention span

As this diagram shows, some children are merely intense.

Is It Just Us or Is ADHD Prevalent in Other Countries?

Many parents have asked me if ADHD is as prevalent in other countries, or if this explosion in ADHD diagnoses is purely a U.S. phenomenon. The answer depends on how one looks at it. If the answer were based just on surveys asking parents or teachers to evaluate children via standardized questionnaires, then ADHD exists in all countries surveyed, sometimes at much higher rates than here in the U.S. However, ADHD is practically an unknown problem in some of these same countries, and treatment with medication is even rarer. For example, the incidence of ADHD in Germany was found to be in the 16% range, yet the rate of diagnosis and medication treatment in Germany is, in fact, less than in the United States.[5] Is this because they don't adequately diagnose and treat children with ADHD, or because they don't jump so easily from a set of "symptoms" to the diagnosis and treatment of a "disease." The answer depends upon your point of view.

The Other Side of the Coin: The Strengths and Talents of the Child or Adult with ADHD

Up to this point we have discussed only the limitations of the child we suspect of having this "disorder." Yet many children (as well as adults) diagnosed with ADHD have a tremendous upside that should not be overlooked.

energy. What may look like distractibility may also be the ability to multitask and "think outside the box." Creativity and spontaneity are the flip side of "impulsivity." So the child or adult with ADHD may be spontaneous, artistically talented, and highly social. They may be highly empathetic, with above average abilities to work successfully with people, whether in the arts, business or the healing professions. It is very important to see the strengths and talents of these people rather than just their limitations.

Here is a great example:

Most people have never heard of Paul Orfalea, but you probably have heard of Kinko's, the chain of copying stores he founded. Paul Orfalea started Kinko's with a single tiny storefront and grew it into an empire that he eventually sold to Federal Express for hundreds of millions of dollars. The remarkable fact is that this man had severe ADHD and Dyslexia and was a D student who was kicked out of four different high schools. Yet he attributes much of his success to his inability to sit still and pay attention in the usual way. The title of his book says it all: *Copy This: Lessons from a Hyperactive Dyslexic Who Turned a Bright Idea into One of America's Best Companies.*

Here are his own words:

"Well, I personally was very lucky not to be a very competent person. I can't read well. I really don't know how to run the machines in Kinko's. But I was always looking at what came out of the machine, and I knew I could sell it. And so my job was really leaving the store. By leaving the store, I told people I trusted them…. My job was really being in the moment, looking at opportunity….

"My restlessness propelled me out of doors. How many managers do you know who really understand what is happening at the frontlines of their business?… And as far as ADD, think about a hundred years ago. Was it normal to sit still and be quiet? And now we have executives that try to sit still and drink coffee at their desk. It doesn't make any sense."[6]

Paul Orfalea is just one of many very successful people with ADHD. In fact, successful entrepreneurs are more likely to have ADHD or some type of learning disability than non-entrepreneurs. Many wonderful artists, counselors, physicians, and other highly successful people have profited from traits that all too often are seen as only weaknesses.

To look at it from another perspective, here is a question I ask at my presentations and lectures: **Is the ability to sit quietly in a classroom and do the same work, at the same time, as everyone else, the highest goal and measure of human development?** I don't think so, and I believe many of you do not either.

I will close this section with the words of Edward Hallowell, author of the best-selling ADHD book *Driven to Distraction*:

"A final note: You may not be able to prevent your child from developing ADD, and that's just fine. I have ADD, and two of my three kids have it as well. With proper interventions, ADD need not be a liability. In fact, it can be a tremendous asset. While a person can learn the skills to compensate for its downside, no one can learn the gifts that so often accompany ADD: creativity, warmth, sharp intuitive skills, high energy, originality, and a 'special something' that defies description."[7]

The Bottom Line on the ADHD 'Epidemic'

The tremendous increase in the diagnosis of ADHD in our country constitutes a real yet complex problem. To some extent, the increase is a function of looking more carefully for the diagnosis and broadening the diagnostic criteria. Or there may well be more children who have the symptoms of ADHD because of environmental factors such as exposure to toxins, nutritional changes, and excessive electronic media bombardment. Finally, I believe that ADHD is seriously over-diagnosed due to lack of precision in our diagnostic methods and society's desire for quick fixes to complex problems.

This book is for the parents of children who really do have ADHD, as well as for those parents whose child has milder symptoms that make the diagnosis less clear. In either case, you are reading this book because you need help, and that is what this book will provide: ways for you to help your child function to his or her optimal potential, hopefully without the use of pharmaceutical drugs.

The next chapter explores the *neurobiology* of ADHD — what science has discovered about what is actually going on inside the brains of ADHD children. I believe the neurobiology of ADHD is both fascinating and informative and that most parents will find it so as well. But if you want to skip ahead to a program for helping your child, then feel free to go directly to Chapter 3. You can return to read Chapter 2 later if you are interested.

Chapter 2
The Neurobiology of ADHD

What is actually going on in the brains of children with ADHD? Because of the recent development of highly sophisticated technology such as functional MRI, PET scans, and quantitative EEG, we can learn a great deal about the structure and function of the brain in children with and without ADHD. Further, by comparing these two groups, we can determine if biological factors account for the differences in ADHD children.

In a way, it may come as a relief to some parents that their child's ADHD may be explained by some biological or biochemical difference. This helps rationalize why their child behaves as though *wired differently* from other children, despite their best efforts. By understanding the neurobiology of the disease, parents can stop blaming themselves or their child for behaviors or weaknesses that are very hard to control.

However, it is important to remember that the human brain, especially a child's brain, has tremendous capabilities for change and adaptation. Just because a child may tend to have lower levels of some neurotransmitters (often referred to as the dreaded "chemical imbalance") or some difference in the relative size of one part of the brain does not mean that there is some permanent defect that can never self-correct, or that he or she needs a lifetime of medication to "correct" the imbalance.

I believe these imbalances can be corrected by many types of more natural and safe interventions than psychostimulant medications, and these will be discussed in great detail throughout this book. So as you read on about the biological differences we have found in children with ADHD, keep in mind that there are many ways to help your child deal with them and even use them to his or her advantage.

Genetics

Science has made enormous progress in our ability to analyze *genes*, the building blocks that make up the DNA we inherit from our parents. This has resulted in an explosion of information that aids our understanding of the genetic basis of ADHD as well as many other conditions.

Many studies have sought to quantify the effect of genetics on a child's ADHD symptoms. How much of a child's ADHD behavior can be explained by genes, and how much is due to environmental factors? These genetics studies are usually done with twins, identical or fraternal, who have the exact same or similar genetic makeup. Although the results of these studies vary a little, there is substantial agreement overall: the results show "a mean heritability of ADHD of 77 percent."[1] This basically means that the tendency to develop ADHD is about 77 percent genetic, with environmental factors comprising the remaining 23 percent.

This comes as no surprise to me or to anyone who works with families that have a child with ADHD. In the vast majority of cases of true ADHD, there is one parent — usually, but not always, the dad — who either had the diagnosis or had similar problems in childhood that went undiagnosed. If it is not one of the parents, then it is usually an uncle or aunt.

It is also true, however, that *severity* of ADHD can be very different from one generation to the next — even if it is clearly passed, for example, from father to son. While the child's ADHD might be severe enough to cause real academic problems, Dad might say he also was hyperactive and had a hard time focusing but got through school without difficulty. This variation could be due to genetics or environmental influences (some of which I discussed in the previous chapter) or nutrition or a number of other factors covered later in this book.

What Is a Gene, Anyway?

I know everyone reading this book has heard of genes and chromosomes. Here's a brief review for those who've forgotten (or never quite learned) the details.

We all have 46 chromosomes: 22 pairs of regular chromosomes and two sex chromosomes — an XX for females or an XY for males. Chromosomes are very long strands of a chemical called DNA, and they constitute our genetic blueprint. Each child gets one of each of these 46 pairs of chromosomes from each parent.

A gene is a particular section of DNA that carries the code for a particular trait or function of the body. Each of us has at least 30,000 genes. Some traits, like eye color, are controlled by one, two, or three genes. In contrast, the gene for making a chemical that clots blood is so specific that, should that single gene have a mutation, the person will have hemophilia. Other traits, like blood pressure, may be associated with and modulated by more than 50 genes. Complex personality traits are probably associated with hundreds of genes. The physical manifestation of a gene — the color of one's hair, the existence of a genetically linked disease, or ADHD — is known as a *phenotype*.

Many different genes are associated with ADHD. At least 18 genes on five different chromosomes have been identified as influential in this disorder, and many of these interact with each other.[2]

It's quite clear that further research will find even more genes associated with ADHD. So far, we don't know which genes on which chromosomes are the most influential. We do know that each gene that has an effect has only a small impact on how a particular child develops and manifests the syndrome — how the phenotype emerges from the genes.

What does all of this mean for a parent of an ADHD child? Will this information help us at all once we have a child with ADHD? Unfortunately, aside from knowing the basic fact that ADHD runs strongly in families, the practical role of genetics is very limited. At this writing, genetic research has little effect on our ability to assess and treat the syndrome. There are just too many genes involved and their individual influences on the development of ADHD are impossible to discern. Therefore, there is little chance that gene therapy will have any role in the immediate future in the prevention or treatment of ADHD.

Nor do I foresee a role anytime soon for investigating the genotype of a particular child in order to help make treatment decisions. I would certainly not advise parents to waste any time or money obtaining any of the 'genetic scans' that have become so popular lately. They are of no practical help.

Brain Differences in ADHD

New technology has enabled us to learn a great deal about both the structure and the function of the brain in children with ADHD. While I believe it is important for parents to understand something about this topic, it is also important to understand that the research has its limitations. In other words, parents cannot necessarily make assumptions about their own child's brain characteristics based on this research.

The research findings presented herein give information about the differences between *groups* of children — specifically, how their brains may look on an MRI, PET scan, or EEG. However, *this does not necessarily mean that any particular child will have any or all of these differences.* The other thing to remember about this research is that, because of the expense involved, many of these studies were done on very small numbers of children, which may limit their accuracy.

Here is an example. If MRIs were given to any group of children, some with and some without ADHD, one would find that, on average, the children with ADHD have a smaller frontal lobe volume than those without ADHD. However, this does not mean that every ADHD child in the study had a

21

smaller frontal lobe, or any other brain difference, as compared with every non-ADHD child — because the study's results reflect the *average* measurements of the group.

One way to understand this is to consider that the average of five and five is five, but the average of two and eight is also five. When we have a small group of subjects, diversity between them is easily lost when we average the results. The smaller the group of subjects is, the greater the chances that the measurements taken vary widely between members of the group.

With these caveats in mind, we can still draw some conclusions. One is that the area of the brain that seems to be consistently affected in ADHD is called the *frontal lobe*, especially the part of the frontal lobe called the *prefrontal cortex*. The prefrontal cortex tends to be less well-developed in the ADHD child than in the child without ADHD.

The frontal lobe is the part of the brain right behind the forehead; it is mainly responsible for what is termed *executive function*. As the name implies, this refers to higher-level operations that help us control and regulate overall brain activity:

The term 'executive function' describes a set of cognitive abilities that control and regulate other abilities and behaviors. Executive functions are necessary for goal-directed behavior. They include the ability to initiate and stop actions, to monitor and change behavior as needed, and to plan future behavior when faced with novel tasks and situations. Executive functions allow us to anticipate outcomes and adapt to changing situations.[3]

Does this ring a bell? Does your ADHD child seem to act without thinking of the consequences or to have a hard time changing behavior when it is required? It is the frontal lobe that is supposed to put the brakes on — to get the child to think for a second before impulsively doing the first thing that comes to mind. How good is your ADHD child at planning future behavior? A lack of executive function due to an underdeveloped prefrontal cortex could explain why she never seems to remember to have her backpack ready for school or why he never seems to put his homework in a place where he can find it for school.

Not only does the frontal lobe tend to be smaller in size in ADHD children when viewed through an MRI, but when studied via other techniques, the frontal lobe's connection to other parts of the brain also seem to be weaker. In addition, one of the main neurotransmitters (we'll talk more about these shortly) in the frontal lobe, which is dopamine, is thought to be abnormal in ADHD.

Other parts of the brain have been found to be abnormal in structure and function in ADHD: the *parietal lobe*, the *cerebellum*, and the *caudate nucleus* are examples. However, none are as significantly different from the norm as the frontal lobe. And many of the studies demonstrating brain differences between ADHD and non-ADHD brains show contradictory results, particularly in the areas outside the frontal lobe.

Frontal Lobe Differences: Deviation or Delay?

There is great controversy as to whether these differences in brain structure and function represent a true deviation from normal development or just a delay in the *rate* of development.

We know, for instance, that the thickness of the prefrontal cortex increases with age from early childhood into adolescence. This makes intuitive sense; how much executive function does the average three-year-old have? For this reason, research studies must compare children of a similar age and usually only examine the children at a single point in time.

However, one fascinating study that did follow brain growth over a period of years found that ADHD children appeared to have a *delay* rather than a *deviation* in frontal lobe development.[4] In that study, 223 children with ADHD and 223 controls about 10 years old were followed with sensitive MRI studies over several years. The researchers measured the thickness of the cortex — the 'gray matter' of the brain responsible for higher-order brain functions — in several areas, including the prefrontal cortex. When compared to controls of the same age, the children with ADHD initially had a thinner cortex in several areas of the brain, but *the cortex continued to grow normally*. Overall, peak thickness in most areas was attained 3.5 years later than in the controls. **In other words, the children with ADHD had brains that developed in the same way as the non-ADHD children, just more slowly.** Interestingly, the only part of the brain that developed more quickly in the ADHD kids was the motor cortex, which is responsible for basic movement. So we had kids with fully developed motor systems and underdeveloped everything else. Does this seem to reflect your own experiences with your ADHD child?

The message from this study is that the brains of ADHD children, at least as far as the thickness of the cortex — the part of the brain most consistently linked with ADHD — will catch up to those of non-ADHD children. There are, however, some other studies that arrived at contradictory conclusions, although none have followed children as carefully over a number of years.

We do know that adults can have ADHD and that the relationship between cortical thickness and ADHD seems to apply to adults as well. One study found more cortical thinning in adults with ADHD as compared to adults without ADHD.[5] It therefore seems that differences in the prefrontal cortex may persist in some adults.

Fact or Fiction? Effects of Medication Are to Blame for Brain Size Differences in ADHD Studies

One question that often comes up is whether or not ADHD-related brain abnormalities are a result of medication treatment, since most of the kids in these studies have taken medication in the past. Those who seek to answer this question in the affirmative cite research that seems to show brain atrophy (shrinkage) with long-term use of stimulant drugs. The answer to this question might influence parents' decision of whether or not to give the medication to their children.

Although total brain volume has been found to be three to four percent less in kids with ADHD than in normal kids, the most recent research on the effect of ADHD medication does *not* indicate that it reduces the size of the brain structures most likely to be related to the disorder. In one study, children who had taken medication were compared with those who had never taken prescription drugs for ADHD and there were no significant differences in brain structure between the groups.[6]

So far, it appears that treatment with medication is not the cause for smaller prefrontal cortices in children with ADHD.

Neurotransmitter Abnormalities in ADHD

There is a great deal of discussion in the scientific literature, in the media, and on the Internet regarding neurotransmitters and ADHD. Evidence of differences in neurotransmitter activity between ADHD and normal children is often cited as proof that children with ADHD (or depression or anxiety for that matter) have a 'chemical imbalance' that must be addressed in order to treat the disease.

Although it is true that there seem to be abnormalities in neurotransmitter metabolism in children with ADHD, the situation is not nearly as simple or clear cut as one might think. Before going into the research, however, let's make sure we understand what a neurotransmitter is and how it works.

How Neurotransmitters Work

A brain is composed of billions of nerve cells whose job it is to transmit information quickly and efficiently. Each nerve cell has a *cell body* and a long filament called an *axon*, which moves information along very quickly in the form of an electrical current. These axons can be several feet in length!

FIGURE 4: **Neuron**

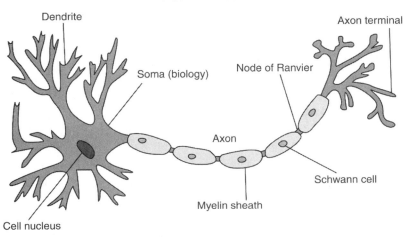

Dendrite

Axon terminal

Soma (biology)

Node of Ranvier

Axon

Schwann cell

Myelin sheath

Cell nucleus

Each nerve cell has to communicate its information to one or many other nerves; this happens at the synapse, or the connection point between neurons. A synapse looks like this:

FIGURE 5: **Synapse**

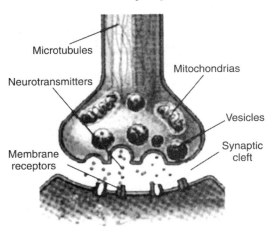

Microtubules

Mitochondrias

Neurotransmitters

Vesicles

Membrane receptors

Synaptic cleft

Here is where the neurotransmitters come in. These are the chemicals in the miniscule space (*synapse*) between the neurons; in figure 5, the neurotransmitters are depicted by tiny balls or dots in the synaptic cleft. Their role is to transmit information across the synapse between neurons. No neurotransmitters, no transmission. If there are not enough neurotransmitters, information may be transmitted more slowly, causing that part of the brain to function less efficiently.

Of the numerous neurotransmitters active in the human body, the most important are *acetylcholine*, *dopamine*, *noradrenalin* (also known as *norepinephrine*), *epinephrine*, *serotonin*, and *GABA* (short for *gamma-aminobutryic acid*). Certain neurotransmitters seem to be most important for certain brain functions, or to be predominant in specific regions of the brain.

Neurotransmitters and ADHD

What do we know about neurotransmitters and ADHD? Studies so far seem to indicate that there is indeed some 'dysregulation' of the dopamine and noradrenalin systems in the ADHD brain. This has been demonstrated by studies in both animals and humans, some of which are quite sophisticated.[7]

More practically, evidence of the roles dopamine and noradrenaline play in ADHD seems to be confirmed by the use of ADHD medications. Every drug that has been successfully used for ADHD has an effect on either the dopamine or noradrenalin systems. Methylphenidate (Ritalin) and dextroamphetamine (Dexedrine), the main drugs used for ADHD, both tend to increase the amount of dopamine available in the synapses. Medications that affect serotonin, on the other hand, generally have no effect on the symptoms of ADHD.

But all of this is much more complex than it seems at first glance. It is definitely not a simple situation of a lack of available dopamine or norepinephrine. In fact, some animal studies suggest that ADHD may involve *overactivation* of dopamine systems. The science is not clear, mainly because we can't go into the living body and measure the amount of neurotransmitters in the brain synapses.

From my review of the literature, the most accurate assessment is this: **Children with ADHD tend to have an imbalance or dysregulation in the systems that control the amount of dopamine and norepinephrine available in the synapses of specific parts of the brain. This imbalance contributes to the deficits we see in activity level, concentration, and impulsivity.**

Here we come to an interesting crossover between neurotransmitter and genetic studies. Earlier we discussed how a number of genes have been identified as contributors to ADHD. It turns out that one of the most prominent of these genes is called DRD4, which is a dopamine receptor gene. This gene would contain the code for producing dopamine receptors, which are necessary for dopamine to be effective.[8]

Keep in mind that we are examining the amount of neurotransmitters available in the synapses *in the brain*, not the amount available to the entire body. Noradrenaline, for example, is produced in the adrenal glands. When large amounts of it are produced (along with epinephrine), one experiences the 'fight or flight' response, which results in a pounding heart, fast breathing, dilated pupils, increased blood pressure, and general shakiness. This is hardly the reaction you would like in your child with ADHD. So the solution to the problem is not as simple as giving large amounts of dopamine or noradrenalin to your child in the diet or in some other fashion.

It is also important to realize that the neurotransmitters in your child's brain are continually being affected by other factors in the environment. Take motivation, for example. Motivation is just one of the psychological factors that influences brain function, and it surely has an effect on the production of dopamine, norepinephrine, and the other neurotransmitters. Think of how well your son or daughter might be able to focus on finishing a homework assignment in 30 minutes if he or she knew a trip to Disneyland was the result! This kind of strong motivation to a child will cause a change in his or her neurotransmitter activity. Other psychological factors that might influence neurotransmitters include self-confidence, relaxation, stress, and anxiety.

The critical point about neurotransmitters and ADHD is that *medications are not the only way to alter or affect any imbalance.* They are one way, to be sure, but many other interventions may produce similarly positive effects on ADHD behavior, probably influencing neurotransmitter balance in some fashion.

Brain Waves and ADHD

We have just explored potential differences in frontal lobes and neurotransmitters in ADHD cases. The third way in which ADHD children's brains tend to differ from those of children without ADHD is in brain wave patterns.

Recall that the brain works by sending signals through neurons, or nerve cells. Nerve cells are long and thin, and wherever they link up with one another, nerve impulses can pass through. These signals are electrical in nature. At any point in time, whether we are asleep or awake, billions of nerve cells operate throughout every part of the brain.

You can think of a brain wave as a set of organized electrical discharges that fall into predictable patterns based on their frequency — how many cycles per second they occur. We have named these brain waves with Greek letters instead of English letters (just to make ourselves sound really smart). So brain waves can be *alpha, beta, gamma, delta,* or *theta.* Different types of brain waves are associated with different functions of the brain and different states of arousal.

This is where it gets really interesting. Beta waves, which have a higher frequency, are associated with normal waking consciousness. As you are reading this, your beta waves should be firing away, making them the predominant rhythm occurring in your brain right now. Theta waves, on the other hand, have a lower frequency and are associated with drowsy or idle

FIGURE 3: **Brain Wave Frequencies and Their Associated Mental States**

EEG Rhythm	Frequency (hz)	Associated Mental States
Delta	1-4	Sleep; dominant in infants
Theta	3-7	Drowsiness; "tuned-in;" inner-directed insights
Alpha	8-12	Alertness; meditation; dominant when eyes closed
Sensory Motor Rhythm (SMR)	12-15	Mentally alert; physically relaxed
Beta	13-21	Focused; sustained attention; problem solving
High Beta	20-32	Intensity; anxiety; hypervigilance
Gamma	38-42	Important in learning

states. If I didn't lose you 10 minutes ago, this should not be your predominant brain wave right now.

So what does this all have to do with ADHD? The fact is that most kids with ADHD have very different brain wave patterns than kids who do not have ADHD. In general, children with ADHD have fewer beta waves and more theta waves when they are in a normal waking state than children without ADHD. In fact, **the ratio of theta to beta waves is probably the most accurate measurement of the difference in brain waves between ADHD and non-ADHD kids.** These brain wave differences are so common that looking at EEG patterns can predict those children who have ADHD with enough accuracy to produce an 80 to 90 percent agreement with the usual methods of diagnosis.

It turns out that most kids with ADHD are in a chronic state of under-arousal, at least as far as brain waves go, when reacting to the same stimuli as others. So when Melissa is sitting in class, her beta waves are reduced compared to most of the other kids and her theta waves are increased. (A small percentage of children with ADHD have *too much* beta firing off in their normal state; we refer to this as over-arousal, which can cause problems as well.)

Although the research is not entirely clear about different subtypes of ADHD, it may be that kids with the inattentive subtype of ADHD — those without hyperactivity — have yet another characteristic brainwave pattern. They might have more alpha waves, which are associated with relaxation and daydreaming, than do ADHD kids with hyperactivity or children without ADHD.

The evidence of this difference in brain wave patterns in ADHD kids is, overall, quite strong. I want to emphasize again, however, that these differences are general tendencies that might not apply to all ADHD children. Your particular child with ADHD could be under-aroused, over-aroused, or normal from a brain wave perspective. And on top of this, children are almost constantly changing their brain wave pattern in response to external events or internal motivation.

The brain is a remarkably flexible organ, and there are ways to beneficially change the way it operates — without medications. Think again of the child who is promised a trip to Disneyland in exchange for finishing his or her homework promptly. I can guarantee you that he or she is firing up those beta waves beautifully, racing through homework that might have otherwise taken two hours!

In Chapter 10, you'll learn about EEG neurofeedback for ADHD, which takes advantage of the child's ability to alter his or her own brain wave function. With EEG neurofeedback, we can actually teach children to influence their own brain waves!

Biological Differences May Represent Strengths as Well as Liabilities

As we have seen, children with ADHD, compared to those without, tend to have significant differences in the growth and size of various brain structures, in the balance of certain neurotransmitters in specific areas of their brains, and in their overall brain wave patterns during certain tasks. We have a great deal more to learn about the neurobiology of ADHD — about how these apparent differences in how the brain is functioning affect various behaviors. I would not be surprised to see much of what we think we now know change significantly with further research, especially in the area of neurotransmitters.

One final word about these differences: **It may be that many ADHD children use other parts of their brain more effectively than non-ADHD children, and that these differences result in actual strengths and talents that we have not yet adequately measured.** Perhaps the ADHD child with reduced frontal lobe function uses another part of the brain to multi-task or to be creative in ways we simply haven't figured out yet. Perhaps the ADHD child's unique neurotransmitter function has the potential to serve him well in some essential aspect of his life. In fact, certain brainwave patterns may uniquely equip the child with ADHD to succeed where others cannot.

As I will emphasize throughout this book, it is important to continually be mindful of the strengths and talents of children with ADHD and to help them use these attributes on their path to happiness and success.

Chapter 3
The ADHD Evaluation

Few things about the "epidemic of ADHD" in this country concern me more than the brief, careless, and medically inadequate evaluations that take place every day in making the diagnosis. Here is a typical situation.

William is eight years old and in second grade. He is not doing well in school: he doesn't seem to pay attention when the teacher is speaking, doesn't always finish his work, and often gets into trouble for talking to other kids or frequently getting out of his seat. Although he is at the high end of his class academically, his grades are poor because he doesn't always turn in his homework and sometimes doesn't finish his tests.

The teacher calls William's mom with news that her son is not "working up to his potential." She recommends that he be taken to a pediatrician for a medical evaluation for ADHD.

Mom is somewhat puzzled because he can concentrate for hours on books he likes or on building things, but she is aware that he has little patience for homework and is very disorganized about his schoolwork in general. Whenever she asks William about school, he just says it's boring and he doesn't like it and doesn't want to go there. In fact, all he likes about school is PE and recess.

So Mom makes an appointment with the pediatrician and is scheduled into a 15-minute visit. She tells the doctor what is going on. He listens for about five minutes, spends five minutes doing an exam, and says he agrees that William might have ADHD. He then gives her two standardized questionnaires — one for her to complete and one for the teacher — and a follow-up is scheduled in two weeks for review of the results and a final decision on the diagnosis.

Dutifully, Mom gets the forms filled out and returns — again, in a 15-minute slot. The doctor takes a few minutes to score the forms and tells her that they are "positive for ADHD." His suggestion: a trial of Concerta, a long-acting Ritalin formulation, to see if it "works." Concerned about side effects, Mom asks a few questions but is told to just watch out for weight loss and return in a month to see how things are going.

Mom gives William the medication, and sure enough the teacher says there is a big improvement. He is much quieter and more organized. He is more willing to do what he is asked. His grades go up. At home, he is more willing to sit and do his homework and finds it a little easier to keep focused while getting ready for school. Mom appreciates these changes but also notices that her son is unusually quiet and has lost a bit of his spark. She is concerned about this but assumes it is a necessary part of the treatment.

Thus, a child begins what will likely be at least five to 10 years of daily medication, a medication that may have significant negative effects on his physical, emotional, and psychological development.

Certainly, William's teacher, doctor, and parents were trying to do what was best for William. The medical evaluation was done. The diagnostic questionnaires were filled out. Everyone followed the appropriate protocols to make this diagnosis. Didn't they?

In fact, this type of evaluation *was completely and totally inadequate!* There is no way in the world that any doctor could obtain enough history to diagnose ADHD in five or 10 minutes of talking. The standardized forms, although a necessary part of the evaluation, cannot replace a thorough and complete history and appropriate testing where necessary.

But the Ritalin "worked," didn't it? Well, of course it helped William's focus and concentration. It would help anybody's, whether they had ADHD or not. It would help yours and it would help mine. That is just the effect that Ritalin has on people. Does that mean our entire nation needs to be taking Ritalin? I don't think so.

Let's look a little more closely at William. If the doctor had bothered to obtain a more complete history, he would have found that William was an extremely precocious toddler. He began reading pretty much on his own at age three and by first grade was reading at the fifth-grade level. He is an excellent artist and loves to build fantastic creations out of Legos. He can sit for many hours drawing, reading, or building things. He writes imaginative stories, far beyond what the average child his age can do. Through first grade, he attended a very small preschool where his teachers adored him and found him wonderfully talented and creative. Sure, he was sometimes a bit of a challenge behaviorally, but they were able to manage him without much difficulty.

A few months after beginning William on the Concerta, Mom runs into John, her son's former preschool teacher. Having become increasingly worried about the changes in her son's personality — he seems "flat," or at least not as happy as before — she brings up the diagnosis and medication. John is absolutely shocked.

"There's no way William could have ADHD," he exclaims. "His concentration span is excellent....I've never seen him unable to focus well on whatever he likes!" He wonders whether William might just be bored in the public school. "He's going to have a difficult time sitting still if he's being taught things he already knows or can learn much more quickly than other students." He urges William's Mom to discontinue the Concerta and have further testing.

For Mom, this encounter is like an alarm bell going off. She had already felt the truth of this intuitively, and the words of this trusted teacher triggered her to take action immediately. She consults an educational psychologist, who performs a more in-depth type of testing on William called "psychoeducational testing" (more about this later).

The results are dramatic: William has an overall IQ of 145, placing him squarely in the "gifted" category. Verbal and nonverbal scores are equally strong, and he has no learning disabilities. After spending some time with William, the psychologist's overall impression is that the youngster is simply bored in school and needs to be challenged.

As a result, Mom stops medicating her son and considers some private schools, but they are just too expensive. So she meets with William's current teacher, shows her the test results, and asks that he be tested for the gifted program. Although initially it takes a while to get the school to act, he is tested, qualifies for the program, and is placed into an accelerated class with a teacher trained specifically to work with gifted students.

It isn't long before all of William's "problems" resolve. His grades shoot up, the behavioral issues cease, and Billy is much happier. A childhood of unhappy school experience and years of taking unneeded medication were avoided because of a chance encounter with a teacher who really knew this child and a parent who was willing to listen to her feelings and fight for what was best for her son.

William's story is not an unusual one. In this case, we get to enjoy a happy ending because the family was willing to persevere with a full evaluation despite medical and educational advice to the contrary. Unfortunately, some children who are misdiagnosed with ADHD continue taking unnecessary medication for years, and many do not ever receive a proper evaluation or diagnosis.

One other thought here. Is it too hard to imagine that a genius like Michelangelo or Leonardo da Vinci could have been a lot like William? If they had been forced to stay in boring classes and given medication throughout their childhood, would the world have the great works of art or science that these people produced?

Susan's Story

Susan is an 11-year-old in fifth grade who has always done well in school, with no problems with inattention. She is, perhaps, a bit day dreamy compared to her siblings, but she is a happy child, has friends, and receives mostly B grades with an occasional C.

Rather suddenly, six weeks into her fifth-grade school year, the teacher calls Mom to report: "Susan is having a very hard time focusing. She isn't hyperactive or impulsive; she just isn't able to focus on the task at hand." Poor test scores, failure to finish her work, and a general state of distraction are causing Susan's teacher to become concerned that something might be wrong. She doesn't necessarily think it's ADHD but wants Susan's mother to take her to the pediatrician to be evaluated.

Mom takes Susan to the doctor, who hones in on the inattention symptom. He conducts the same type of brief evaluation described in William's case, advises that Susan probably has ADHD, and recommends Adderall, another longer-acting ADHD medicine. When Mom mentions that there are some stresses in the family, the doctor replies brusquely, "The questionnaires do show that your child has ADHD." "Couldn't the family problems be causing her symptoms?" asks Mom. "Susan's ADHD should be treated," says the doctor, "but it wouldn't hurt for you to seek out counseling as well."

So, in July, Susan begins to take Adderall. It seems to help at first, although the dose has to be increased twice in the first four months. Mom is very busy, so she doesn't get around to the counseling that had been suggested. Six months later, Susan begins to show signs of serious depression: she's sleeping poorly, stops wanting to see her friends as much, and becomes very irritable.

Around this time, Susan's sister Lora tells her school counselor that her stepfather has been physically abusive to her mother for the past year. When the situation is investigated, it becomes clear that the stepfather is an alcoholic who becomes violent and physically abusive to his wife when he's intoxicated. Those "stresses" Mom had mentioned stemmed from a dysfunctional relationship with her second husband in which she feels trapped and helpless. The children have not been physically abused but have been witnessing domestic violence on a regular basis. They are afraid for themselves as well as for their mother.

I wish this were a rare situation, but physical and sexual abuse are both more common than we all like to think, and children often will not speak about it. Of course, Mom could have been more forthcoming with the doctor, but he was rushed during their appointment, and she wasn't sure that was an appropriate time to discuss her relationship with the children's stepfather.

In reality, Susan's poor school performance was not just a result of her emotional reaction to the abuse; it was also a cry for help. Perhaps if someone had taken the time to really talk to her when the problems in school began, the truth would have surfaced much sooner.

Common Denominators in Misdiagnosis of ADHD

Although these children were totally different, their stories exhibit a couple of interesting similarities: they both were performing poorly at school, and they both had some symptoms of attention deficit disorder that were amplifications of natural tendencies each had as part of their personalities. Those natural tendencies were exacerbated by their particular situations.

In William's case, he did have a mild tendency to be disorganized and perhaps a little impulsive; this part of his personality became exaggerated and dysfunctional because he was bored. Susan had a somewhat "dreamy" aspect to her character that had never been a problem before but became more intense in the face of her depression and fears. Notice that Susan did not start talking out of turn or leaving her seat and William did not quietly stare off into space; *they both reacted according to tendencies in their baseline personalities.* It is also noteworthy that this tendency had not previously caused significant problems in either of their lives.

The other thing to pay attention to here is that, in both cases, the medicine "worked" to improve their school performance, even though the children did *not* have ADHD. It is very important to remember that:

- **A trial of Ritalin is not an adequate substitute for a thorough diagnostic evaluation.**

- **Just because a medication seems to "work" to improve a set of symptoms does not mean that ADHD is the correct diagnosis.**

These two points are very important. Stimulant medications will improve concentration and focus in most people, whether they have ADHD or not, so *the fact that a child shows the expected response to Ritalin or some other stimulant does not mean that the child has ADHD.*

Throughout college campuses in the U.S., there are students who have no symptoms of ADHD but who illegally use Ritalin or other stimulants strictly to be able to study longer and harder. A thriving black market for these medications exists on every college campus. Most students use them to aid studying and working, just as many of the rest of us use caffeine, another stimulant, for the same purposes. Others abuse these drugs, taking them in high doses — even crushing and snorting the drugs or injecting them intravenously — to achieve a high.

Conditions Commonly Misdiagnosed as ADHD

Here's a short list of some of the conditions that can be and often are misdiagnosed as ADHD, at least in part because of inadequate evaluations.

Psychological or learning issues:
   Depression
   Bipolar disorder
   Anxiety disorder
   Learning disabilities
   Boredom in the gifted child
   Intense or difficult temperament
   Oppositional defiant disorder (ODD)
   Sensory integration disorder (especially in younger children)

Medical or physiological problems:
   Sleep apnea or upper airway obstruction (leads to loss of quality
      sleep, which then affects daytime behavior)
   Iron deficiency (much more on this in Chapter 8)
   Lead toxicity
   Poor nutrition (covered in Chapters 4 & 5)
   Food sensitivities (covered in Chapter 6)

Social Issues:
   Inadequate parenting
   Sexual or physical abuse
   Mismatch between child and school or child and teacher
   Discrepancy between parental expectations for behavior
      or performance and child's ability or temperament
   Bullying

How does a parent, teacher, therapist, or diagnosing physician determine whether the child merits an actual diagnosis of ADHD, or whether the child has one or more of these other issues at the forefront of his or her problems? Let's explore how an adequate evaluation for ADHD is performed — an evaluation that will effectively rule out all of these other factors and avoid misdiagnoses and unnecessary medication.

The ADHD Evaluation

The most important aspect of an ADHD evaluation is that it must be done by a health care professional (or team of professionals) with experience, knowledge, and interest in the area of ADHD and related disorders. In my opinion, it is impossible to do an evaluation like this in less than two sessions, the first session at least 60 to 90 minutes and the second at least 45 minutes in length.

Why should it take so long? Why two sessions?

It is important to examine every aspect of a child's physical, social, and emotional history, from birth on, as well as the family dynamics. In cases of children who are old enough — usually age 5 and up — the examiner needs to talk with the family, the parents alone, and in most cases the child alone. He or she needs to note the child's emotional state, how he relates to the parents and to the examiner, his facility with language, the degree of motor activity, and many other factors. There are literally thousands of small details that well-trained observers must notice as they view and interact with the child and his family. The evaluation must also include a thorough physical exam with special attention to coordination and neurological issues. (One cannot even imagine doing all of the above in 15, 30, or even 45 minutes.)

And yet there is still another important part of life for a school-aged child: the school and the teacher. This is why a second visit is essential for a thorough ADHD evaluation. After the initial encounter with the family, the pediatrician must get feedback from the teacher, the counselor, or anyone else who has important knowledge of the child.

I find speaking with the teacher, especially in the elementary grades, to be extremely helpful. Teachers often spend more time than anyone with the children being evaluated, and their feedback can be vital. The standardized questionnaire is simply not an adequate substitute for actually speaking with the teacher because things come up in directed conversations that just don't fit into a standardized form.

I can remember more than one case where the standardized questionnaire the teacher had filled out indicated that a child had ADHD, but the teacher, it turned out, did not actually think that was the case. The simplified answers on the form may have pointed one way, but the teacher's more in-depth and personal knowledge of the child indicated something else. Think about William, our bored, gifted child. A teacher who understood what was happening to him might have realized he did not have ADHD, but just filling in the numbers on the standardized form would have "proven" — to some observers, anyway — that he did.

A conversation between diagnosticians and teachers may be a little more difficult during the middle school years because a child may have six or eight different teachers, none of whom know the child very well. In that case, a school counselor, principal, or other professional who has been involved may be of great help.

Following all this interaction with the family, the child and the school, the professional evaluating the child then must take the time to synthesize all the available information to form an opinion about the child's diagnosis and to suggest a course of treatment. Then the information should be presented to the family in an organized and coherent manner. Whether the recommendations are dietary or behavioral — even if they include prescribing stimulant drugs like Ritalin or Concerta — they need to be discussed in depth, and parents need to have plenty of time to ask questions about the diagnosis and recommended treatment.

I did not personally devise the method of evaluation I have just described. It is the one recommended by the American Academy of Pediatrics, a very conservative organization when it comes to ADHD treatment. However, in practice, it is far more often ignored than followed by most doctors.

More about ADHD Questionnaires

Standardized questionnaires are used as tools in the evaluation of ADHD. The most common questionnaires used with parents and teachers are the Conners and the Vanderbilt, but there are a number of others. These forms ask the person filling them out to rate the child (usually on a scale of 1 through 3 or 1 through 4) in a number of characteristics. Generally, they ask whether the child exhibits the problems a little bit, sometimes, or often. Here are some examples from the Vanderbilt teacher's questionnaire.

There is no doubt that these questionnaires are a useful part of the evaluation for ADHD. They ask the parent or teacher to consider the child's behavior from a number of different perspectives, and they can be scored in

---

Frequency Code: 0 = Never; 1 = Occasionally; 2 = Often; 3 = Very Often

1. Fails to give attention to details or makes careless mistakes in schoolwork 0 1 2 3

2. Has difficulty sustaining attention to tasks or activities 0 1 2 3

3. Does not seem to listen when spoken to directly 0 1 2 3

4. Does not follow through on instruction and fails to finish schoolwork . . 0 1 2 3

5. Has difficulty organizing tasks and activities 0 1 2 3

6. Avoids, dislikes, or is reluctant to engage in tasks that require sustaining mental effort 0 1 2 3

7. Loses things necessary for tasks or activities (school assignments, pencils, or books) 0 1 2 3

8. Is easily distracted by extraneous stimuli 0 1 2 3

9. Is forgetful in daily activities 0 1 2 3

10. Fidgets with hands or feet or squirms in seat 0 1 2 3

---

a quantitative way that compares one child with large groups of children who have been evaluated via the same questionnaire.

These questionnaires have their limitations, however. First, it's easy for the parent or teacher to consciously or subconsciously manipulate the results. Clearly, on all of the examples above, a score of 3 will tend to show that the child has ADHD; a score of 0 will show that he doesn't. Second, the questionnaire only lists a set of visible behaviors, with no attempt to look at the "why" — the reasons behind the behaviors. In William's and Susan's cases, both were diagnosed with ADHD based on these overt behaviors, but neither really had the disorder.

So the bottom line is that you should expect to see these questionnaires if your child is being evaluated for ADHD, but they should be only one part of a thorough and careful evaluation, not a single tool to give a simple yes or no answer.

Who Should Do the Evaluation?

As mentioned earlier, an ADHD evaluation should be done by someone who has a great deal of interest and experience in the evaluation and treatment of ADHD and doesn't necessarily have to be performed by a physician.

Ideally, the process of ADHD diagnosis would be performed by a multi-disciplinary clinic that includes a pediatrician, a psychologist, a nutritionist and perhaps other professionals, all of whom would participate in the evaluation — a setup that isn't easy to find. Of course, in my ideal, the professionals would be highly interested in non-pharmaceutical treatment of ADHD and in the central role that can be played by diet and nutrition. Now we're talking about something that is really, *really* hard to find.

The most common situation, in reality, is one health care provider performing the evaluation. Most often, the choice is a pediatrician/family practice physician, a child psychiatrist, or a psychologist, so what follows is a guide to what to expect with these providers.

A pediatrician (or less often, a family practice doctor) may have watched the child and family grow and therefore is likely to have good background knowledge of the family/child. This may be a very good choice **if this doctor is very interested in the evaluation and treatment of ADHD and willing to set aside the time to do it correctly.**

As I indicated at the start of this chapter, however, pediatricians too often try to fit the evaluation into a brief time slot in which it is impossible to do an adequate job. Also, many pediatricians are just not that interested in ADHD; maybe their real passion is sports medicine or allergies. Too often, these well-meaning doctors do an inadequate job in the ADHD realm.

ADHD isn't a simple childhood illness like a cold or ear infection. Not every pediatrician is able to competently mange this syndrome without special training or interest. Unfortunately, insurance companies often think the pediatrician or family practice doctor *should* be the one to diagnose ADHD, but that's another story. (See "Time Out for a Brief Rant" on managed care in Chapter 7 for more on this facet of the diagnosis issue.) As a parent seeking an evaluation, it is your job to find out whether ADHD is an area of interest and expertise for your pediatrician or family doctor.

A child psychiatrist has an advantage in skillfully diagnosing ADHD because he is, or should be, well trained in ADHD and likely to have a great deal of experience dealing with this disorder. The child psychiatrist usually takes (or should take) at least an hour for an initial evaluation, should be able to diagnose the medical as well as the behavioral aspects, and be in a position to follow the child carefully on a long-term basis.

Unfortunately, in most cases, my experience of child psychiatrists evaluating ADHD falls far short of the ideal. I have found that many, but certainly not all, child psychiatrists are very quick to prescribe medications and conduct evaluations that are just as inadequate as those of primary care doctors. I see many children who have been diagnosed with ADHD by child psychiatrists; very rarely have they performed the complete evaluation as outlined in this book. Most made the diagnosis and started medication on the very first visit.

I often see young children who have been placed on two or three different medications for ADHD, usually under the care of a psychiatrist. Child psychiatrists are often quick to prescribe a second or even third medication if a stimulant is not working, or prescribe other medications to counter the side effects of the stimulants. Pediatricians tend to be more reluctant to do this.

Also, after the initial visit, many child psychiatrists spend very little time with patients — again, often due to our friends in the managed care industry. Most insurance plans only reimburse psychiatrists for 15-minute "med checks" after the initial visit. They are faced with a dilemma: should they fail to take adequate time with their patients, or should they choose to stop accepting insurance?

A clinical child psychologist is a professional who is trained in psychology rather than medicine. There are some real advantages to selecting this type of professional for ADHD issues.

Clinical psychologists are usually well-trained in the area of ADHD evaluation and treatment and are accustomed to taking the time necessary for a complete evaluation. They are competent in administering a variety of tests, including those used for learning disabilities (discussed in more detail below). Many psychologists actually go to the school and observe the child in class, noting how well he or she is paying attention, interacting with other kids, and staying on task. If a child does have attention issues, the clinical psychologist often makes solid recommendations for both home and school interventions.

The clinical psychologist does have one serious limitation, however. He or she is not medically trained and therefore not generally able to assess for allergies, nutritional issues, or other medical factors that may be affecting a child's development. They are not able to order appropriate laboratory testing and they cannot prescribe medication; if medication is indicated, they must refer to a medical doctor.

If a clinical psychologist performs the initial evaluation on your child, be sure to also consult with a provider of medical care before initiating any treatment, especially pharmaceutical treatment. One good combination would be that of a psychologist and a pediatrician knowledgeable about ADHD.

Learning Disabilities

We have discussed various factors that can contribute to an incorrect ADHD diagnosis. One of the most important is a learning disability. Learning disabilities and their relationship to ADHD is a topic that is often very confusing to parents, which is not surprising given that most medical doctors aren't that clear about this either.

A learning disability refers to a difference 'from the norm' in how a child's brain works in one or more areas of learning; specifically, when there is a problem with the basic brain processes involved in understanding or using spoken or written language. A learning disability affects a person's ability to listen, think, speak, read, write, spell, or do mathematical calculations. The best estimate is that about 15 percent of children in the United States have a learning disability. Being diagnosed with a learning disability does not reflect on the child's intelligence; children with learning disabilities are as intelligent as those without them. If a child has a below-normal IQ, difficulties in reading or writing are not defined as learning disabilities.

ADHD is *not* generally considered a learning disability. However, learning disabilities and ADHD often go together. One recent estimate is that 25 to 70 percent of children with ADHD have a learning disability, while 15 to 35 percent of children with a learning disability have ADHD.

Here are some common learning disabilities:

- **Dyslexia** is a language-based disability in which a person has difficulty understanding written words. It may also be referred to as reading disability or reading disorder.

- **Dyscalculia** is a mathematical disability that makes the grasping of math concepts or solving of math problems difficult.

- **Dysgraphia** reflects difficulty writing letters or writing within a defined space.

- **Auditory and visual processing disorders** are sensory problems that make it difficult to understand language despite normal hearing and vision.

- **Nonverbal learning disabilities** are characterized by problems with specific processing functions, including intuitive function, visual and spatial function, and organizational and evaluative function.

To understand more about learning disabilities, let's take a closer look at dyslexia, probably the most common one. If one thinks about it, learning to decode all the squiggles and shapes you're seeing right now on this page and to give them meaning is a pretty special skill. I find it amazing that most people can do it without difficulty, and it's not surprising that up to 20 percent of people are not "wired" to do it that easily. They can all learn to read eventually, but it is significantly harder for a person with dyslexia. A dyslexic person may eventually get quite comfortable with reading or may never really enjoy reading because it is just too much work. The same would be true of dyscalculia or dysgraphia. In school, faced with tasks that seem far too difficult, a child with these disabilities could begin to "give up" in a sense; this could manifest as poor attention or even acting out. Without a correct diagnosis, that child might seem to fit perfectly into the diagnostic criteria for ADHD.

How do you know if a child has a learning disability? The first sign is when a child who is otherwise intelligent and has developed normally does not learn reading, writing, or math as easily as he or she should. Of course, we have to realize that there is a large variation in how quickly children learn these things, but when the difficulty seems significant, learning disability should be considered as a possible cause.

It is rare to detect a learning disability before school age because preschoolers typically are not that interested in reading. It can be difficult to judge whether learning disability is present even in kindergarten or first grade. But the bigger the gap is between a child and everyone else his or her age, the more suspicious one should become. Most school districts define a learning disability as a gap of two grades between a child's achievement and his expected ability, a measurement that would be hard to demonstrate in kindergarten or first grade.

If there is evidence that a child has a learning disability, then he should be tested by a clinical or educational psychologist. The child will be given an intelligence test (both nonverbal and verbal) and tested for achievement in reading, writing, and math. Various other areas, such as short and long-term memory, attention, sensory, and visual-motor skills, will also be tested. This testing will answer, with reasonable accuracy, the question of whether a child has a learning disability.

Learning disabilities can easily be confused with ADHD. Imagine a seven-year-old child who has a significant but undiagnosed reading disability. Unlike nearly everyone else in class, for this child the words are just not making sense. Progress is slow. So what does he do? He starts fidgeting, looking around the room, maybe bothering his neighbor. He tries to avoid reading as much as possible. But since reading is part of almost everything one does at school except simple arithmetic, this quickly becomes a problem. From the outside, this can look just like a child who is distractible and has a short attention span. The only way to tell the difference between ADHD and learning disabilities is a thorough evaluation.

LD testing is time-consuming and costly for school districts. If a child does prove to have learning disabilities, he or she will qualify for special education services and an Individual Education Plan (IEP), which are also costly for the school. It therefore is not surprising that schools can be very reluctant to order learning disability testing. It's much easier and less expensive for a school to assert that a child only has attention issues, for which he can be referred to a physician for possible medication. This doesn't cost the district a penny. Sometimes, the school is right, and the child *does* have an attention rather than a learning issue. Either way, it takes a clinician with knowledge and experience to know when and if the learning disability evaluation is really needed.

Does every child with ADHD need a learning disability evaluation? Definitely not. Kids who are keeping up academically despite poor concentration, distractibility, and hyperactivity don't need to be evaluated for LD, as long as they are learning well while having those difficulties. If a child is so hyperactive and distractible that she can't focus for two minutes, it's probably useless to do an LD evaluation. A child can't learn in that state, nor would she likely be able to settle down enough for accurate testing to take place. A child with less pronounced ADHD symptoms who is falling behind academically should have an LD evaluation at some point.

Bottom-Line Advice

If the possibility is raised that your child may have ADHD, first and foremost make sure you obtain an adequate evaluation as described in this chapter. It could be the most crucial thing you do for your child's long-term health and development.

Once this is accomplished, and if ADHD is indeed correctly diagnosed, you can then begin to assess which modes of treatment make the most sense. As you'll see in upcoming chapters, there's a lot more to ADHD treatment than stimulant medications. There are many options for nutritional, behavioral, and educational interventions, as well as various alternative therapies that may be effective. In fact, there are so many choices that most parents find them hard to sort through. My aim in the remainder of this book is to make sense of these possibilities and guide you in choosing what is best for your child.

Chapter 4

The Importance of Good Nutrition; or, When Did Pop Tarts Become Breakfast?

One of the single biggest factors contributing to ADHD behavior is lack of proper nutrition. I'm constantly amazed at the poor quality of foods children are eating. We are allowing our children to start their day with breakfasts that are often nothing but sugar in various disguises. And the lunches they eat at school are, for the most part, equally disastrous. It's no wonder that so many of our kids are having a hard time sitting still, concentrating, and learning.

Much of this stems from the fact that people are confused. Good parents who want their children to eat well are not sure what is good food, nor what constitutes a good diet. We live in a society in which mass media is bombarding us with never-ending streams of misleading and contradictory information about which foods are healthy for families. It's hard for anyone without training in nutrition to separate the truth from the lies. Should we eat low fat? High fat? High protein? What are "whole grains" anyhow? Are they important? Is fruit juice good or bad? Isn't white bread OK if it's enriched? (Hint: No.)

But there's another important factor contributing to our kids' poor eating habits: many parents have given up their authority and responsibility for what their children eat. I can't tell you how many times I have heard a parent say something like this: "I know that Josh shouldn't be eating pop tarts for breakfast, but it's all he'll eat. That's better than nothing, right?"

No! It's *not* better than nothing.

By allowing children to eat whatever they like, parents abdicate one of their primary responsibilities: raising healthy children. Our children are being raised in a "toxic food environment" where they are constantly bombarded by advertisements and commercials for every conceivable kind of junk food. Foods that are least healthful for kids are presented with colorful, child-attracting packaging and images of their favorite characters, beginning when they are toddlers. How can they possibly develop a healthy sense of what is good for them to eat?

The Toxic Food Environment

In our society, we are connected in more ways than ever before with a never-ending flood of information about everything, especially about food. Most of the diet and nutrition information we are bombarded with comes not from objective sources, but from corporate food producers who are interested only in their stockholders and profit margins. Children are most vulnerable to this onslaught, which in turn has a strong negative influence on their food desires and choices.

Did you know that the average child between ages two and seven sees 4,400 food ads per year on television? And the average 8- to 12-year-old sees 7,600 hundred food ads a year! Teenagers see slightly fewer: 17 a day, or about 6,000 a year. The overwhelming majority of these are for candy, snacks, fast food, and cereals. A Kaiser Foundation study found that 34 percent of food ads targeted to children are for candy and snacks; 29 percent are for cereal, often processed and sweetened (many of which are not much better for them than candy or snacks); 10 percent are for beverages. Another 10 percent of food ads targeting children are for fast food.[1]

This exposure is especially harmful to preschool-aged kids. Research shows that preschoolers can't tell whether they are watching a commercial or the program itself; in fact, they have no concept that what they are seeing is a "commercial." Often, the star of the program is hawking the junk food they want the children to buy. How can children possibly know what is healthy for them to eat?

Every time I refer to these numbers in an article or lecture, I have to force myself to look them up again because I can't believe them myself. How can parents fight back against thousands of advertisements produced by people who are professionals at convincing children to want things and to relentlessly nag their parents for them? Is there something to be done about this?

For this and many other reasons, it's crucial to limit the amount and type of programs your children are watching, especially younger children. If you choose to allow children to watch TV at all, put on a video or educational programming without advertisements. You'll help your child and save yourself a lot of arguing about why Cocoa Puffs aren't really a good breakfast.

We can help as a larger community as well. Here's what transpired in England: In 2006, a total ban on junk food advertising was placed around all children's programming, on all children's channels, and around all programs that have a particular appeal to children under 16. If this seems like too much government interference, consider that cigarette advertisements used to monopolize the airwaves until enough people protested and the government listened. Few of us would ask that those be brought back to children's television.

Subsidies and the Toxic Food Environment

Beyond the factors contributing to the toxic food environment already mentioned, there is another that may surprise you: our government's farm and food policies, which strongly affect our food costs, which in turn impacts the food choices we're drawn to make.

Ever wonder how Burger King or McDonald's can produce a huge meal for two or three bucks? One reason is that the U.S. government greatly subsidizes the production of corn and soy. Because large corporate farms can produce them cheaply, they feed these foods to cows and chickens, which in turn reduces the price of meat. Corn and soy are also turned into the high-fructose corn syrup and corn and soy oils with which many junk foods and fast food products are made. The end result is that American tax dollars help to make the least healthy products cheaper to buy. If we gave these same subsidies to small farmers producing fruits, vegetables, and other healthy whole foods, the bad stuff would suddenly become far more expensive, and it would be easier for families to make healthier choices.

The take-home message is this: our poor nutrition is a problem that needs to be attacked at every level of society. The individual choices of a family are, of course, most important, but we all need to work at the school, community, state, and federal levels to give our children and families the best chance to choose, and to afford, nutritious food.

Obesogens – Toxicity and Obesity

As if our poor eating habits aren't bad enough, new research indicates that the toxins in our environment, which we discussed earlier, may be contributing to the epidemic of obesity in our country. (Toxins that increase the tendency to become obese have been termed "obesogens" in some recent medical publications.) It turns out that when pregnant women are exposed to toxic chemicals like pesticides, fungicides, and plastic byproducts like Bisphenol-A, it may program their infants toward obesity. Apparently these compounds cause a gene named PPAR gamma to turn precursor cells into fat cells rather than connective tissue cells. So the infant ends up with more fat cells, which cause changes in metabolism, more hunger, and more tendency to retain fat. The research on this subject is in the early stages but very worrisome; for a simplified yet well done summary, see the September 21, 2009, issue of *Newsweek*. This is another good reason to pay very careful attention to the chemicals in your environment.[2]

Good Nutrition Is Especially Crucial for ADHD Kids

Children who naturally do fine at school may be able to do so even on the worst diet, providing they get a minimal amount of calories and nutrients. They may not do as well as they would on a nutritious diet, and they may be at higher risk of developing various chronic diseases, but they'll get by in school.

For children whose ability to pay attention and concentrate in the classroom is not their strongest asset, nutrition can make all the difference. In fact, it can make the difference between success and failure. If you don't believe this, let me tell you the story of Appleton Central Alternative High School in Appleton, Wisconsin.

As an alternative school, Appleton Central is for "at-risk" students. These students have exceptional personal needs and are characteristically credit deficient, continually disruptive in class, and/or frequently truant. Often they struggle with psychological and emotional problems and come from dysfunctional home environments. Some struggle with issues of teen pregnancy/parenthood, drug addiction, homelessness, and trouble with the law.[3]

Obviously, these children have a lot more problems than the average child with ADHD, but I'll bet that many began with untreated ADHD symptoms.

Initially, the students at Appleton Central received the typical poor quality breakfast as part of the school breakfast program. They spent the rest of the day snacking from vending machines full of junk food. In 1997, Appleton Central's administration contracted with Natural Ovens, a bakery and producer of natural and nutritious food, to begin a new food program. All the vending machines were removed, and the students began receiving a breakfast and lunch consisting of nutritious whole foods without food additives of any kind. They were not allowed to bring food to school, and if they did not eat what was offered, they did not eat. (Almost all of them ate.)

The results were nothing short of astounding. The students' attitudes, behavior, and ability to learn improved dramatically. In the words of principal LuAnn Coenen, "I can say without hesitation that it's changed my job as a principal….Since we've started this program, I have had zero weapons on campus, zero expulsions from the school, zero premature deaths or suicides, zero drugs or alcohol on campus. Those are major statistics."[4]

Teacher Mary Bruyette had this to say: "Since the introduction of the food program, I have noticed an enormous difference in the behavior of my students in the classroom. They're on task; they are attentive. They can concentrate for longer periods of time."

The students themselves noticed a big difference in their ability to focus and learn and were almost uniformly enthusiastic about the program.[5]

This dramatic change came from **simply changing the diet** of children who previously had a lifetime of difficulty with school and home behavior.

By the way: the school was *not* asking these kids to eat seaweed sandwiches on rice bread and drink rutabaga juice! Here are examples of meals from the typical weekly menu; I think you'll agree that most kids could handle this without much trouble.

- Tacos, fresh fruit, salad bar, energy drink, whole-grain breads
- Scalloped potatoes and ham, corn, Texas toast, fresh fruit, salad bar, energy drink, whole-grain breads
- Chicken noodle soup, turkey sandwiches, ham or egg salad, fresh fruit, salad bar, energy drink, whole-grain breads

I hope you can see how absolutely crucial good nutrition is for a child with ADHD.

The rest of this chapter will discuss nutrition in a way that will give you the tools to make the dietary changes your child needs. You will learn which foods and nutrients are necessary for optimal nutrition in general, and especially for children with ADHD. In Chapter 5, I will discuss how to get your children to eat these foods and give you some great, easy recipes for healthy meals and snacks.

Good Nutrition for Children with ADHD — and the Rest of Your Family

Before going into the specifics of nutrition, let's ponder a very basic question. Why do we have such a hard time figuring out what to eat? In our society we spend an incredible amount of time worrying about food, reading about food, dieting, and generally obsessing about what we should eat, yet we keep on getting more confused and less healthy. Why?

One reason is that we have an incredible array of choices as to what to eat — more than anyone in the history of the world — and no good way to choose. Think about what was available to your great-grandmother, whether she was on an Iowa ranch, a village in Italy, or small ranch in Mexico. Only a limited amount of foods was available in each of these cultures, and there were a limited number of ways to prepare them. She didn't have to worry about convincing Sara not to demand McDonald's for dinner because there was no McDonald's, and there were no fast food commercials. Great-Grandma didn't worry about whether vegetables were organically grown because *everything* was organically grown. Life in the food choice arena was pretty simple. Best of all, she didn't have to worry about whether there was enough folate, fiber, or iron in the family's food because we didn't know anything about that stuff back then.

This is not to say that nutrition was optimal in all cultures a century ago. Certainly, there may have been deficiencies or excesses that contributed to health problems. Still, the diets of traditional cultures had evolved over many thousands of years based on wisdom handed down from generation to generation. If people had enough food, they tended to eat pretty well.

Today, the situation is entirely different. We have enough choices to make our heads spin, and we have less and less time to think about these choices. Somehow, from all the diet plans and nutrition books and Internet claims and government reports — which appear to reverse themselves and contradict each other with regularity — we're supposed to figure out, in the limited amount of spare time we still have, which foods are right for us and our children.

Unfortunately, we're not doing a very good job of it so far. Despite the avalanche of nutritional information and advice, Americans continue to eat poorly. As a result, we are getting fatter and fatter and developing significantly more of the chronic diseases caused by poor diet.

This chapter will simplify the whole thing for you. There are some basics of good nutrition that most experts know to be true, and these are especially important to children with ADHD. After reading this chapter, I think you will be confident about the basic principles you need to improve your child's diet and give her or him the best chance to succeed.

Michael Pollan's Perspective on Food and Nutrition

Some of the best books on food and nutrition are those by journalist Michael Pollan, including *The Omnivore's Dilemma* and *In Defense of Food* (see Appendix B). Pollan offers two excellent general food rules that you can use to guide your family's choices:

1. **Eat food, mostly plants, and not too much.** The advice to "eat food" might sound self-evident, but many of the highly processed food-like items in our stores are put together like synthetic chemicals. They aren't really "food" at all.

2. **Never eat anything your grandmother would not have recognized as food.** What would she have said if you handed her a heaping helping of pasteurized cheese spread? You get the idea.

The Essentials of Good Nutrition

Despite the incredible amount of complicated and confusing information out there, the principles of sound nutrition in childhood start with some basic concepts about calories, protein, carbohydrates, and fats.

Total calories

A child needs enough calories to grow. This is rarely a problem in the United States (although it can arise with children on psychostimulants, which artificially reduce the appetite). Many children consume too many calories of the wrong kind and do not get enough exercise. Childhood overweight and obesity are rampant in the U.S. However, unless your child is overweight, don't worry too much about total calories. If you concentrate instead on providing healthy food choices as outlined below, the issue of calories tends to resolve itself.

Protein

Likewise, children need protein to maintain health and to grow. Proteins are crucial for almost every biological function of the human body. Most people know the most common protein sources such as meat, fish, and dairy, but you don't have to eat those foods to get plentiful protein; beans, nuts, soy, and some grains are also good sources. As is the case with total calories, most children in our country get plenty of protein overall, although they often don't acquire it in the one meal where they need it most, which is breakfast.

Why is it so important to get adequate protein at breakfast time? Protein is digested and metabolized into sugar fairly slowly, tending to produce relatively stable blood sugar levels — which helps to stabilize behavior and focus. A sugary breakfast that doesn't contain adequate protein, on the other hand, causes blood sugar to soar, then crash, with potentially negative effects on the child's ability to sit still and pay attention, whether she has ADHD or not! I'll tell you more about the importance of this later.

Children need about ½ gram of protein per day for each pound of body weight. A 50-pound 6-year-old, for example, would need about 25 grams of protein per day. A 3.5-ounce chicken breast has 32 grams; an ounce of cheese has 7 to 8 grams; a half-cup of beans has about 8 grams. A child could easily get 19 grams of protein in a simple breakfast consisting of a cup of milk (8 grams) and a slice of whole wheat toast (3 grams) with peanut butter (8 grams). You can see it is not hard to get adequate protein unless your child has an unusual diet.

Carbohydrates

Carbohydrates are large molecules built from various combinations of simple sugars. They are primarily used for the production of glucose, the simplest sugar, which fuels the basic energy needs of all the cells in our body, especially the brain. They are present in grains like wheat and rice, fruits, vegetables, and beans. Carbohydrates make up a major part of the human diet. Most people obtain more than half of their daily calories from a variety of carbohydrate sources.

Despite the clamoring of food faddists that carbohydrates are somehow bad for you, the bottom line is that carbohydrates are absolutely essential for good health. The notion that 'carbs' are bad is complete nonsense. Adults who want to lose weight can do so — at least temporarily — on high protein, low carbohydrate diets, but this is not relevant here. **The *kind* of carbohydrates we eat is what is crucially important.** We need to distinguish between healthful and non-healthful carbohydrates. In the most general sense, we can divide carbohydrates into two types: whole, unprocessed foods, which provide *complex* carbohydrates; and processed foods, which provide mainly *simple* carbohydrates. Let's use bread as an example. A slice of dense multi-grain bread would be a less processed complex carbohydrate. A slice of white bread would be a highly processed simple carbohydrate.

Does it really matter? Yes — it matters *a lot*. The difference between these two types of carbohydrate may explain many of the health problems of our society, as well as some of the problems of children with ADHD symptoms.

Here's why. When your child eats any carbohydrate, it is digested — broken down — in the stomach and intestines, becoming transformed from long or short 'chains' of carbohydrates into very small molecules of glucose. This glucose is the simplest form of sugar, the form in which it passes through the intestinal wall into the bloodstream. Glucose then floats around in the blood until it passes into individual cells, where it can then be metabolized ('burned') to produce energy.

The difference between complex and simple carbohydrates is how fast they are converted into sugar. White bread, our example of a simple carbohydrate, is digested very quickly into sugar, causing a quick spike of the sugar level in the blood — the phenomenon some call a *sugar rush*.

Blood sugar levels are closely regulated by the body, primarily by the pancreas in the form of the hormone *insulin*. In the case of a sugar rush, the pancreas basically overreacts and overproduces insulin in an effort to bring that level back down quickly. Blood sugar then drops too low. When blood sugar falls below normal in this sudden fashion (this is termed hypoglycemia), we can get stressed, fidgety, and nervous. We crave another round of simple sugar to set the cycle going again.

If we had chosen that good multigrain bread instead, things would have gone differently. Because the carbohydrates in it are not processed, the digestive enzymes have to work for a longer time to break them up. The sugar is released more slowly into the bloodstream; there is less of a sugar spike, the pancreas does not need to overcompensate, and there is no corresponding dip in blood sugar. Simply choosing a more dense, whole-grain, minimally processed bread has the effect of balancing out energy and sugar levels.

FIGURE 7: **Blood Sugar and Insulin Response to High and Low Glycemic Meals**

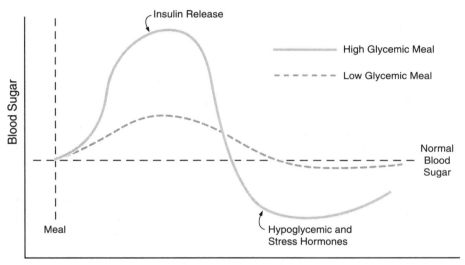

Eating too many highly processed carbohydrates doesn't just lead to ups and downs in blood sugar. Over time, with too many repetitions of this cycle of rising and falling blood sugar, the body can actually become resistant to insulin. More insulin is produced, other hormones are activated, and the final result can be obesity and diabetes. Diabetes is occurring in epidemic proportions in our children, and insulin resistance may be one of the important causes. The role of processed foods containing an overabundance of simple carbohydrates is a major factor in this huge increase in diabetes and obesity.

Glycemic Index: Low Is Good, High Is Bad

The *glycemic index* (GI) is a measure of the speed at which foods are turned into sugar in the body. For the most part, highly processed, simple carbohydrates are generally turned into sugar quickly and are high on the glycemic index. Relatively unprocessed, complex carbohydrates are turned into sugar slowly and are low on the glycemic index. When it comes to glycemic index, low is good; high is bad.

The glycemic index of glucose is 100 and serves as a comparison point for all other foods. Generally, everything over 70 is considered high on the glycemic index. Below 55 is low. (Beans are an excellent carbohydrate source, most with a glycemic index between 20 and 50.) Between 55 and 70 is the middle ground. (Check out the web site www.mendosa.com/gilists.htm for a complete chart of the glycemic indices of the most commonly eaten foods.)

Let's look at a couple of the cereals widely regarded to be healthy choices for breakfast. Corn flakes are highly processed and have a glycemic index of 83; Rice Krispies have a GI of 82. Neither of these is considered to be a sugary cereal, and it's true that neither has frosting or icing or ingredients that turn milk chocolatey. Still, the carbohydrates in these cereals are so processed, it's just like eating sugar. Slow-cooked oatmeal, on the other hand, has a glycemic index of 49. Big difference.

Having said this, I should point out that whether or not a food is processed is not the only factor in determining the glycemic index. Potatoes are a good example. Potatoes are an unprocessed complex carbohydrate, but they are high on the glycemic index, with a baked potato coming in at 85. *However, the vast majority of fruits and vegetables are low to medium on the glycemic index*, so you really don't have to worry about one or two oddities. (Parsnips, for another example, have a GI of 97, but I doubt you'll have much trouble keeping your kids from eating too many of them.)

Glycemic Load

Finally, there is one more term we have to consider, and that is the *glycemic load*. (Stay with me…we are near the end of the carbohydrate science lesson!)

The glycemic load refers to the actual effect that high- and low-glycemic index carbohydrates have on the body. It takes into account whether a food contains a lot of carbohydrates, or just a little. Really, this is just common sense: if a food has very little carbohydrate overall, it won't produce a big blood sugar surge — even if the carbohydrate is digested quickly. Cooked carrots (not raw), for example, have a high glycemic index but have so few carbs that the glycemic load is very low. White bread has a high glycemic index *and* a high glycemic load because it is mostly carbohydrate.

Here's the take-home message: you're doing well if your child's carbohydrate intake consists mainly of an assortment of whole grains, beans, fruits and vegetables. To further slow the transformation of carbohydrates into glucose and to help keep blood sugar within healthy limits, include some protein and fat in each meal (we're getting to fats next).

Dietary fiber also slows digestion and decreases glycemic load. Since dietary fiber tends to be high in whole grains and less processed foods, you don't need to worry about that separately. The sources of carbohydrate that are low on the glycemic index almost always come packaged with plenty of fiber.

By the way, one can't always predict the glycemic index of a food by how sweet it is. The glycemic index of strawberries is 32, peaches 30, and cherries 23, all very low for fruits that taste very sweet.

A high glycemic index breakfast can bring on ADHD-like symptoms. When children eat a breakfast high on the GI and with a high GL, they're going to experience an early or mid-morning drop in blood sugar. This can lead to symptoms that are very similar to ADHD. David Ludwig, Director of Optimal Weight for Life program at Children's Hospital in Boston, describes it this way:

Here's what happens: A child eats a breakfast that has no fat, no protein, and a high glycemic index — let's say a bagel with fat-free cream cheese. His blood sugar goes up, but pretty soon it crashes, which triggers the release of stress hormones like adrenaline. What you're left with, at around 10 a.m., is a kid with low blood sugar and lots of adrenaline circulating in his bloodstream. He's jittery and fidgety and not paying attention. That's going to look an awful lot like ADHD to his teacher. The possibility exists that in children predisposed to ADHD, quality of diet may have additional impact.[6]

At this writing, at least two studies have confirmed the theory that a low-GI, low-GL breakfast promotes better attentiveness and achievement in school.

Nineteen normal children ages five to seven were given a breakfast that was either low, medium, or high on the glycemic index. Two to three hours afterward, those who ate a low-GL breakfast performed better on tests of memory and sustained attention, showed fewer signs of frustration, and spent more time on-task when working individually in class.[7]

College students were given either a low or high glycemic index meal; those given the healthier, low-GI meal did better on tests of memory over three hours later. In this study, glucose levels did not drop significantly in either group; it may be that the insulin produced by the high sugar spike was somehow responsible for the cognitive problems.[8]

Research into the effect of the glycemic index on concentration and learning is just beginning, but one thing is certain: parents' observations support these studies. I have had a number of parents tell me that, when their child eats a healthful breakfast and lunch with low-glycemic carbohydrates, protein, and healthful fat (more on these good fats later), they notice definite and significant improvements in behavior and attention.

Here's the bottom line. **Switching to less processed, lower glycemic carbohydrates is good for the whole family's health. It may also make a big difference for your child with ADHD or ADHD symptoms. So why not go ahead and do it?**

Fats

Like protein and carbohydrates, fats are absolutely essential for good health. These nutrients:

- Provide energy (nine calories per gram)
- Are the building blocks of cell membranes (the outer boundary of each cell, through which nutrients pass in and wastes pass out)
- Modulate immune function
- Serve as 'carriers' for certain nutrients (including vitamins E, D, and A)
- Are sources of many compounds produced by the body

Before the nutrition gurus decided that carbohydrates are bad for our health, they told us for many years that all fats were bad. They were just as wrong about this as they are about carbohydrates.

For decades, people were encouraged to switch to a low-fat diet to shed excess weight. Unfortunately, they substituted processed carbohydrates for fat. Guess what happened? Everyone got even fatter — because eating high on the glycemic index, without balance from proteins and fat, basically primes the human body to gain weight.

Fats, like carbohydrates, are found in foods in a few different forms. Most of them are necessary and healthful in reasonable amounts. Some should be consumed in moderation. Others should be avoided whenever possible.

Saturated fats are present mainly in dairy, red meat, and certain oils like coconut oil. They are solid at room temperature. Saturated fats, in excess, tend to raise cholesterol levels and may be associated with insulin resistance. A little saturated fat is fine, but it should be consumed in moderation. Choose foods rich in monounsaturated and polyunsaturated fats as your primary sources of fat.

Monounsaturated fats are fats that remain liquid at room temperature. Put simply, they're really good for you! Good sources include olive oil, canola oil, products made from these oils, nuts, avocados and olives. Meat and poultry have some monounsaturated fatty acids as well. Monounsaturated fats tend to reduce the risk of heart disease and diabetes. I recommend doing most (if not all) of your cooking with olive oil.

Polyunsaturated fats are also liquid at room temperature, and so are also referred to as oils. They come from foods such as seeds and grains, corn oil, safflower oil, and sunflower oil. Generally speaking, polyunsaturated oils are both healthful and necessary — but things get a bit more complicated here. Omega-6 and omega-3 fatty acids are two classes of polyunsaturated fats. Both are necessary, but most of us get way too much omega-6 and too little omega-3, and this sets up a state of imbalance in the body that has far-reaching effects — effects that may be dramatic in the child with ADHD. (This topic is complex enough to merit its own chapter: see Chapter 7.)

Trans fats **are just plain bad for you.** They are man-made (they don't occur in nature except in the digestive tracts of cattle). Humans consume trans fats because industrial food producers alter naturally occurring liquid fats (oils) to make them solid at room temperature.

It must have seemed like a good idea when this process called hydrogenation was first developed; after all, this process makes the oil more stable and less prone to spoilage. A hydrogenated oil (think old-fashioned Crisco) behaves like a saturated fat. It can be kept at room temperature without spoiling and can be used to repeatedly fry foods without breaking down and becoming rancid. Hydrogenated oils lend a desirable texture to margarine, shortening, and commercial baked goods and snacks like cookies, crackers, chips, and French fries.

Unfortunately, these fats also cause inflammation, increased risk of heart disease, and may be associated with increased rates of certain types of cancer. The National Academy of Sciences has written that there is *no benefit* and *no safe level of dietary intake* of trans fat. **Try not to eat any. If the labeling says it contains hydrogenated or partially hydrogenated oil on the list of ingredients, don't buy it and don't eat it.**

Here's the catch: the manufacturer is allowed to say that the product is 'trans fat free' if there's less than ½ gram of trans fat per serving! In other words, the labeling can be misleading. To avoid the possibility of consuming trans fats 'accidentally,' one must pay close attention not only to the label details, but also to the amount of the product that is consumed. For example, if a package of cookies has just under ½ gram of trans fat per serving, and you eat more than a serving (which is probably far less than the average person would consume at a sitting), you could end up consuming many more grams of these dangerous fats than you planned to or should — all because the labeling was misleading.

Thus far we have covered the major nutrition categories (or macronutrients): calories, protein, carbohydrates and fats, all of which have both a good and a bad side. That's why parents need to be able to distinguish between the healthful and unhealthy aspects of these nutrients in the foods their children consume. In addition to the basic macronutrients, there are several other components of food that are essential to good health and we cover them next.

Vitamins, Minerals, Phytochemicals, and Additives

Vitamins

It's common knowledge that vitamins and minerals — substances that naturally occur in the foods we eat — are needed for good health. Severe vitamin deficiency causes serious disease. Severe vitamin C deficiency, also known as scurvy, is serious and can even be fatal; a deficiency of vitamins B-6 or B-12 can cause anemia.

Although children rarely develop severe vitamin or mineral deficiencies in the United States, some — particularly those who eat a typically poor modern diet — can develop mild deficiencies that may affect optimal functioning.

For example: vitamin D, which comes mainly from sun exposure, certain fish, and fortified foods, promotes good bone health in growing children. You might know that a severe deficiency of vitamin D in a young child leads to a condition called *rickets*. What you might *not* know about vitamin D is that even a non-severe deficiency has been associated with increased risk of cancer, heart disease, and autoimmune disease…or that a large percentage of the U.S. population is vitamin D deficient. In one study, over 55 percent of children were found to be vitamin D deficient. The numbers could prove to be even worse in the more northern latitudes and among people of color (darker skin means less absorption of ultraviolet rays into the skin, which is the catalyst for formation of vitamin D in the skin). Such widespread deficiency may be due to people spending less time in the sun and using more sunscreen (which prevents vitamin D formation), but we don't yet understand the entire picture.

There is not much direct research relating vitamin deficiencies to ADHD at this point, but this doesn't mean that no relationship exists. The research has just not been done. **Unless a child with ADHD eats extremely healthfully, I always recommend a multivitamin.**

Minerals

Just like vitamins, minerals are essential to health. Severe mineral deficiencies can cause serious disease, and subtler deficiencies can cause subtler health issues. Calcium, iron, zinc, and magnesium are a few well-known minerals.

Severe mineral deficiencies are rare in this country, as minerals are abundant in a wide variety of foods. Milder mineral deficiencies, however, are common. Iron deficiency is not unusual and can lead to anemia.

Some very interesting research has been done on the relationship of the level of certain minerals, specifically zinc, iron, and magnesium, to ADHD symptoms. We will discuss this in a separate chapter.

Phytochemicals

Phytochemicals are naturally occurring substances found most predominately in fruits and vegetables. They have many health-promoting effects. Perhaps you recognize the names of some of these: carotenes, lycopenes, resveratrol, or flavonoids. They're less well known than vitamins and minerals but are still crucial for good health.

Many of the phytochemicals are powerful *antioxidants*, which help protect the body against wear and tear and damage from the environment. As research into phytochemicals expands, we are seeing that they work in other ways, too — reducing inflammation, for example, or promoting better functioning of the immune system. We are just beginning to understand the importance of phytochemicals in the prevention of cancer, heart disease, and other illnesses.

Fresh fruits and vegetables are the best source of phytochemicals; in fact, these chemicals are the compounds that give these foods their rich and beautiful colors. A good example is the carotenes, which are responsible for the orange color of carrots and squash.

The current recommendation is for children to get five to nine total servings of fruits and vegetables each day. Don't worry, this isn't as hard as it sounds, and your child may already be getting more than you think. We'll talk more about how to do this in the next chapter.

One important point: no matter what's said by advertisers for costly nutritional products, *a pill cannot replace the phytochemicals and other nutrients in fruits and vegetables*. There are thousands of these compounds in fruits and vegetables, and we are constantly discovering new ones or learning new information about the importance of old ones. Try to get your child to eat as many servings of deeply colored fruits and vegetables as you can. Try to hit every shade in the fruit and vegetable rainbow. And if your child won't eat them plain, there's always a smoothie!

Stealth Veggie Attacks

Getting kids to eat fruit usually isn't too hard; vegetables, however, can be a much bigger challenge. Here are a few other tricks for sneaking phytochemical-rich vegetables into a recalcitrant child:

- Cook some leafy greens (chard, spinach, or kale) in olive oil with garlic until soft. Puree into red pasta sauce and serve over your child's favorite pasta. You can do this with zucchini, too.
- Puree cooked butternut or yellow summer squash and add to macaroni and cheese.
- Add carrot juice to smoothies.
- Add *very* finely chopped celery or cucumbers to tuna or chicken salad.

In recent years, a few books have been published on this very topic: how does the concerned parent ensure that the kids are getting their five-to-nine a day? Jessica Seinfeld's *Deceptively Delicious* is one such book; another is *The Sneaky Chef* by Missy Chase Lapine. I encourage making use of their helpful suggestions if your child is not a great vegetable eater.

Artificial Colors and Flavors and Preservatives (Additives)

This topic is discussed in depth in Chapter 6, so here we will discuss it only briefly.

Artificial colors and flavors make 'normal' kids more hyperactive, which means they can exacerbate ADHD symptoms in kids with the disorder. These chemicals are not healthy for anyone. They aren't really even food; our bodies did not evolve to be able to tolerate them. Avoid them as much as possible.

Also avoid certain preservatives such as nitrites, BHA and BHT, sodium benzoate (which can combine with vitamin C to make benzene, a carcinogen), and artificial sweeteners. Other food additives are more benign; some, like ascorbic acid and beta-carotene, are simply vitamins used as preservatives. The excellent web site of the Center for Science in the Public Interest (CSPI) maintains a complete list of food additives and their relative hazards. Go to www.cspinet.org/reports/chemcuisine.htm, print out the list, and keep it on your refrigerator. As you begin to watch out for these additives, you might also want to keep a copy on hand when grocery shopping.

Organic Foods: Are They Worth the Expense?

When I talk with parents about the best dietary choices for a child with ADHD, they often want to know whether they should be using only organic foods. This is a tough question because the expense can be high and the benefits of going organic are not dramatic. Still, there's enough evidence to merit a close examination of what you might hope to gain by feeding your family organic foods.

Many people think that any food producer can call its product organic — that the term is essentially meaningless. This isn't true in the U.S., where organic standards are quite strict. The official definition, from the USDA:

Organic food is produced by farmers who emphasize the use of renewable resources and the conservation of soil and water to enhance environmental quality for future generations. Organic meat, poultry, eggs, and dairy products come from animals that are given no antibiotics or growth hormones. Organic food is produced without using most conventional pesticides; fertilizers made with synthetic ingredients or sewage sludge; bioengineering; or ionizing radiation. Before a product can be labeled 'organic,' a Government-approved certifier inspects the farm where the food is grown to make sure the farmer is following all the rules necessary to meet USDA organic standards. Companies that handle or process organic food before it gets to your local supermarket or restaurant must be certified, too.[9]

Increased consumption of organics is better for the health of the air, soil and water that surround us, and certainly this will promote better health in future generations — but this benefit may not be seen in our own children. We've got a long way to go to clean up the messes created by standard, non-organic agricultural practices. There are, however, two kinds of immediate benefits you might reap if you go organic:

1. **Organic foods, especially fruits and vegetables, tend to be more *nutrient-dense* than conventionally grown products.** In other words, organic vegetables and fruits contain more vitamins, minerals, and phytochemicals per ounce than conventional versions. This isn't the most important benefit you're likely to see, however. The difference in nutrient density probably isn't dramatic enough to have direct impact on your child's overall health.

2. **Organic foods are free of pesticides, sewer sludge, antibiotics, and other harmful substances found in and on conventionally produced foods.** This is the most compelling reason to 'go organic.' Dozens of the chemicals found in conventionally produced foods have been found to cause harm on their own, and we know very little about their effects in combination — which is how they enter the bodies of even our youngest family members.

A study that we discussed in Chapter 1 found 287 different industrial chemicals in the umbilical cord of newborns. This means that these chemicals were in these babies' bloodstream throughout fetal development.

What impact this might have on a child is something we simply don't know, although some research points to these chemicals having true potential to do damage. In one study, babies with high levels of certain organochlorines (from pesticides) in their blood were found to have delayed motor and mental development.[10]

We know that when a child eats organic foods, the level of pesticides in his or her body changes. This was proven by another research study that demonstrated that children who ate organic fruits and vegetables had one-fifth the level of organophosphate pesticide metabolites (chemical 'fragments' of these pesticides) in their urine compared to children who did not eat organics.[11] Another study showed that the incidence of ADHD was two to three times greater in those with detectable concentrations of certain *persistent organic pollutants* (POPs) in their blood.[12] Such POPs are found on and in conventionally produced foods.

The evidence is compelling enough for me to support organic foods for children when possible and practical for your budget. Keep in mind that certain fruits and vegetables tend to have less pesticide residues than others, even when conventionally grown; you can then choose to use your food dollars to buy organic where it counts the most. The boxed section below entitled "Fruits and Vegetables Highest and Lowest in Pesticides" can help you choose where to best spend your dollars on organically grown produce.

Fruits and Vegetables Highest and Lowest in Pesticides

This list comes from the excellent web site maintained by the Environmental Working Group (foodnews.org).

Highest in pesticides. These 12 popular fresh fruits and vegetables are consistently found to have the highest levels of pesticide contamination. So it's best to always buy organic versions:

Peaches	Nectarines	Lettuce
Apples	Strawberries	Imported grapes
Bell peppers	Cherries	Carrots
Celery	Kale	Pears

Lowest in pesticides. The following 12 popular fresh fruits and vegetables have the lowest levels of pesticides so it's much safer to buy conventional versions:

Asparagus	Bananas	Cauliflower
Avocados	Broccoli	Sweet corn

Onions	Pineapples	Mango
Papaya	Sweet peas	Kiwi

So the message is, make every effort to buy organic apples and peppers, but don't worry as much about the avocados or bananas. It's also often possible to find products that are pesticide free but are not certified organic. These are often grown locally, perhaps found at farm stands or farmer's markets. Some small farming operations choose to use mostly organic practices but can't afford to obtain organic certification.

At your local farmer's market, for example, you might find eggs from chickens that received no hormones or antibiotics but didn't necessarily eat organic feed every day for their entire lives. You might find milk or meat from cows that are grass-fed but do not meet full organic certification requirements.

If your family eats dairy products, eggs, and meat, keep in mind that in animal-derived foods like these, pesticides and other chemicals become more highly concentrated through a process called *bioaccumulation.* If the food given to a chicken or cow is highly processed and contains conventionally farmed ingredients, those harmful chemicals will actually become more concentrated in its meat, eggs, and milk, delivering a higher concentration of these chemicals into the body of the person who eats them. Whenever possible, choose organic versions of these foods.

As of this writing, seafood is regulated under different rules; you won't find organic seafood, but you will find farmed and wild-caught versions.

The bottom line: feeding your children food that's free of pesticides and other chemicals is good for their health. Please try to do it when it is financially practical — but don't feel guilty when it isn't.

Keeping It Simple...and Keeping It Light

In this chapter, I have tried to cover the basics of good nutrition to help you plan a practical, healthy diet for your children, whether or not they have ADHD. But it wouldn't be possible to tell you everything about nutrition even in a thousand pages. Other chapters in this book deal with ADHD-specific dietary concerns such as food sensitivities, sensitivities to additives, and the use of omega-3 fatty acids, all with the aim of helping your child achieve better focus and better behavior without drugs. By all means, if you'd like to know more, check out a few of the other excellent books on nutrition in Appendix B.

I want to make clear, though, that I do *not* recommend becoming too dogmatic or too severe about diet and nutrition! I am not against treats, and I fully expect that most children will sometimes eat foods that are not perfectly nutritious. Unless your child has severe food reactions, there's no harm in allowing him to have ice cream at a birthday party, a soda at a soccer game, or those highly processed waffles with syrup and jelly for a Sunday breakfast. In fact, I think that excessive rigidity about controlling every morsel of food a child eats is likely to cause rebellion and a kind of psychological over-reaction that cancels out any good you might be doing with a strict dietary regimen.

Few people can attain perfect nutrition for themselves, even as adults. I don't think it is wise to force it upon children. If you can maintain the guidelines laid out in this chapter most of the time, and especially around school hours, you'll be doing a great job. Now onto the next chapter for some strategies to get your child to eat well most of the time.

Chapter 5
Practical Guidelines for Feeding Your Child

Now that you recognize how important diet changes can be for the well-being of your child, the next step is to make them happen. You may be wondering what you can do to get your child to actually eat the healthy diet that I just recommended. Perhaps your child refuses to eat anything but a few highly processed foods; maybe he has a fit if he doesn't get what he wants to eat. You might already be making two or three different meals at dinnertime to accommodate everyone's preferences. Maybe you're in a single-parent or two-working-parent family, leaving little time to cook after tired parents and their tired child arrive home at 6:00 or 6:30 in the evening. The last thing you need in your life is more complexity in the meal-preparation department or more complaints from the kids that they hate the food you're giving them and want something else.

I certainly don't have an answer for every situation, but I'd like to offer a set of guidelines and principles to help you manage your child's eating behavior in a way that will improve overall health, lead to more family harmony, **and in the end make your job easier, not harder.** This can be a sensitive area to talk about because people have deeply ingrained attitudes toward food, mealtimes, and the feeding of children. However, I believe that this approach will result in both healthier children and more enjoyable mealtimes.

First and foremost, I urge you to apply the following principle as much as you are able. This comes, and I'm paraphrasing, from Dr. Ellyn Satter, one of the leading feeding therapists in the U.S., and if you really stick with this one, everything else becomes much simpler.[1]

> **Your job is to offer your child the food you want to offer, at the time you want him or her to eat it. The child's job is to decide what and how much of it to eat.**

This sounds simple, but it has profound implications for how we feed children. If followed, it could help correct many of the mealtime problems regularly confronted by frustrated parents.

Let's say that after reading the previous chapter, you notice that your seven-year-old son Seth is often wired, irritable, and inattentive within an hour of his usual breakfast, which is always frozen low-fat waffles with syrup and a glass of orange juice. Realizing that this is a high-glycemic, low-protein, low-fat, low-fiber breakfast, you decide to make a change. So you go to the store and buy high-fiber multigrain waffles and serve them with milk. Seth comes in and throws a fit. He won't taste them, doesn't want them, and demands his normal breakfast. Now you have a choice:

1. You can try to persuade, bribe, or threaten him to eat what you have served, or demand that he stay at the table until he finishes.

2. You can give in, give him back his old breakfast, and try to figure something else out for tomorrow.

3. You can simply and calmly let him know that this is what is available; he can eat it or not, as he likes. If he doesn't eat it, you allow him to leave the table after a reasonable amount of time (maybe 10 minutes) and assume he will be fine until lunch.

Clearly, the third choice is the one I'm looking for based on the principle presented above. You have done your job by serving him nutritious food at a time you'd like him to eat. He has done his job by deciding whether or not to eat it.

But what will happen if he skips meals? Won't he become hypoglycemic (a blood sugar drop) and have even worse behavior? He might become a little hypoglycemic, but *probably less so than after eating the sugar-on-sugar that was his normal breakfast.* His blood sugar won't peak and crash but will stay low and maybe go a little lower by lunchtime. He will remember how hungry he got before lunch, and the next day (or the next, or the next, depending upon how stubborn he is), he'll probably eat the breakfast he's given.

This doesn't mean you cannot offer Seth a *choice* of healthy breakfasts. You could ask him if he wants the "new" (healthier) waffles or a slice of whole-grain toast with peanut butter or oatmeal or some whole-grain breakfast cereal with milk and a piece of fruit. You can even put a box of that cereal on the table, along with some milk and a loaf of the good bread, and let him take what he likes. The point is that you are still deciding what healthy choices to serve for breakfast, and he is still deciding what and how much to eat.

Virtually every parent has some version of this reaction when faced with a child who won't eat what's on his plate: "Oh no, I'm not feeding my child and she's going to starve to death!"

If you feel these pangs, keep reminding yourself that this approach can end up removing much of the stress most families experience around mealtimes. After a few days, Seth will realize that arguing with you about what you serve isn't doing any good, and he'll stop. You won't have to fight with him about eating, finishing, or staying at the table, wasting time you probably don't have in the morning. You'll simply serve the food, let him eat what he eats in the time he has, and move on. In the vast majority of cases, children will sooner or later begin to eat a reasonable amount of healthy foods.

In a way, you're actually giving power back to your child. After all, he or she still has the major decision-making power in the situation. You're not putting any pressure on her to make her eat. It turns out that children are surprisingly adaptive in this situation; most of them come around quite well to eating what is offered. I'm even amazed at some of the kids I see who learn to read labels at very young ages and figure out what's okay for them to eat and what isn't. I know four- and five-year-olds allergic to nuts who, when given a cookie, always remember to ask whether it has nuts in it.

But what should you say on that first day, or the night before the first day, to explain to your daughter why she isn't getting her chocolate rice puff cereal anymore? Try something like this:

"You know, Eva, it's daddy's and mommy's job to feed you food that will help you grow up to be strong and healthy. We've found out (after reading a book by mean old Dr. Newmark) that some of the food we've been giving you isn't as good for you as we thought. We've bought some other foods that we really think you are going to like for breakfast, and we'll see which ones work for you. So you're going to get to decide which of the new breakfast foods you'd like to eat tomorrow."

Of course, what you say to your five-year-old will differ from what you say to an older child. Depending on the child's level of understanding and interest, you might discuss how you think food might affect his or her ability to concentrate and stay out of trouble at school or home.

Keep in mind as you apply this first principle:

Don't label it as an experiment. Presenting it something like "Let's see if this helps you concentrate; if it doesn't, we'll go back to the old meals" almost guarantees that the child will decide it doesn't help at all.

Do get rid of any food in the house you do not want your child to eat. This is very important! It's not fair to change Eva's diet and let her brother Paul continue to eat Cocoa Puffs because he doesn't have behavior issues. For that matter, if we don't want Eva eating sandwiches on white bread, then there shouldn't be any white bread in the house, period. Yes — this means *you* will end up changing your diet, too, at least at home. This may indeed involve some sacrifices on everyone's part, but isn't that what a family is for, to support each other? Dad can always get his doughnuts 'on the outside,' and the teenager will, unfortunately, eat whatever she wants when she's out with her friends. But in the home, set a good example and remove temptation.

Using the same strategy, let's explore the after-school snack, which is sometimes the worst meal a child eats. Perhaps Seth is accustomed to coming home and heating up a Pepperoni Hot Pocket full of nitrites, dangerous trans fats, and white flour. As his parent, you've decided that he needs a healthier snack. Go ahead and put out a bowl with some baby carrots, cashews or peanuts, dates or figs or raisins, yogurt, and some peanut butter or healthy salad dressing for a dip. There's nothing to cook, and nothing that can't easily be put back in the refrigerator.

When Seth gets home and demands his Hot Pocket, say they are all gone and you are not buying anymore because they are not a healthy food. (Tell him why you think this is so, if you like, modulating the message to his level of understanding.) Show him what you are offering and ask him if he'd like to eat any of it. If he does, praise him for his adventurousness and willingness to try something new. If not, let him leave the room. If he throws a tantrum or whines, handle it just as you would handle a tantrum or whining about wanting a new toy he can't have — which I'm assuming does not entail just giving in and buying it.

Again, I would not advise begging, bribing, or pleading with the child ("it would make Mommy so happy if you'd just try some"). Remember, he is in charge of what he decides to eat. However, also remember that he can't have anything else to eat until dinner — because your job is to decide what foods are offered and when they are eaten. It would not be unreasonable to offer some other healthy snacks in the course of the afternoon, such as a smoothie, an orange, or celery sticks.

Here's a tip that might help you during after-school snack time: in our house (and this seems to be an almost universal parenting experience), the kids never went into the refrigerator to seek out fruit. But if we cut it up and put it on the table, it disappeared completely. Many other parents who've put forth the extra effort to cut up fruit and leave it out report the same result.

When it comes to dinners, things can get a little more complicated. If you are cooking a dinner for the family, do you make a substitute if Kristy refuses to eat any of it? If the rest of the family likes a spicy Chinese noodle dish and she just can't stand it, do you simply say, "Eat this or nothing," or should you have something else on the table?

Some experts advocate being dogmatic about holding to your stance, but

I believe it's reasonable to put out a simple, healthy substitute when a disliked dinner is being served. In my family, it would have been a bowl of yogurt or some tofu, or maybe even whole wheat bread and peanut butter. And then it was our daughter's choice whether she wanted to eat the alternate food or not. In any case, I would recommend against any substitutes that involve extra cooking. Life is hard enough these days. If you're cooking a family meal regularly, I congratulate you — and the last thing I want to do is make doing so more difficult.

Some parents pressure, cajole, or force children to taste everything on the table. Dr. Satter definitely recommends against this, as it violates the power-sharing arrangement. *Remember: They get to decide what and whether to eat.* There's nothing wrong with encouraging a child to try something new, but forcing the issue will backfire. If you are able to instill good eating habits when your children are toddlers, they will usually turn out to be adventurous eaters on their own. If your child is picky and hates new things, just keep offering and he or she will try some things eventually. As long as what they do eat is healthy, all is well.

Get Kids Involved in Shopping and Cooking

Another way to get your children more positively involved in the food selection and eating process is to have them shop and cook with you. Ask them to help you by reading the ingredients and choosing from a selection of healthy foods. You can make the process even more rewarding by letting them throw a favorite treat or two into the cart.

Teach children to cook simple meals with you and encourage them to take pride and ownership in what they've created. There's no reason you can't create a wonderfully healthy oatmeal cookie recipe with raisins, nuts, or apricots that your child will love to cook, share, and eat.

You can take this even further by getting your children involved in gardening. Even the time-constrained parent can grow herbs, tomatoes, berries, greens, zucchini, or a few 21-day radishes in a pot or in a simple garden plot. The experience could change their image of vegetables forever.

Make a Family Meal a Priority

I know it is very hard for some families, but **I strongly recommend assembling the family for a daily meal if at all possible.** I can't overemphasize the importance of the social aspect of mealtimes, especially the evening meal. Mealtimes should bring the family together at the table in a relaxed, pleasant atmosphere.

Please don't be afraid to keep it simple. I would much rather see a parent put together a very simple, easy-to-fix meal that allows the time and energy to sit down and eat it in a leisurely way than feel the need to cook something time-consuming and then be too frazzled or rushed to enjoy it. Anyone can prepare healthy meals that are fairly easy and fast, and the added benefit is that mealtime becomes a family event in which even the cook can partake.

And the family meal absolutely should not be a time that includes watching TV or videos, nor should this time be used for discussions or arguments about sensitive topics. When mealtimes are fun, sociable times where adults feed themselves healthfully, happily and adventurously, children will follow suit. If they have not experienced power struggles about what they are eating, they will eat even better. Mealtimes are definitely *not* a good time to raise questions about how things went at school, whether he behaved, how he did on the math test, or whether he finished his work. For the child with ADHD, school is probably not all that fun or relaxing an experience in the first place, so mealtime should not add to the unpleasantness. Instead, start conversation with questions such as: "Do anything fun today?" "What did you do after school?" "How's soccer going?"

Keep meals light and enjoy yourselves! Someday they'll move out of the home and you'll be eating alone, wishing you had those dinners back.

Pack Your Child's Lunches

I continue to be amazed at the abysmal quality of the food most of our schools serve for lunch. Although some schools are improving their food, and you might be fortunate enough to have your child at a school that serves healthy, organic fare, schools have an overwhelming tendency to serve high-fat, high-sodium, low-fiber, processed foods with few or poor quality fruits and vegetables. I know this isn't necessarily the fault of those who prepare the food. Some schools even try to streamline the lunch process and cut costs by contracting with fast-food providers for a new and different junk food meal for each day of the week. Many factors, mostly economic, contribute to the appalling current state of most school lunch programs, but we should not tolerate the situation. In almost every school district that has switched to healthier foods, the kids have eaten them and done very well.

Unless your child is lucky enough to attend a school with an unusually enlightened school lunch program, I strongly suggest a lunch brought from home. It doesn't have to be fancy or complex; pack something simple and relatively quick to eat, low in glycemic load, and with some fat and protein. For some reason, schools are giving kids less and less time to eat anyway, so you might as well make something that can be eaten quickly and easily. Even a high-quality nutrition bar (I'm partial to the organic Cliff Bars myself, but there are many good ones) and a piece of fruit might be better than what they would eat if they went through the lunch line and bought what the school was offering.

Feeding the Teen

Control over what is eaten or when it's eaten dissolves for parents of teenagers. Teens will find ways to eat what they want when they are not in the house. They'll stop at Starbucks or McDonald's; they'll trade with their friends to get foods forbidden at home; they'll buy chips and a Monster Drink from a vending machine. You still can and should control what food is served at home, and you should apply the same principles about mealtime as when they were younger. But trying to completely regulate their food intake is just about impossible.

If you start these good nutrition practices with your children when they are young, then by the time they are teens you will have instilled good eating values, tastes and habits that will carry them through these years. Still, even previously good eaters may rebel and begin meeting friends at Denny's for the super sausage breakfast, in which case there may not be much you can do. Just continue to demonstrate healthy eating habits at home. Keep open the dialogue about food without developing a power struggle over every morsel they eat.

If your teenager has ADHD symptoms and is open to discussions, try to point out the ways in which food may be affecting her success at school and/or her emotional state. One idea might be to invite your child and some of his friends to view the video produced about Appleton Central High's amazing results with its new school food program that was covered in Chapter 4 (see Appendix B for how to obtain it). Another approach may be to share a research study you've read on the topic of nutrition and ADHD. Or you can try leaving an interesting quick-read publication where your teen might stumble upon it (such as "Nutrition Action Newsletter" or Andrew Weil's newsletter "Self Healing"; see Appendix B). If your child happens to read it, he can enjoy the feeling of discovering nutritional principles for himself rather than having to hear them from you.

In the end, you'll have to allow teenagers to accept some responsibility in their food choices, just as with their other choices. Most likely, as you and I did back in our own teen years, they'll make some less-than-healthy choices...and hopefully they eventually will return to healthy eating.

Some Simple Meal Suggestions

Now that I have given you the principles for how best to provide healthy food for your ADHD child and your family in general, this next section offers a few easy, healthful, and tasty meals and snacks that most kids will like. For those who have time to cook, excellent recipe books are available (some are listed in Appendix B). But my objective here is to emphasize simple, nutritious foods that require no recipe and little time or effort to prepare.

If your child turns out to be sensitive to ingredients used in these meals and snacks, rest assured that you'll learn to work around this. As food sensitivities become more accepted as a contributing cause to a long list of health problems, many products are entering the market (for example, non-gluten flours, non-dairy cheeses, and egg substitutes) that accommodate people with food sensitivities. Similarly, cookbooks and web sites have emerged to help keep cooking and eating safe, interesting, and delicious even for those with limited diets.

Breakfast Ideas

Yogurt: Plain or naturally flavored, organic. Add fruit, nuts, ground flax seeds, healthy granola (a brand with little added sugar). Note: Flax seeds are an excellent source of fiber and omega-3 fatty acids and have a nutty taste; some kids like them and some don't. See if yours do.

Fruit: Organic if possible, especially for those most liberally doused with pesticides as listed in Chapter 4. Don't be afraid of frozen fruit, which is both easy to prepare and keep on hand. It's nearly as nutritious as fresh fruit and kids especially love to eat it when the weather's hot. Mixing frozen blueberries into plain or vanilla yogurt makes a simple ice-cream-like dessert for anytime of the day!

Bread: Whole grain, high fiber, with peanut or almond butter or cream cheese.

Eggs: Organic if possible, with whole-grain toast, but avoid serving eggs every day.

Non-breakfast food: Breakfast does *not* have to consist of what we normally think of as "breakfast foods!" Any nutritious food or combination of foods will work fine. In many countries, the concept of breakfast foods doesn't really exist. Any of these could also serve as breakfast food: leftover refried beans with tortilla; turkey burger with cheese, lettuce, tomato, and all-natural ketchup; or a bowl of leftover chicken noodle soup. The possibilities are limitless, just keep it healthy.

Cereal: Choose minimally processed, low-sugar cold cereals and serve with milk, rice milk, or almond milk. All-Bran or Bran Bud cereals are good choices. If preparing oatmeal, avoid highly processed instant oatmeal, which is high on the glycemic index; instead, use whole grain rolled oats, which can be cooked on the stove or microwaved in just a few minutes. Add whatever your family likes: dried fruit, fresh fruit, nuts, shaved coconut, a dollop of yogurt.

Waffles or pancakes: Try homemade or frozen multigrain waffles or pancakes with some protein and not too much sweetener. If you use maple syrup, offer a small bowl of it for dipping instead of pouring it all over the plate.

Smoothies: These drinks present an amazing opportunity to induce kids to eat a variety of healthful foods, especially fruits. A homemade smoothie is a dramatic departure from the overly sweetened versions available at the average smoothie shop. Start with blueberries or strawberries, whatever your child likes; frozen berries work well. Toss them into the blender, then add yogurt, water, juice, or milk, even a little honey or other sweetener if needed for taste. You can adjust consistency and sweetness to your child's preferences. Once you get the hang of creating a smoothie your child likes, you can experiment with other additions: cashews or other nuts, different fruits, flaxseed, even vegetables (celery) or vegetable juices (carrot). For a very young child who cannot or will not take the vitamins or supplements that he or she needs, they can be added to the smoothie as well. If your child can't or won't consume dairy products, other types of protein in powdered form can be mixed in. With a relatively simple drink, your child can start the day with a couple of healthy fruit servings, a good amount of protein, and adequate calories. Just remember to start slow, getting them to really enjoy the drink before beginning too many new additions.

Lunches for School

Sandwiches: Use only whole grain breads along with peanut or almond butter and jelly, unprocessed meats, cheese, tofu. Try corn tortillas or whole-grain pita bread for making sandwiches, or as an accompaniment along with any of the vegetables, fruit and dips listed below.

Cheese and crackers or chips: Use whole-grain crackers and experiment with different kinds of cheese. Lots of whole-grain chips and crackers are available now. Seek brands made with small amounts of healthful fats and be sure they don't include any hydrogenated oils (even if they say 'trans fat-free,' the presence of these oils on the ingredients list means that they could contain up to 0.4 grams per serving).

Fruit: Sliced apples or pears, orange slices, berries.

Tuna or canned salmon: Because of mercury content, give tuna only once every two weeks; use chunk light instead of albacore. You can also prepare canned wild salmon in the same way you prepare tuna, and it has much less mercury.

Vegetables: Use cut-up carrots, celery, green or red peppers, with or without a dip.

Nuts: Any kind. Store them in the fridge to keep them fresh, as nuts can go rancid easily when kept at room temperature for long periods.

Bean dip: Try hummus or black bean with cut-up vegetables or crackers.

Snacks

Cut-up fruit or vegetables: Serve alone or with some type of healthy dip.

Healthy dips: Peanut butter, almond butter, yogurt, low-fat Ranch dressing, bean dip (or use canned beans, smash them up with some additive-free salsa, and serve with tortillas).

Cookies: Homemade with raisins, dried fruit, and/or nuts. I admit this takes some preparation, but reasonably healthy store-bought cookies can also be found these days. Read labels carefully.

Tofu: As I did with my son when he was young, try lightly sautéing it and serve plain or with soy sauce or a bit of ketchup.

Dried fruit: Raisins, cranberries, dates, figs, mango, apple.

Others: Choices listed in the other categories will work here, too. Hummus, smoothies, crackers with cheese or dips, tortillas with beans, and yogurt all make great snacks. So, too, do healthful leftovers.

Dinners

My best advice for dinner foods is to try to find healthy modifications of dishes you're accustomed to serving to your family, based on the advice given in the last three chapters. Substitute healthful foods for less healthful ones. Emphasize protein, healthful fats from olive oil and canola oil, whole grains, and vegetables. For dessert, offer fruit, healthful homemade or store-bought cookies, sorbet, or even some chocolate without additives.

This may represent a big change, but remember that you don't have to do it all at once. Every small change you make will contribute that much more to the health of your child. If you keep steadily working toward a healthy diet and stay open to trying new foods, you'll develop a version of this food plan that will work for your family. The slow and steady way, with progress over time, leads to the goal of healthful eating. Finally, remember that no family eats perfectly 100% of the time; allow yourselves the occasional splurge and enjoy it fully and guilt-free!

Chapter 6
ADHD and Food Sensitivities

In my experience, food allergies and sensitivities are surprisingly common in children with ADHD. Identifying and eliminating these sensitivities can be one of the most beneficial treatments, often resulting in dramatic changes in behavior. My best estimate, from research and my own clinical experience, is that 25 to 50 percent of all children with ADHD have some type of food sensitivity and show significant improvement when the food or foods are removed. Before going into more detail about this subject, let me tell you about Joshua and how eliminating foods that affected his behavior made a major difference in his life and that of his whole family.

From the time Joshua was an infant, he was a challenge to his parents. He was colicky and had difficulty breastfeeding. His weight gain lagged behind what was expected. His parents tried substituting formulas but things appeared to get worse. His nose always seemed to be congested, and he did not sleep well.

Some improvement occurred when Joshua became a toddler. He was able to tolerate regular foods well and he gained weight. But he also became extremely active and restless and was in constant motion. He could not sit and listen to a book or focus on any one task for more than a few minutes. His parents struggled to get him to bed at any regular time. Night after night, Joshua would only give in to sleep when he collapsed from exhaustion on his own accord. His parents hoped it was just a phase and that he would calm down as he grew older.

Yet his preschool years were pretty much the same, and on top of the other issues, he became oppositional, arguing and throwing temper tantrums whenever he didn't get his way. Sometimes he threw tantrums for no obvious reason at all. Despite his parents' encouragement, he never sat still to draw or play with Legos. A television show or video could catch his attention for 10 or 15 minutes; but even then, he was constantly moving. Dinnertime was a real strain, as Joshua would be out of his seat and back at least a dozen times before finishing.

Taking care of Joshua dominated the family's life. His parents were not only frustrated, but also feared that their other two children were being neglected because of the demands placed on them by Joshua's behavior. In addition, Joshua's nasal congestion seemed constant, and he seemed to catch every bug that came around, getting sick more often than most other children.

His pediatrician prescribed allergy medicines, which helped a little but did not solve the problem. In preschool, Joshua refused to obey instructions from teachers, never sat still, and often was aggressive with the other children. Joshua was asked to leave two separate schools because of concerns about his own safety and the safety of other children.

His parents held their breath and waited to see what would happen in kindergarten. Unfortunately, it was just as they feared. Within the first week, the teacher was sending home notes about his inability to pay attention, sit still, or participate in class activities. After a month, Joshua's teacher suggested that he might benefit from a medical evaluation for ADHD.

Joshua's parents were wise enough to know that a medical evaluation meant he would be diagnosed with ADHD and placed on Ritalin or a similar drug. They didn't like the idea of his being on a medication long-term. They knew about the possible side effects and chose to investigate more natural treatments, which is how they ended up in my office.

At our first appointment, my impression was that of a boy in constant motion. Throughout the entire 90-minute interview, he barely sat still. I couldn't get him to stop to draw a picture or look at a puzzle, and he needed frequent redirection. He was thin and pale, with large dark circles under his eyes. Otherwise, he was a bright child with normal coordination and language skills for his age.

There wasn't much doubt about the diagnosis. If ever a child actually had the syndrome we call ADHD, Joshua did. His behavior was going to cause serious difficulties at home and school, and I believed that he would have major challenges with schoolwork and social relationships if nothing was done to help him.

As I talked through Joshua's history with his mom and dad, a couple of "red flags" became evident. When asked whether any foods seemed to set him off, they replied, "He's even worse than this when he drinks Gatorade or any other colored fruit drinks." They also commented that once when Joshua had stomach flu, he was fed only Pedialyte for 36 hours. They had been amazed at how quiet and focused he became but had attributed it to being ill. Both of these reports strongly suggested to me that Joshua was allergic or sensitive to certain foods and that these sensitivities were a major cause of his difficulties with attention and behavior.

We started Joshua on an elimination diet. I'll discuss this in more detail later in this chapter, but here are the essentials: first, we did a 14-day trial during which time we eliminated from his diet all the foods that commonly cause allergies. This included dairy, wheat, soy, corn, eggs, nuts, and all artificial colors and flavors. After that, the plan was to re-introduce these foods one at a time to see which foods he was reacting to.

Five days into the trial, Joshua's parents called me to report that they were astounded at the change in their son. "He's like a different child!" they said. His hyperactivity was tremendously decreased; he was more willing to listen; and for the first time in his life, Joshua sat on Mom's lap and let her read him an entire story. Needless to say, his parents were very happy with the change they saw in Joshua.

They had more good news: Joshua's congestion had decreased and the circles under his eyes were lighter. His mother added: "Within three days of starting the diet, Joshua's teacher called to ask if he had been placed on medication for his hyperactivity." The teacher informed them that he was able to sit more quietly, was paying attention to what was taught, and was beginning to play better with the other children. The teacher was very happy with how well the 'medication' was working!

The next step was to reintroduce, one by one, the foods we had removed from Joshua's diet. But before we get to that part of the story, let's talk more generally about food allergies, food sensitivities, and children with ADHD.

This can be a complicated subject, and in some circles is not considered important in ADHD treatment. However, my experience proves otherwise. While it is true that not every child's symptoms will respond to dietary changes, cases like Joshua's — where an alteration in diet makes all the difference — have taught me that it is always worthwhile to consider the role of diet in a child's ADHD symptoms.

ADHD and Food Sensitivities: The Big Picture

Medical research has firmly established that food allergies or sensitivities are a real and surprisingly common problem in children with ADHD. You would never know it from reading the standard recommendations for treatment of ADHD, but as early as the 1980s, medical researchers were demonstrating that a significant percentage of children with ADHD were allergic or sensitive to one or more foods and that these sensitivities affected their behavior significantly. Over and over again in my practice, I have seen that identifying and eliminating the foods to which the child has sensitivities can result in rapid and dramatic changes in behavior.

In 1985, a research team led by Joseph Egger placed 76 children with ADHD symptoms on an *oligoantigenic* diet, which is a diet in which only a few non-allergenic foods can be eaten.[1] ADHD symptoms improved in 62 of these children, and 28 of those improved children were then placed in a *double-blind placebo controlled trial* to further test these results. Those 28 received one of two types of drinks: either a drink that had an allergenic food in it, or a drink without the allergen (the placebo — which is what made the study 'placebo-controlled'). No one — not the children or their parents or the researchers — knew which children got which drink (that's the double-blind part). This type of study is considered to be the 'gold standard' in medical research, and a positive result in a study like this is quite significant.

Observers who did not know which drink the children received were assigned to observe their behavior. Not surprisingly, the children who took the allergen-containing drink had worsening behavior, while the children who had the placebo drink had no deterioration in their conduct.

The substances that caused the most reactions were artificial colors and flavors (no surprise there! — more on this in the next section), as well as wheat, dairy products, and soy, all of which are common foods children eat. This study was published in the *Lancet*, one of the world's most prestigious medical journals.

Dr. Egger repeated a similar study in 1992, this time using a desensitization treatment, and again a high percentage of children responded positively to dietary changes.[2] In 1993, another researcher named Carter did a similar study, and 59 of 78 children responded positively.[3] In 1994, Boris followed suit, using a multiple food elimination diet (a diet that will be described in detail later in this chapter).[4] Nineteen of 26 ADHD children responded favorably. Carter further proved his point by then giving children on the diet a placebo or an allergenic food. The study was again double-blinded so that neither the child nor the research team nor the parents knew which food had been given to which child. The results showed that the allergenic food caused many of the children to have more ADHD-like behaviors while the placebo did not.

I could mention several other studies but by now you surely get the idea. These were generally small studies, but all had similar results. Certainly, the evidence is strong enough to merit trying an elimination diet of some type in children with ADHD.

Of special importance, it seems, is the avoidance of artificial colors, flavors, and preservatives.

Put Down That Blue Lollipop and Read Your Book:
ADHD and Food Additives

Eliminating commonly eaten foods like wheat, dairy, and soy can dramatically impact the ADHD child. The evidence is even stronger regarding the role of artificial colors, artificial flavors, and preservatives. Several studies, some of them quite recent, have demonstrated that these substances clearly increase hyperactivity:

- In 2004, a researcher named Bateman studied 273 hyperactive three-year-olds. They were given one of two drinks: either one with food colorings and sodium benzoate (a common preservative); or a placebo drink that contained only juice. Children who took the artificially colored and preserved drink became more hyperactive.[5]

- A study published in 2006 involved two groups of children who were *not* hyperactive, one group aged 3 to 4 and the other aged 8 to 9. All of the children who received the artificial substances became more hyperactive. In other words, these substances not only make hyperactive kids worse, they make "normal" kids more hyperactive![6]

The evidence in this area is so convincing that officials in England and the European Union have already recommended a ban on six of the most common food colorings. Unfortunately, the United States is slower to make changes regarding food safety issues.

I received this note from the mother of one of my former patients about her personal experience regarding this issue: *"My son is 11 now and doing wonderfully! We tried him on Concerta when he was 8 but the side effects with his stomach and the weight loss was not worth it to me! He is now in the 5th grade, getting all A grades. We have him on a diet free of red dyes and as natural as I can 80% of the time! The food alone makes a HUGE difference to his personality and hyperness. We are also doing the omega-3 vitamins and I can tell if we skip a few days."*

A Method for Reducing Food Sensitivities

You may have heard of Doris Rapp, MD, a pediatric allergist who has done a great deal to bring public attention to the importance of food sensitivities in children with ADHD. She has written several books on the subject and treated thousands of children with ADHD and related problems. She has appeared on the Phil Donahue show and other TV shows, demonstrating the reactions of children given allergenic foods right in front of the audience. She also has documented the impact of environmental contaminants on children, a topic I'll discuss later in this book.

Dr. Rapp created an interesting treatment for children who had food allergies and ADHD. She would prepare a liquid to be placed under the tongue that was a very diluted preparation of the food the particular child was allergic to. This is a desensitization process, which is the rationale

behind allergy shots. Given this liquid on a regular basis, most children developed a tolerance to the foods to which they were sensitive. They were
then able to eat them without changes in their behavior. Unfortunately, it is
rare to find physicians who are skilled in this type of treatment approach.

Why Isn't This Link Between Foods and ADHD More Widely Known?

Many people ask me why more doctors don't talk about the relationship
between ADHD and food allergy or sensitivity when good research backs it
up. The reason is simple: they are not familiar with it. Physicians get most
of their information from pharmaceutical representatives and medical con-
ferences, which are sponsored by — you guessed it — pharmaceutical companies.

If a new drug with almost no side effects were created for ADHD, and it
had as big an impact as the interventions used in the studies I have described,
two things would happen. First, pharmaceutical representatives would de-
scend on every pediatrician's office with study results on this "new drug."
Second, enormous amounts of research money would be poured into more
and larger studies to confirm its efficacy.

In actuality, pharmaceutical companies stand to make absolutely no
money finding treatments for food sensitivities, so they do not ply doctors
with glossy reprints on these studies or sponsor dinners at which these results
will be discussed. Pharmaceutical companies are not in the business of promoting therapies that might help people circumvent the need for their products. This is one reason that the studies I cited were small: research money
is difficult to acquire without the backing of drug companies.

So if your pediatrician or child psychiatrist hasn't brought up the possibility of food sensitivity as a major influence on your child's behavior, don't
let it stop you from experimenting with this on your own. Determining
whether your child is sensitive to certain foods is not difficult — aside from
the angry fit the child may throw at not being able to eat his favorite foods
for a while. At best, testing changes in your child's diet will yield great improvements, and it will have been well worth any displays of temper your
family will have to weather for the initial few days of the experiment. At
worst, the diet changes won't make a significant difference and you can revert to giving the child the foods he prefers. Not a bad risk-benefit profile,
especially compared to the one you face with drugs like Ritalin.

Is Allergy Testing Important?

How does one go about finding out if a child is allergic or sensitive to certain foods? To begin with, we need to define our terms — terms like *food allergy* and *food sensitivity*, as well as a few terms related to the immune system overreactions that are often (but not always) behind the effects these foods have on sensitive children.

In usual medical practice and research, a true food allergy refers to an allergy that can be demonstrated by laboratory or clinical testing. If one were to visit an allergist for allergy testing, laboratory testing would be done via either a skin test or a blood test.

In a skin test for food allergy, small amounts of protein extracted from various foods are injected into the subcutaneous layer of the skin. If an antibody to that food is present, specifically one type of antibody called Immunoglobulin E (or IgE), there will be redness and *"induration"* (a swelling of the skin that can be felt with the hand) in a circular area around the site of the injection. This area is measured at each injection site. Pure histamine, the immune system chemical that is produced in response to allergens, is also injected for the sake of comparison, since it always causes an allergic reaction. The size of each red bump is then measured and compared to the histamine reaction to gauge how strong an allergic reaction has been mounted against each food.

In a blood test, blood is drawn in the standard way and placed into very small samples of food protein and some type of labeling material. If there is IgE antibody in the blood to that particular food protein, then there will be a visible reaction. This reaction is then graded on a scale, usually from 0 to 6, with 6 being the most severe.

Sounds pretty straightforward, right? It would seem that if your child has ADHD, you have the blood test or the skin test done and, if it is positive for a certain food, you remove the food from the diet. If it is negative for all foods, then food allergy is not a problem, and you seek other interventions. I wish it were that simple, but it isn't. Many food allergies and sensitivities do not involve IgE and therefore are not detected via standard allergy testing. In fact, some food sensitivities don't involve antibodies at all.

To understand this, we'll have to discuss some relatively complicated immunophysiology, but I will try to keep it as simple as possible.

What is an antibody, anyway? Antibodies are proteins produced by a type of white blood cell called a B cell, and they occur in response to some substance perceived by the body as "foreign" and therefore as a threat. The body produces antibodies to viruses like a cold and flu, as well as to allergens like pollen, molds, or foods. The IgE antibody, the only antibody measured by most physicians to test for allergies, is usually responsible for what we call immediate hypersensitivity reactions. This is what happens when a person eats a peanut, for example, and within a short period of time develops hives or begins to wheeze. Worse yet, he or she might develop anaphylaxis, which begins with swelling of the lips and tongue and can produce life threatening shock. IgE antibody is also mostly responsible for allergic rhinitis, often called hay fever.

Here we come to a crucial point: the human immune system has many ways of reacting to foreign substances in an allergic manner, and the IgE antibody we just discussed is only one of the ways. Our immune systems produce a number of different antibodies that can be involved in allergy, including IgE, IgA, IgM, and IgG (with subclasses from IgG1 to IgG4).

Further, antibodies are not the only way in which the immune system can react to an allergen. *Cell-mediated immunity* is another form of immune response that does not involve antibodies and works in an entirely different manner — and can be involved in immune reactions to certain foods. Not only that, the body is also capable of toxic reactions to foods that do not even involve the immune system. In other words: not all allergies to foods have to do with antibodies, nor even with any aspect of the immune system. When we test for IgE antibody alone, we are only testing for one of a number of possible ways in which the body can be "allergic" to a particular food.

Because IgE reactions are more or less immediate, they are not what we're looking for in children with ADHD. We already know that they do not have hives or wheezing when they eat certain foods. We are looking for more chronic, behavioral reactions to foods, and these reactions can often be significantly delayed. In ADHD, the symptoms we are looking for are the common symptoms of ADHD itself — hyperactivity, poor focus, impulsivity and other behavioral problems. It is also true that delayed food reactions can cause chronic congestion, dark circles under the eyes, eczema, and various gastrointestinal problems like diarrhea or abdominal pain.

I am reminded of a young patient of mine named Jenny. Every time Jenny ate anything with soy, her cheeks turned red and she vomited within minutes. Yet blood and skin tests for soy allergy came back negative, and she was told she did not have an allergy to soy. Her mother was understandably confused and frustrated by this. I reassured Jenny's mother that she could trust her own observation and common sense more than these particular laboratory tests. She simply avoided giving Jenny any soy foods. Problem solved.

The next question that a reasonable person might ask is, "Why, then, don't we just do blood or skin tests for these other types of allergic reactions as well, instead of just for the ones triggered by the IgE antibody?" The answer is twofold. First, for some of the ways in which the body can react to foods, we simply don't have any laboratory test at all. And second, although we do have tests for some of these other reactions, they are not accurate enough to be useful.

For example, another antibody called IgG is the most prevalent antibody in the body and is responsible for a wide range of reactions, many of which are delayed or chronic reactions — more typical of what we are looking for in children with ADHD. This would seem to be an excellent antibody to test for, right? Food tests for IgG are available, and there are even some for the subclasses of IgG mentioned above.

But there's an obstacle: *everyone has lots of IgG antibodies to food running around in their bloodstreams.* It is a normal thing. To be useful, the test would have to distinguish a *normal* level of IgG for a certain food from an *abnormal* level. The test would also have to give a reasonable idea of whether an abnormal level of IgG for a food — for example, wheat — is what is actually causing symptoms in a specific child. In my opinion, and that of most researchers, this test has not been refined to the point where it can achieve this end. The studies done on this test so far fail to prove that they can accurately predict whether high IgG levels for certain foods actually are associated with real clinical problems, including ADHD.

Here's a practical example. Let's say Evan has ADHD. Suspecting food allergy, an IgG test is ordered and shows that he has high levels of IgG antibody to 14 foods. How sure can a parent be that these 14 foods really are causing ADHD symptoms? Also, how sure can a parent be that foods showing up as negative on this test (no allergy) are *not* causing ADHD symptoms? If, for example, the test shows that the IgG antibody to milk is very high, does that mean that milk is at least partially related to Evan's ADHD symptoms? And if it says that the IgG antibody to eggs is very low, does that mean that eggs are not involved in causing these symptoms?

The test simply isn't accurate enough for parents to be sure of either of these things, and they cannot be sure until the food is actually removed from their child's diet.

To illustrate this, consider Jessie, a 10-year-old who had great trouble concentrating in school. Her mother came to me with a thick folder of medical records, including several sets of IgG food allergy tests and skin tests from an allergist. Jessie's mom had spent the last couple of years changing her child's diet in response to the results of these tests — but had found no real improvement in Jessie's ADHD symptoms. When I looked through her chart, I saw the problem: the IgG and IgE tests didn't agree with each other, and the results of the IgG tests changed with each repetition. Needless to say, this family was pretty frustrated with the whole business. After we sat down and talked about what they had both been able to actually observe about

Jessie's response to foods, we came up with a reasonable plan to see which foods really affected her ability to concentrate, regardless of the laboratory results. Within a couple of months, two or three problem foods were identified. With those foods eliminated from her diet, her schoolwork improved, and she was also able to eat a reasonably normal diet.

IgG testing remains a subject of much controversy. Many very good physicians and other professionals who take a holistic or integrative approach to ADHD believe that these tests are useful and order them frequently. I do not think that many of them believe the research is sufficient to prove these tests accurate. Rather, they feel that using these tests has worked for them in *predicting* what foods a child with ADHD may be sensitive to and adjusting the diet accordingly. That has not been my experience, but I respect this as a reasonable approach when the tests are used in this way.

A number of other, even less proven, tests for food allergy can be obtained. Some of them measure different antibodies; others measure the extent to which white cells deform in the presence of certain food proteins. All of them claim to be accurate, but there is no research to back these claims.

For me, any form of laboratory food allergy testing for ADHD, including the standard IgE testing, must be used only as a guideline — a clue that indicates which foods might or might not be affecting behavior. Lab tests need to be followed by careful clinical testing and observation to verify their accuracy. After all, does it matter if a child has a highly positive IgG or IgE test for corn if removing corn makes no difference in his ADHD symptoms?

None of the studies I quoted in the early part of this chapter used food allergy testing as a criteria for removing foods from the diet. The ones that used allergy testing as part of the study showed that it was of no help in predicting the results.

Food Allergy or Food Sensitivity?

There is much confusion and controversy about whether to use the term "food allergy" or "food sensitivity" to describe this potentially important cause of ADHD symptoms. To some medical doctors, a child only has a food allergy if some type of medical test demonstrates a measurable antibody reaction to a food. From this point of view, even if a child vomits every time he eats soy or his behavior worsens with the ingestion of dairy, it is not an allergy unless a blood or skin test can prove it.

To me, it is largely a question of semantics. It seems more accurate to use the term food sensitivity to describe behavioral reactions to foods in the absence of any laboratory proof of allergy. This will keep our friends the allergists from getting upset when we claim that food allergies are important in ADHD.

Multiple Food Elimination Diet How-To

I believe that the only real way to know if certain foods are affecting the hyperactivity, concentration, or impulsiveness of your child is to *remove the food from the diet and carefully observe the results*. You can use one of three different strategies to do this:

1. Eliminate just one food at a time.

2. Give the child only a few foods for a certain period of time — a stringent and difficult approach called the oligoantigenic or "few foods" diet.

3. Eliminate a number of the most likely allergic foods at once — an approach called the multiple food elimination diet.

Which strategy do I recommend? It depends. But first we'll discuss the pros and cons of each approach.

Single food elimination diet. To do this, you would pick a commonly allergenic food — for example, dairy products — and eliminate it entirely for a period of two to three weeks while closely observing the child's behavior. If there is no change at all, you can assume that there is no sensitivity to milk. You would then add dairy products back to the diet and try the next allergenic food on your list. Eliminating only one food at a time is simple and easy both for the parent and the child, but there is one major problem with this approach. What if the child is actually sensitive to two different foods? If Billy, for example, is sensitive to both wheat and dairy, you might not see much of a difference in his behavior when only wheat is removed from the diet because the dairy is still having a negative effect.

Doris Rapp, MD, who is mentioned earlier in this chapter, called this the *two-tack principle*. If you have two tacks stuck in the bottom of your foot, and you only remove one of them, your foot is still going to hurt, and you might not notice a lot of difference in how much pain you have.

Oligoantigenic or "few foods" diet. This diet narrows the child's food choices down to a bare minimum, usually including meat, rice or potato, one type of fruit, and one type of vegetable. Children may rapidly improve on such a diet, but it's quite stringent, hard to stick with, and may not be nutritionally adequate long-term. It may be suitable for children in whom there is a high suspicion of allergy and they have not responded to the other elimination techniques.

Drugs

ɔd elimination diet. This approach is the one I prefer. In this
ιe foods that most commonly cause food allergies is eliminated
ατ υιιτ. πιι υther foods are allowed. There are many variations on this diet,
but in the rest of this chapter I will discuss the one that has worked best in
my medical practice.

First, I recommend eliminating the following foods — all at once:

Dairy *(and any product with casein, which is the main protein in milk)*
Wheat *(and any product with gluten, the main protein in wheat,*
   rye, and barley)
Corn
Soy
Eggs
Nuts
Citrus
Any product with artificial colors, flavors, or preservatives

The first question most people ask when they hear about this is, "What
in the world *can* my child eat?" This is understandable because these foods
are certainly the most common items in most diets. However, don't fear —
there's plenty left to eat when these foods are eliminated. Your child can eat:

1. Any meat
2. Any fruit except citrus
3. Any vegetable
4. Any type of bean or bean flour
5. Rice, oats, quinoa, amaranth, buckwheat, millet, tapioca, and teff (these
   grains do not contain gluten); or flours made from these grains

Most children should stick with the diet for 14 to 21 days. **During this
elimination diet, it is *very important* to adhere to it strictly.** It is definitely not
enough to just "reduce" the amount of dairy or wheat your child is eating. To
be an accurate test, there must be complete avoidance. It is important to read
all labels thoroughly and be as vigilant as you can about keeping these foods
out of your child's body for the duration of the elimination period.

These days, it is easy to find an incredible array of substitutes in many
grocery stores and health food stores for most of the eliminated foods. There
are gluten- and casein-free crackers, cakes, cookies, and candy bars, which
often are free of other foods not allowed on the diet as well. There are waffles, pancakes, and brownie mixes made from rice or tapioca flour. My wife
makes a rice-based, dairy-free brownie mix that is quite delicious. If your
child really needs some kind of milk — although nutritionally, this is not

necessary — rice milk or hemp milk is widely available.

During the elimination period, watch your child carefully for changes in behavior, attention, activity level, and stool consistency. Take note of any other changes that may be important in your child's case. It can be very helpful to keep written notes during this time on a calendar or some other type of daily chart.

Again, I remind you that, during this trial period, it is crucial to be strict about avoiding these foods.

If, after the trial period, you have seen a significant change in your child's behavior, begin to add the foods back **one by one.** (If you've seen no change, refer to the section titled "What If My Child Does Not Respond During the Elimination Diet?") Wait three days between each addition of a food group and watch carefully to see if any food triggers or worsens the problem behaviors.

This is a good time for us to check back with Joshua, the boy I introduced at the beginning of this chapter. When we left the story, Joshua had just spent 14 days on his multi-food elimination diet, with major changes already evident. On day 15, Joshua was allowed to have all the milk and dairy products he wanted. He was watched carefully for that day and two more days, and there was no regression in his behavior. Dairy was OK for this child.

On the fourth day, wheat was introduced, and he ate all the bread, crackers, and pasta he wanted. By the end of this day, his hyperactivity had returned; by the next day, he was almost back to his usual hyperactive state. All wheat and gluten products were discontinued again. In a couple of days, the behaviors resolved. Wheat and gluten were definitely implicated in his symptoms through this test.

The same process was repeated for soy, corn, eggs, nuts, and food coloring. In the end, wheat/gluten, eggs, and food additives turned out to be the culprits in provoking Joshua's ADHD-like symptoms. When Joshua stayed away from these foods, his behavior was better. He could cooperate and learn at school, and life at home became a joy rather than a nightmare. He wasn't a perfect child, and even on his diet was more active than many children, but it was all within the realm of normal, reasonable behavior for a child of his age.

If possible, enlist professional help during the elimination diet. I do not recommend that parents undertake the elimination diet on their own. This is not because of any nutritional shortfalls your child might suffer; this won't happen over such a short period of time. My rationale for recommending outside assistance is primarily because of the difficulty parents often encounter in sorting out the results. It helps a great deal to have a professional, such as a pediatrician or other specialist, involved to discuss the results of the diet with you from an objective standpoint.

When I recommend an elimination diet, I give the parents my phone number and e-mail so that they can contact me to ask questions or resolve confusing issues. The parents contact me often — especially during the phase where foods are added back. Sometimes, assessing which foods are really the culprits can prove difficult. So can discerning which behavior changes have to do with reintroduced foods versus changes that are normal variations in behavior.

Nutritional Issues When Foods Are Eliminated

Many parents ask me if they have to worry about nutritional deficiencies when children are on elimination diets or later on when certain foods are eliminated long-term. They wonder if their child will get enough protein or calcium or vitamins. In most cases, nutritional issues are not a significant problem, as long as a knowledgeable health care professional is monitoring the situation. This is another reason to have a health care practitioner along on this journey.

The elimination diet covers a relatively short period of time — two to three weeks for the full elimination and a few more weeks as foods are added back. As long as the child is eating a reasonable amount of food, nutritional deficiencies are unlikely. He or she will probably get the basic protein, carbohydrates, and fats needed to maintain health, and it is unlikely that vitamin content will be appreciably affected since the foods that are removed are not generally significant vitamin sources.

Concerned parents also ask, "What if my child turns out to be sensitive to one or more of these foods? Will it be hard to get good nutrition without milk, wheat, or nuts?" Again, the answer is generally no, with the exception of nutrients usually obtained through dairy products: calcium and vitamin D.

If your child turns out to be dairy sensitive, consider alternate sources of calcium and vitamin D. To make up the calcium gap in a child who is sensitive to dairy, load up on leafy greens, cabbage, tofu, and molasses, and give the child calcium-fortified rice milk or orange juice. A chewable calcium supplement appropriate for your child's age is a fine alternative.

Dairy is a source of protein as well, but protein is rarely an issue for children in our country unless their diets are very restricted. One example might be a vegetarian family that has used dairy as a main protein source, which could cause the elimination of dairy for sensitivity reasons to pose a problem. In that case, particular attention would need to be paid to other sources of protein, such as soy, beans, and nuts.

Vitamin D is added to cow's milk as a supplement, and recent research has shown that this vitamin is very important for good health and disease prevention. Lack of vitamin D is believed to be related to diseases such as asthma, autoimmune disease, Type I diabetes, cancer, and depression. Vitamin D can only be obtained through sunlight or foods supplemented with vitamin D.

Surprising numbers of children are vitamin D-deficient, especially in the northern latitudes. Why the increased numbers of vitamin D-deficient children up north? Since vitamin D is produced in the skin when sunlight strikes it, folks with less sun exposure produce less. The sun is the best source of vitamin D, and sunscreen-free sun exposure a few times a week — short of the amount of time required to cause sunburn — will help produce adequate levels of Vitamin D. Children are increasingly deficient in this vitamin because they are outside less; when they are, they wear sunscreen and hats that block vitamin D production. At this writing, Canada has already raised the recommended daily requirement of this vitamin from 400 international units (IU) to 1000, and it is likely that the United States will do so soon.

For children who do not drink milk, a multivitamin that contains the minimum daily requirement of vitamin D for their age group is an excellent idea.

Aside from these considerations, there is no reason to be concerned that a child who is avoiding certain foods while on the elimination diet will have any significant nutritional deficiencies.

What if My Child Does Not Respond During the Elimination Diet?

What if you don't see any positive changes during the elimination diet? This is a tricky question. One might conclude that the child's problems must not be related to these foods and that it's time to return to the normal diet.

However, this conclusion is premature. A number of parents have told me they didn't really notice significant changes in behavior while their child was on the elimination diet, but when they started to add back the foods, they observed a significant *worsening* of behavior. In other words, the child may not seem to improve much on the elimination diet, but when the foods are reintroduced into his diet, the ADHD symptoms get significantly worse than they were to begin with or during the elimination phase. I'm not totally sure why this happens, except that changes during the elimination phase can be on the subtle side and may not be so obvious until the behavior worsens again. It is also possible that some other foods not on the list for elimination are causing the problem. But in my experience, if a child with ADHD is not improved when these major food allergens are removed from the diet, she is unlikely to respond to the removal of other foods.

This is the point at which lab test results might prove useful. If, for instance, tomatoes have shown up as a highly positive food sensitivity on some food test, then tomatoes can be added to the list of foods to eliminate along with the other foods in the elimination diet. The same is true if mom or dad suspects any other particular food that is not on the list.

Are Some Children More or Less Likely to Respond to the Elimination Diet?

Some children seem to me more likely than others to respond to the elimination diet (in other words, more likely to show behavior changes during one of the two phases of the diet). This would mainly include children who have other significant allergy symptoms such as asthma, hay fever, or eczema. It would also include children with significant gastrointestinal symptoms like stomach aches, constipation or diarrhea. However, children without any of these symptoms do sometimes respond to the diet as well, so I might still recommend elimination diets for children without any allergy symptoms. I also have observed that elimination diets seem less successful in children who have the inattention type of ADHD without the hyperactivity aspect. For some reason, these kids just don't seem to respond as well to the elimination diets, so I often do not conduct them unless other factors point to food sensitivity.

"But My Child Will *Never* Stick to This Diet!"

I know this is not an easy intervention. It takes determination and persistence. Many parents are very concerned that their child will refuse to eat anything at all or will become ill. The fact is that, in all my years of practice, I have never seen a child simply refuse to eat or become ill from undergoing the elimination diet. Certainly, I have seen many kids become upset because they are not getting what they are used to eating.

This is quite understandable, but as a parent, you need to weigh the short-term frustration your child is feeling against the possible long-term benefits. If you can find and eliminate a food or foods that cause the chronic behavioral and neurological difficulties of ADHD, surely it is worth the two or three weeks of effort it will entail.

What if you do find a food that significantly increases ADHD symptoms? Does that mean your child will never be able to eat that food again? Will you have to be a strict and stringent member of the Food Police until your child turns 18?

Not at all. Once you see the pattern of reaction that a child has to a certain food, you can decide whether it is worth giving it to him or her at certain times. For instance, let's say that Laurie gets hyperactive and loses focus for three or four hours after eating wheat. Her parents may decide that it is OK to let her have wheat at a birthday party on a weekend. They know what kind of reaction to expect and can make the choice to let her ride it out instead of depriving her of birthday treats. If, on the other hand, the behavioral reaction is too severe, or lasts for three days instead of three hours, they might decide it is rarely worth allowing.

Also, some children who demonstrate sensitivities to foods in the elimination diet seem able to tolerate one or more foods to which they are sensitive as long as they don't eat them too often. They have no reaction, for example, if they consume the food only once every few days or once a week. If they start to eat that food daily, however, the ADHD behaviors come back in full force. In these instances, it appears that whatever reaction the child has to this food needs to build to a certain level before behavioral symptoms appear. This is the basis of what is known as a "rotation diet" in which foods are rotated so that no one food is eaten daily. Full rotation diets are very difficult to follow on a long-term basis, but some people do use them.

Whether you follow a structured rotation diet or take a more casual approach, you may find that giving an allergenic food only at intervals will allow the child's sensitivity reaction to dissipate before symptoms occur. This can all be worked out by trial and error once the initial sensitivities and reactions are determined. The only way to reach this point is by carrying out the elimination diet in as strict a fashion as possible.

Finally, even with the best of intentions, mistakes will be made. At some point, the school or Grandma will either forget or take pity on the child and give him a cookie or a slice of pizza. This does not mean that all is lost. Just go on with the diet as planned, noting carefully any type of behavioral changes that occur.

What about the Feingold Diet?

Many parents have heard, somewhere along the line, about the Feingold diet as a treatment for ADHD. This diet was one of the first attempts at treating children with ADHD with nutritional intervention.

In 1973, Feingold published a study claiming that 50 percent of treated children improved after elimination of all artificial food colorings, flavors, preservatives, as well as naturally occurring *salicylates*. Salicylates are chemicals that are naturally present in a number of foods, including many fruits and vegetables.

Here is a partial list of foods and medicines that contain natural salicylates as would be found in the Feingold diet:

Almonds	Currants	Plums
Apples	Grapes	Prunes
Apricots	Nectarines	Raisins
Aspirin	Oil of wintergreen	Rose hip
Berries	Oranges	Tangelos
Cherries	Peaches	Tangerines
Cloves	Peppers (bell, chili)	Tea
Coffee	Pickles	Tomatoes
Cucumbers		

After a certain time on this diet, the fruits and vegetables could be added back, leaving the child on a fairly normal diet. Artificial colors, flavors, and preservatives would be eliminated permanently in the Feingold plan.

This diet became the focus of great controversy. A number of follow-up studies were done, many of which could not replicate Feingold's initial findings. It is difficult to do studies of such a complicated diet, and this may be the reason subsequent research didn't support the Feingold hypothesis.

The general consensus of scientific opinion at this point is that the Feingold diet probably works for some percentage of children with ADHD, but not for as many as originally claimed. The Feingold Diet is now presented as the Feingold Program, which has been updated from the original version.

My own opinion is that the Feingold Diet probably does work for a percentage of children with ADHD, but this is mainly because of the elimination of artificial colors, flavors, and certain preservatives, and not because it eliminates the salicylate-containing fruits and vegetables. It does not seem reasonable to me that a high percentage of children would be sensitive to so many perfectly healthful fresh fruits and vegetables. I have, however, had at least one family tell me that their child did much better when avoiding all of these substances and relapsed when just the fruits and vegetables were added, so there may be a small subset of children who do have this salicylate sensitivity.

In any case, Ben Feingold deserves much credit for being the first researcher to focus on the importance of nutrition and food sensitivities as factors that contribute to ADHD.

The Bottom Line

The bottom line for me is that many children with ADHD are sensitive to foods they eat, and removing the offending foods from the diet can produce significant improvement. In some children, it will be dramatic; in others, not so dramatic. Although the task of pinpointing which foods may be affecting your child is not simple and takes a real effort, I believe that the payoff is well worth it. Any time I see one child whose nervous system is compromised by the foods he or she is eating eventually become calmer, more focused, and live a happier life without medication, it is immensely rewarding for me and for the whole family. This is why I believe that every child with ADHD deserves at least serious consideration of whether food sensitivities are playing a significant role in his or her difficulties.

Chapter 7
Omega-3 Fatty Acids and ADHD

Let me start this chapter with a recommendation as unequivocal as any you will get in this entire book: **In my opinion, *every single child who has ADHD* would benefit from taking, or needs to have at least *tried*, a daily omega-3 fatty acid supplement.**

I say this based on two strong bodies of evidence: the extensive research that exists about omega-3s and ADHD, and my own personal experience with many children who have taken omega-3s. Time and time again, parents have noticed significant and positive changes from this single supplement.

What kind of changes? Parents report that their children demonstrate improved ability to focus and concentrate, decreased hyperactivity or emotionality, greater cooperativeness, and less oppositional behavior — in fact, there can be improvements in any aspect of ADHD-related behavior simply from adding this supplement.

I am not saying that every child will have a dramatic response to omega-3s. In some children the results will be subtle or there may be no effect at all. However, the possibility of significant positive results is high and the risk of adverse effects is extremely low. Coupled with the fact that research indicates that children with ADHD have abnormally low levels of omega-3s, I see no reason not to recommend at least a trial for every child with ADHD.

Omega-3 Basics

Remember how I let you off easy in the discussion on polyunsaturated fats, promising to get back to it later? Well, now is later. While this information can get a bit complicated, understanding at least the basics is important — not only for your child with ADHD, but for your own health as well.

Recall that three major classes of fats are found in foods: *saturated*, *monounsaturated*, and *polyunsaturated*. These classes distinguish between different types of fat in terms of the *number* of double and single bonds they contain in the long chains of carbon that comprise fat molecules (also known as fatty acids). The location of these double bonds alters the shape of the fatty acid molecule, which in turn has an impact on its actions in the body.

Within each class, various types of fatty acid are distinguished from one another by the *location* of double bonds along their carbon chains.

Here, we are most concerned with the polyunsaturated fats, a class that includes the omega-3s (which have a double bond at the third carbon), the omega-6s (double bond at the sixth carbon), and the omega-9s (double bond at the ninth carbon). All of these are necessary for the normal function of the human body. Some fats can be built within the body from others that we consume, but **these omega fats, which are *essential*, can only come from our diets.** Some are virtually omnipresent in the human diet (the omega-6s) while others are more scarce (the omega-3s).

I provide these biochemical facts for those who are scientifically-minded but you need not remember the details. Just remember this: *Omega-3 fatty acids are essential for normal brain function; we can't make them ourselves; and most of us don't get enough of them.*

The two main omega-3 fatty acids that are important in ADHD (as well as for immune system health, heart health, and overall well-being) are called DHA and EPA. These omega-3 fatty acids have two vital functions: they are an essential part of cell membranes, and they have *anti-inflammatory* effects throughout the body. Inflammation is an immune system response to an irritant (such as an injury or allergen) or to an *antigen* (bacteria, virus, or other 'bug' that can invade the body) designed to get the 'bad guys' out and restore a state of healthful balance. It usually involves some combination of swelling, redness, pain, and temporary loss of function. A fever is a form of inflammation; so is the swelling of a sprained ankle; so is an allergic reaction. Modern research has demonstrated an important role for chronic, low-grade inflammation in many kinds of disorders, including those of the nervous system and cardiovascular system.

The Role of Omega-3s

First, **omega-3s are a crucial part of the cell membranes that surround the cells of the brain and nervous system.** Cell membranes form a border around cells, separating what is inside from what is outside. They are not just a passive barrier, however; cell membranes are responsible for regulating almost every substance that gets into and out of cells, and this regulation is crucial for normal cell function. In the brain and nervous system, good cell membrane function will affect neurotransmitter levels, signaling between cells, the creation, growth, and development of connections between nerve cells, and may other vital functions. Omega-3 fatty acids are especially malleable, and their fluidity is part of the reason they are the best building material for cell membranes that work optimally. Omega-6s are also present in the brain, but in smaller amounts; they are not as malleable or as fluid as omega-3s, and do not function there as efficiently.

The second basic characteristic of omega-3 fatty acids is that they are *anti-inflammatory* — **that is, they tend to decrease inflammation wherever they operate in the body.** This can be in the brain, the gut, the skin, the immune system — really, just about anywhere. Omega-6 fatty acids, on the other hand, are *pro-inflammatory* — they tend to promote inflammation. This isn't all bad; there has to be a balance between the ability to mount an inflammatory response and to suppress it.

The balance between O-3s and O-6s is the most crucial aspect of this fatty acid picture. These two classes of fats compete for the same enzymes in the body — and those enzymes are the biochemical keys that enable these fats to do their many jobs. It is not only crucial to get enough of each type of fat, but for *the balance of what is ingested to be correct.* Although omega-6 deficiency is all but unheard of, lack of omega-3s is practically guaranteed in the average American child's diet.

Omega-3s Are Lacking in Almost Every Modern Person's Diet

Ready for a shocking but indisputable fact? **Practically the entire modern, industrialized world is deficient in omega-3 fatty acids, and this may be one reason that epidemics of chronic disease have overtaken our society.**

How could this be? To answer this question, we'll need to look back in history at the diets of our ancestors and at the massive changes that have occurred in our food supply in only the last century. When we look at the modern diet in the context of what our species has consumed since it first walked the planet, the current imbalance becomes quite easy to understand.

The omega-3 fatty acids are most highly concentrated in fish and other seafood. But they are also present in animals that spend their lives grazing on brush or grass; in eggs from chickens that eat natural, wild diets; and in dairy products from grass-fed cows. Other sources of omega-3s in the human diet are flaxseed, avocados, walnuts and some other nuts. A few vegetables are also good sources, especially purslane (which is considered a weed in the U.S. but is known as an edible in many other parts of the world).

It is important to realize that the vast majority of human evolution occurred before we even had agriculture. Paleolithic (Stone Age) people did not cultivate grain — one of the major sources of omega-6 fats in the modern diet — and ate very little of it. A Paleolithic person's estimated dietary ratio of omega-3s to omega-6s was about 1:1 or 1:2. And then, suddenly, about 10,000 years ago, with the advent of agriculture, more and more grains loaded with omega-6s were being produced. Omega-6 fatty acids come from seeds, grains, and the animals that eat them. Wheat, rice, corn, and soy are all full of omega-6 fatty acids. Until quite recently, however, there was still more of a balance, as many staple foods, such as meat and dairy, were still raised on wild grass, brush, and other natural feed.

Over the last 100 years, this ratio (lower omega-3s to higher omega-6s) has gotten even worse. For many people, almost everything they eat is somehow tied to grains. We now eat wheat and corn and soy and cook with their oils. Our beef cows and pigs and chickens are fed on these grains. Our milk and diary comes from grain-fed cows. We hardly ever eat some of the wild vegetables containing omega-3. We don't eat enough seafood and even the farmed fish are lower in omega-3s than wild fish. The result is that we have an omega-6 to omega-3 ratio of 15 or 20 to 1 instead of 1:1.

Why This Ratio Matters

An imbalance between omega-3 and omega-6 fats in the body has very serious implications for our overall health:

1. It pushes the body toward an inflammatory state, which has been linked with a large number of health conditions — the same conditions that are rising most meteorically in our population; and,

2. It alters the balance of fats used as 'building blocks' for the brain and nervous system, which in turn impedes our brain's optimal function — an issue of special importance when it comes to children with ADHD and other neurological issues.

In fact, this lack of omega-3 fatty acids (whether due to low intake or too high an omega-6 to omega-3 ratio) has been associated with a mind-boggling array of diseases and health conditions, including heart disease, autoimmune disease, allergy, diabetes and the metabolic syndrome (also known as 'pre-diabetes'), depression, bipolar disease, schizophrenia, and autism. Most importantly for us in the context of this book is the strong association that has been found between omega-3 fatty acid status and ADHD.

A shortage of omega-3s has even been found to have an adverse impact on general infant neurological development. Research has shown that formula-fed babies whose formula was not supplemented with omega-3 fatty acids (which occur naturally in breast milk) had slower neurological development than those who had it added to their formula. DHA, one of the two main types of omega-3, is now added to infant formulas because of abundant evidence that formula-fed infants were at a disadvantage compared to those fed naturally DHA-rich breast milk.

Research on ADHD and Omega-3 Fatty Acids

Researchers have been investigating the relationship between ADHD and omega-3 deficiency for a number of years. Following is a summary of the results.

- **Children with ADHD have lower omega-3 levels in their bodies than non-ADHD children.**

Although we're most interested in the concentration of omega-3s in the child's brain, we can't very well extract them directly from that particular organ — so we measure the level of these fats in the child's blood and/or red blood cells. In almost every study comparing children with ADHD to children without ADHD, children with ADHD have less omega-3 in their blood or some other abnormal imbalance of fatty acids. This is especially worrisome because even the 'normal' kids we are comparing them to do not get enough omega-3s and their "normal" amount is probably way too low.

We really don't know why ADHD children have low omega-3. (It is also true that children with learning disabilities have inadequate blood omega-3 levels.) It doesn't seem to be related to their intake of these fats. Although this has not been carefully studied, we can presume that children with ADHD eat the same (inadequate) amount of omega-3s as children without ADHD. One small study showed that ADHD adolescents ate the same amount of omega-3 and omega-6 fatty acids as those without ADHD, yet still had less omega-3 fatty acids and more omega-6 fatty acids in their blood.[1] If this is so, there must be some abnormality in their ability to digest, metabolize, or retain omega-3s in their systems. This is an area where more research is needed.

- **In most but not all studies, when children with ADHD are given omega-3 supplements, their symptoms improve.**

A number of research studies have been performed to measure the response of ADHD children to omega-3 supplements. Most have demonstrated positive effects, although some have not.

In one study, a British research team gave 40 children with ADHD and learning disabilities either a fish oil supplement or an olive oil placebo every day for three months. At the end of that time, the children taking the fish oil improved significantly in their ADHD symptoms as well as in measures of their learning ability. In fact, on almost every measure, including attention, hyperactivity and cognition, the children taking fish oil had substantial improvements, whereas those taking the placebo had minimal or no improvement.[2]

In another study, this same group of researchers looked at children with Developmental Coordination Disorder, a diagnostic category that includes ADHD, learning issues and clumsiness.[3] This study was bigger, involving

117 children, but the treatment was the same — either omega-3 fatty acids or a placebo. Not only did the children on omega-3s improve in their ADHD symptoms, but their learning rates shot up significantly. Look at these numbers after three months of the research and showing the mean increases:

Reading: Subjects taking omega-3s: **9.5 months increase**
Subjects taking placebo: **3.3 months increase**

Spelling: Subjects taking omega-3s: **6.6 months increase**
Subjects taking placebo: **1.2 months increase**

During the three months of the study, the ones who got the fish oil made a 9.5-month improvement in reading while the ones taking the placebo made only a three-month improvement!

Amazing, right? Whether you're a scientist or not, you can see that the results of this latter study were pretty dramatic. You might be wondering why you haven't heard about this sooner. Well, there's a reason, and if you'll pardon me for going on a brief rant first, I'll tell you what it is.

Time Out for a Brief Rant

Imagine, for a moment, what would happen if a study about a new pharmaceutical medication emerged with these same results. Think of it: a completely safe medication that could dramatically improve learning and decrease ADHD symptoms! I'll tell you what would happen. Pharmaceutical company representatives would be in every pediatrician's office the next day, waving copies of the study and urging them to prescribe the new med. Suddenly, millions of dollars would be available for follow-up studies. Other pharmaceutical companies would immediately start working on their own 'me-too' variations of the drug. They'd make sure this hit the media in a big way; newspaper and television headlines would scream about *The New ADHD Cure*!

Guess what happened when the omega-3 study results came out? Mostly nothing.

There certainly weren't any drug representatives in any pediatrician's office because companies can't patent fish oil and charge big money for it. There weren't any headlines, and although there have been a few small follow-up studies, this didn't cause the big research money to start flowing — as it most certainly would have if this study had been about a pharmaceutical product.

As a doctor who tries to treat children with ADHD, I become very frustrated at the lack of adequate research funding available for truly promising natural treatments. Results like those of the last two studies described here should stimulate large-scale studies, which could then, in turn, tell us so much more that we need to know about omega-3s and how to use them in ADHD. That did not happen because of the economics of our health care system — where research is most prominently funded by pharmaceutical companies. And then, of course, critics of natural treatments tell the world that pharmaceuticals are the only good choice because there's 'just not enough research to be sure other treatments are effective.'

Okay...end of rant.

■ **Studies showing little or no benefits from the omega-3 trials tend to have flaws.**

To be fair and present both sides of the evidence, let's look at the research in which children with ADHD were given omega-3 supplements (vs. a placebo) and no improvement occurred in the treated group. Why would this be? First of all, that is just what happens as science evolves; rarely does every study come out the same way. Sometimes, the way a study was designed contributes to a negative result despite testing a substance that has shown benefit in prior studies.

To illustrate, let's use an actual study.[4] In this study, the children were given omega-3s or a placebo for four months, after which their parents filled out rating scales and a questionnaire known as the Continuous Performance Test as the means to determine differences. No advantage was found for the children taking omega-3. However, *all of the children in this study were already on Ritalin or some other psychostimulant* and were **not** taken off their medication during the four-month study. This means that, on average, most of their ADHD symptoms would have been corrected before the study began! It's not reasonable to expect omega-3s to show a measurable effect when children are already on a stimulant.

The research team did take the children off their medication for one day before the Continuous Performance Test, theorizing that almost all of the stimulant would leave their systems in that one day, thus producing a state that would demonstrate the effect of the omega-3s on a medication-free child. Although technically it is true that most of the medication is gone from the blood in 24 hours, anyone who has treated children with ADHD knows they are often not 'back to normal' 24 hours after a long-term medication is discontinued.

Another problem with this study is that only the omega-3 fat DHA was administered, without any EPA. Most of the studies indicating a positive effect from omega-3 used supplements containing both DHA and EPA. Another study that found no benefit — this one from Japan — also used only DHA.[5] Overall, I would say that most of the studies examining the effect of omega-3 fatty acids have shown a significant benefit and that there were some significant flaws in at least two of the studies that did not demonstrate a benefit.

Here a few more relevant points related to the effectiveness of omega-3s for ADHD (and learning disabled) children:

- Recent studies have shown that reduced blood flow in the brain may be at least part of the cause of various neurological and psychiatric issues. Omega-3 fatty acids have been shown to improve blood flow in the brain, possibly due to their anti-inflammatory effect.

- Omega-3 fatty acids appear to promote better learning in *anyone*, whether ADHD or a learning disability exists or there is no disability or disorder at all. In one study in South Africa, second graders were given a piece of bread containing either a fish spread or a placebo spread for six months. Tests of word recall and spelling showed significant improvement favoring the children who ate the fish spread.[6] (I'd like to see them try to get American kids to eat fish spread every day for lunch! School district lawyers would probably ban the idea, calling it cruel and unusual punishment.)

- Omega-3s may also help relieve depression in children. In one study on this topic, omega-3 fatty acids given to children with depression caused positive changes that were not seen in the children who took a placebo.[7]

- These benefits may all start before the baby is even born, at least as indicated in yet another study. It showed that babies whose mothers had the highest levels of DHA in their blood did better on measures of attention as early as **4 months old** and continuing until the middle of their second year of life.[8]

How to Make Sure Your Child Has Adequate Omega-3s

Assuming I've convinced you that your child needs to have more of these omega-3s in his or her system, how do you go about getting that to happen?

You could try getting your child to eat a whole lot of fish — at least one serving of a high omega-3 fish every day such as salmon, sardines, or herring. (First of all, good luck! Secondly, if your child is that cooperative about his or her diet, you probably wouldn't be reading this book in the first place.) But there is another potential drawback to this approach. Many types of fish — particularly tuna fish, which tends to be the most popular type of fish among children — have high levels of mercury, which we know is a neurological toxin. Eating any kind of fish every day without consuming too much mercury might prove to be a nearly impossible undertaking. For most families, increasing a child's fish consumption might be beneficial but eating enough of it to produce adequate levels of omega-3s is unlikely to be practical.

My recommendation for any child who has ADHD or similar issues is a fish oil supplement. Fish oil has two distinct advantages. First, it is the **richest natural source of pre-formed DHA and EPA**, and the labeling on the bottle tells you exactly how much of each of these fatty acids it contains. (Later I will tell you what to look for.) Second, as long as you buy your fish oils from a reputable company, you can be certain that mercury and other contaminants have been almost completely refined out of the oil, down to the nanogram. This kind of processing makes fish oil a much safer DHA and EPA source than fish itself.

Fish oil supplements for children come in a number of forms, including capsules that must be swallowed or liquids that can be taken from a spoon or mixed with anything that your child will eat. Also available are chewable capsules, gummies, and products of various other consistencies.

Why are there so many forms? I hate to say it, but fish oil has the unfortunate quality of tasting like...fish. If a child can't swallow a capsule — and the capsules unfortunately are not small — the liquid and some other forms could have a fishy flavor even though most brands have added ingredients (strawberry, lemon, orange) to make them more palatable to children.

My experience is that more than 95 percent of parents find some form of fish oil that their child will eventually adapt to. Some kids actually like the liquid or chewable tablets a lot; some don't. Some kids learn to swallow capsules much more quickly when given the choice between developing this skill or taking the oil in liquid form. Others will ingest it via some food like peanut butter or a strong juice like orange or grape juice. (Hint: don't try to mix this stuff in water or milk. Oil and water don't mix, and you'll end up with a puddle of oil and fishy-tasting milk or water.)

If you convey the attitude that this is important to your child, just as if he or she was taking a necessary medication, then you will find a way. Kids are adaptable; I often hear that giving the omega-3 oil was difficult at first but that eventually the child learned to like or at least accept some brand, flavor or form. It may take a little persistence and yield a few unused bottles of fish oil — which you can take yourself. You probably need it!

One caution about the little chewable capsules: Kids tend to like them, but you need to be aware that some have very little DHA/EPA per capsule. With one of the best-known chewable brands, for instance, 10 are required to equal ½ teaspoon of liquid, which is a very basic dose for a smaller child.

Therefore, that bottle of chewable pills represents nine days' worth, which makes it about five times more expensive than a liquid.

How about Flax Oil?

Flaxseed oil is touted as an excellent source of omega-3 fats and indeed it is, but there's a drawback. Vegetable sources of omega-3s contain a different omega-3 than those we've been discussing up to this point: they are rich in *alpha-linolenic acid* (ALA). While ALA can serve as a precursor (building block) to produce DHA and EPA, we're currently unclear about how efficient this process is in the human body. In some studies, very little ALA is converted to DHA and EPA after it's consumed; in others, the efficiency of the conversion is greater — that is, more ALA is transformed into DHA and EPA. Few of these studies have involved children. Therefore, you need to be skeptical when commercial food products boast about how much "omega-3" they contain. If you read the label carefully, you will see this is often in the form of ALA, without any DHA or EPA.

There's no arguing the point that DHA and EPA are the most crucial of the omega-3s, particularly for children with ADHD. The research on this is conclusive. It stands to reason that, if we're not sure whether taking flax oil will raise DHA and EPA levels, we're better off giving children the real thing. Ground flax seed, on the other hand, is a good way to supplement a child's diet with needed nutrients and fiber and is worth adding to smoothies, yogurt, nut butters, and hot cereals if your child likes it.

Other foods rich in vegetarian-sourced omega-3 (ALA) have the same potential shortcoming as flax oil in terms of the type of omega-3 they contain. Walnuts and avocados fall into this category, and both are very healthy foods that can only help a child's nutrition levels. But to have real impact on ADHD symptoms, you will need to also supply plentiful EPA and DHA to your child.

Omega-3 Supplements for Vegetarians

Vegetarians can increase the amount of omega-3s in the diet with flaxseeds, flax oil, and other sources of ALA (walnuts, soybeans, omega-3 eggs, green leafy vegetables) and hope that the child can convert these to DHA and EPA. One study done in India showed that children with ADHD who were given flax oil and antioxidants did increase their levels of EPA and DHA and in turn decreased their ADHD symptoms.[9]

The ratio of omega-6s and omega-3s in the overall diet may be an important factor in this conversion. In other words, children whose diets consist of more omega-6s and less omega-3s overall are less likely to convert the ALA into EPA and DHA. I advise those who use a vegetarian supplement to make sure their child gets minimal omega-6 fatty acids. (Primary sources of omega-6 include grains, eggs, nuts, chicken, and especially seed oils like sunflower and soybean oils.)

Another option is to administer supplements made from algae, which is one of the few known vegetarian sources of DHA and EPA. Algae-sourced omega-3 supplements, however, tend to contain mostly DHA and little or no EPA.

Finding the Right Dose

I have a confession. Although I have told you, with great confidence, about the benefits of omega-3 fatty acids for ADHD (and for just about everything else), I have not told you about some things we don't know yet. And there are two important things we don't know. First, we don't know what the optimal dose of omega-3s for ADHD is; and secondly, we do not know the optimal combination of EPA and DHA.

After all this, am I telling you we're clueless about how much to take? Not at all. We do know a lot. From the studies I have cited, we know about some doses and combinations that have worked for ADHD and other conditions. We just haven't been able to do enough research to hone in on what the *optimal* dose would be. This goes back to the funding problem I was complaining about earlier. If omega-3s received the same levels of funding enjoyed by every new psychostimulant that comes off the assembly line, we would have abundant studies in which various doses were given and compared to control groups. We would know which dosage amounts and which ratios of DHA to EPA worked best in most situations. Unfortunately, we are not there yet.

When I recommend a dose, I employ the doses and combinations used in the studies that had positive results as a starting point, adjusting them as needed to optimize the child's response. This can only be done in the context of the physician/practitioner-patient relationship. I can make the basic recommendations below with confidence, but I strongly advise that you work with a health care professional to find the optimal dose for your child.

- Use a combination of EPA and DHA — this is one thing that all the successful studies had in common. These fatty acids seem to have complementary functions; and they don't appear to have as pronounced an effect when used alone. Some studies used three times as much EPA as DHA; some used three times as much DHA as EPA. Since we don't know which is better, I like to use a product with a relative balance of the two. Don't use a product with only DHA or only EPA.

- Some studies also used a small amount of omega-6 fatty acids, especially GLA (gamma-linolenic acid). This may seem odd in light of the fact that our diets generally produce too high a ratio of omega-6s compared to omega-3s. However, gamma-linolenic acid is a unique omega-6 in that it is metabolized to an *anti-inflammatory* fat, which decreases the influence of the other omega-6s. I don't specifically recommend a product that has GLA, but doing so should not cause any problems in children with ADHD.

- I would use *at least* 500 to 1000 milligrams (mg) total DHA + EPA per day, depending on the size of the child. I might start with 500 mg in a four- or five-year-old, increasing to 1000 for most children aged seven and up. Teenagers may need an even higher dose. So, for example, a supplement with 300 mg of EPA and 200 mg DHA would be about right for a smaller child.

- We really don't know what the upper limit of omega-3s should be. In one Japanese study, nine children with ADHD were given a starting dose of 16.2 *grams* of DHA/EPA — that's about 16,000 milligrams! — and received this dose for eight weeks, throughout which researchers tracked their blood levels of these fats.[10] Only one child had slightly loose stools, and no one dropped out of the study. ADHD behaviors improved significantly, although that aspect of the study is open to question because there was no control group. This study demonstrates that you don't really need to worry about giving too much omega-3 to your child; in my medical practice, my concern is that I might not be recommending enough!

Why We Don't Routinely Test Children's Omega-3 Levels

Some studies, like the one in Japan just mentioned, actually measured blood or red blood cell levels of DHA and EPA. So one might wonder why I don't simply recommend this kind of testing to see if children need more omega-3s and whether they are getting enough by taking fish oil supplements. This is a very good question. The answer is that we don't know enough about what the "correct" levels of EPA and DHA should be in the blood, in either normal children or children with ADHD. Recent research does tend to confirm that blood levels of these substances are a good indication of brain levels in animals, but we are not sure of this in humans. We are also not sure if optimal blood levels for ADHD children are the same as those for more typical children. At this point, these measurements are not widely used for determining an individual child's need for omega-3s, but this could change very quickly as new information becomes available.

Are There Any Adverse Effects with Fish Oils?

Fish oils are very safe. When given at a dose of three grams or less per day, they have 'Generally Recognized as Safe' (GRAS) status in the U.S. This means that the Food and Drug Administration considers fish oil to be basically a food and has designated it to be free of safety issues when given in reasonable amounts.

Two types of side effects, both minor, can occur with fish oil supplementation:

Digestive: Fish oils can cause a fishy aftertaste, which can emerge in the form of the dreaded 'fish burp.' They can also cause stomach upsets of various kinds (as can most foods we eat). Loose stools are infrequently a problem for some children. Most kids do not have these side effects, but they can occur. Overall, fish oil is well tolerated by the digestive tract in most children (and adults).

Helpful tips:

- Try a different brand, try taking the fish oil with food, or try changing the time of day the supplement is taken.
- If your child can swallow a capsule, freezing the capsule often prevents the fishy aftertaste or burps.

Decreased blood clotting: Large amounts of fish oil can decrease the ability of the blood to coagulate by inhibiting platelets function. This is often referred to as a 'blood thinning' effect, although there is no actual thinning involved. In children, this side effect occurs in theory only; I have never seen or heard of a child who had a problem with blood coagulation because of fish oil. The exception would be the child who is on an anticoagulant medication such as Coumadin. Always check with your doctor before using supplements if your child is on a prescription medication.

You should discontinue administering fish oil, and almost all other supplements, if your child is scheduled for surgery.

How Long Will It Take to Work?

Theoretically, the full effect of fish oil will take months to develop because it takes that long for EPA and DHA to saturate those all-important nerve cell membranes. So I tend to advise parents that they are not likely to see immediate, dramatic improvement.

Yet it's not uncommon for parents to report fairly immediate results. Moms or dads sometimes tell me that they notice better attention or less hyperactivity within a week of starting the fish oil. This could be just the placebo effect, but it's also possible that some of the benefits — especially the anti-inflammatory effect — occur much sooner than we think.

Once there is improvement, it should continue even if the omega-3s are missed for a few days. However, I've heard from a number of families that they saw a noticeable difference in their children's behavior on the days they missed a dose. I'm even aware of kids who ask mom for their 'brain vitamin' before going to school, saying that it helps them while they're there. Again, this may be a placebo effect or perhaps they really can tell the difference.

A Few Words about the Placebo Effect

Up until now, I've talked about the placebo effect primarily in terms of research studies, which need a 'control group' in order to ascertain whether some medication or supplement is really working or whether the changes are due to the placebo effect. This implies a kind of negative view of the placebo effect — something we need to get rid of or take out of the equation, and for certain types of research this is correct.

Actually, however, the placebo effect can represent something wonderful: the power of belief to influence how a body or a mind reacts to any type of experience or intervention. In terms of health care, if someone believes in the power of any medical intervention, it has a much better chance of working. This belief has the power to change any function of the human body.

If I give someone a sugar pill and tell them it will lower their blood pressure, it very often does! In some way, belief harnesses an innate healing ability of the mind and body. It works at a subconscious level to actually change the body in a specific way — in this example, altering the complex set of mechanisms that control blood pressure.

As parents, we can use this power of belief in very positive ways. Whether you give fish oil or a multiple vitamin or make changes in the child's diet, *the message you send about your faith in the intervention will have a powerful effect on your child and on its success.* I would urge you to be very conscious of how you talk and act in front of your child about any action you take regarding ADHD. Once you decide to do it, let your child know unequivocally that you believe it will really help. By doing so, you will significantly increase the chances of success.

Omega-3 Fatty Acids: A Summary

Just in case you're not completely convinced that your child is likely to benefit from fish oil supplements, allow me to summarize my main points on omega-3s:

- Omega-3 fatty acids are crucial for our health — especially for optimal brain function.
- Most of us do not get enough of these fatty acids in our diets.
- Children with ADHD have even lower levels of omega-3 fatty acids in their bodies than other children, who also tend to have lower levels than they probably should.
- Studies have shown that taking omega-3 fatty acid supplements can improve both ADHD symptoms and learning. I have seen this improvement firsthand with frequency in children whom I have treated.
- Omega-3 supplements have almost no significant risks or side effects.

Did I mention that I recommend these supplements unequivocally for children with ADHD?

Chapter 8
The Minerals: Iron, Zinc, and Magnesium in ADHD

A significant deficiency of minerals can affect virtually every bodily function, including the contraction and relaxation of muscles, the sending of impulses along the nerves, the regularity of the heartbeat, and the ability of blood cells to carry oxygen from the lungs through the rest of the body. When mineral nutrition is inadequate, mood, focus, attention, and ability to sit still can all be affected.

Minerals come from the earth and from the water we drink. They are absorbed into our bodies through the walls of the intestines, where they serve many purposes. Natural, whole foods have abundant mineral content; a person who eats a healthful diet of unprocessed foods is likely to have adequate mineral levels. But with the advent of highly processed diets — from which much of the mineral content has been drained — people are having more difficulty achieving adequate mineral nutrition. When a child subsists on white flour, sweets, junk food, and other modern kid-friendly staples, a deficiency of some minerals is entirely possible. The most common minerals that become deficient in children, and the ones that have been most closely linked to ADHD, are iron, magnesium, and zinc.

Iron Deficiency in ADHD

Although few doctors are aware of it, several research studies have shown that a deficiency of iron correlates with the presence of ADHD and with the severity of symptoms; this means that iron deficiency is often present in children with ADHD, and the more severe that deficiency, the more severe the symptoms. More than one study has shown that ADHD symptoms improve when iron deficiency is treated.

Very few pediatricians or other doctors check iron levels as part of routine child care or in children with ADHD. Many do check for anemia, but this more common test will *not* identify iron deficiency.

Anemia is an abnormality of the red blood cells that sometimes (but not always) indicates an iron deficiency. A number of other medical conditions can lead to anemia. On the other hand, iron deficiency can — and often does — exist in the absence of anemia. Therefore, if your child had a blood count taken and you were told it was normal, it means that your child isn't anemic

— but could still have an iron deficiency.

Testing for iron deficiency is pretty straightforward: a simple blood test is performed to measure the total level of iron stored in the body. The most common and accurate of the handful of tests used for this purpose is the *serum ferritin* test. Ferritin is a storage form of iron, and if its levels are low in the serum (the watery component of the blood), total iron stores are low as well. Research has shown that low serum ferritin is strongly associated with ADHD as well as other learning and neurological issues that we'll cover later.

Proof That Iron Could Be a Factor in Your Child's ADHD

Let's consider the plausibility of the ADHD-low iron connection. Why would low levels of iron be associated with ADHD?

Most of us think of iron deficiency anemia as something that causes fatigue, lack of energy, and perhaps decreased ability to fight off infections. Iron also happens to play some important roles in the neurological system, however. It therefore makes perfect biological sense that iron status affects ADHD symptoms as well as other learning and behavioral problems.

There is a relationship between ADHD and neurotransmitter imbalance, especially imbalances of noradrenalin and dopamine. It turns out that iron is essential for the optimal production of both of these neurotransmitters because it is needed for the most important enzyme involved in their production. And studies in animals have shown that iron levels influence the metabolism and transport of these neurotransmitters in the brain.

We know that iron deficiency anemia, which occurs when iron deficiency affects the hemoglobin in red blood cells, causes significant learning problems in infants and children. At least 16 research studies performed in countries around the world found that cognitive, motor, and/or social/emotional functioning were reduced in infants who had iron deficiency anemia when compared to infants without iron deficiency anemia.[1] A number of studies have related iron deficiency to difficulties with learning and behavior in older children.

In 2004, a physician named Eric Konofal compared iron status in two groups of children: 57 with ADHD and 27 without, using the serum ferritin test.[2] Then he correlated the results with the severity of ADHD in the children who had the disorder. The findings:

1. Average ferritin level was 23 in the children with ADHD...and a robust 44 in the controls (children without ADHD).

2. Serum ferritin levels were abnormally low—less than 30—in 84 percent

110

of the children with ADHD and in only 18 percent of the controls!

3. Within the group of children with ADHD, lower serum ferritin levels correlated with worse scores on the ADHD rating scales, especially in measures of attention and cognition.

In 2008, this same doctor and colleagues reported the effects of giving iron therapy to children with ADHD in *Pediatric Neurology*, a highly respected medical journal.[3] In this study, they began with 23 children who had both ADHD and serum ferritin levels lower than 30. Eighteen of them received iron supplements for three weeks and five received a placebo. The results:

1. The serum ferritin levels in the children given iron supplements increased from an average of 29 at the beginning of the study to 55 at the end of the study.

2. The overall ADHD rating scale and another measure, the Clinical Global Impressions Scale, improved significantly in the group treated with iron, but **not** in the children receiving the placebo.

3. Outcomes on the Conners Rating Scale questionnaire also improved more in the iron group than the placebo group, but not quite enough to reach statistical significance (which means that this aspect of the results might have been due to chance).

Overall, this study showed that iron treatment of those children who had ADHD and low ferritin levels reduced their ADHD symptoms significantly.

I need not review all the other research in detail, but there are at least three other studies indicating that iron deficiency is related to ADHD symptoms in general or in specific aspects of ADHD. Only one such study failed to find a correlation.

Getting Your Child Tested

Given that most studies have found a correlation between ADHD and low iron stores, **I recommend that all children with ADHD have their iron levels checked — specifically by *measuring serum ferritin*.** The standard blood test for anemia, the CBC, should be done as well to make sure your child is not truly anemic.

Should you simply start administering iron supplements without testing the levels present in the child? This is not a good idea and could even be dangerous. Iron is not a totally benign or harmless supplement. Too much iron can have serious health implications. One in every 200 children has a genetic disease called *hemchromatosis*, which causes the body to store too much iron. This condition can exist in childhood without any symptoms, and treating these children with extra iron would be dangerous. **It's very important to test iron levels before giving any iron supplement and to retest after treatment has been under way for two months.**

Why don't most doctors recommend testing serum ferritin in children with ADHD? The simple answer is that most of them are not aware of this information. It is not widely discussed in most medical seminars offered to clinicians or in educational articles for doctors. Again, as with many of the treatments I have discussed, there is not as much research as we might like, but there is certainly enough to warrant more. Once again, however, no one profits from recommending iron testing and therapy for children with ADHD, so the information gets lost amongst the constant promotion of profitable new pharmaceutical products.

What Iron Levels Indicate the Need to Treat
Your Child with Iron Supplements? What Dose to Give?

Once your child has been tested, the question remains: what iron levels indicate the need to treat him or her with iron supplements? There is some disagreement among researchers on what "normal" iron levels should be. Most agree that ferritin levels below 20 are low and those over 30 are normal. There is some disagreement about whether levels between 20 and 30 are abnormal or just the lower end of normal. Eric Konofal used 30 as a cutoff, and since treatment for those children was effective, I use that as a guideline. **I therefore recommend treating children who have ADHD and a serum ferritin below 30 with iron supplements and more urgently recommend it for ferritin levels below 20.**

In order to treat iron deficiency effectively, you'll need to give the child a fairly hefty dose of iron — more than can be obtained in a multivitamin. The usual **recommendation for iron-deficiency anemia is three to five milligrams (mg) of elemental iron for every kilogram of the child's weight; this equates to about 1.4 to 2.3 milligrams per pound.** I recommend treating at the lower end of this range to minimize side effects. **This high a dose of iron should be obtained either with a doctor's prescription or, if over the counter, with a doctor's specific instructions.**

We don't know why children with ADHD tend to have lower ferritin levels. Just as with omega-3 fatty acids, we have no reason to believe ADHD children consume less iron than those who have adequate levels, so there may be a problem with their bodies' ability to absorb or metabolize iron. Thus, it sometimes takes a significant amount of iron over a long period to correct that problem. However, in other cases, the ferritin levels go up within a month or two. This is why I recommend rechecking the iron level about two months after starting treatment and adjusting the dosage accordingly.

After iron levels are normalized, or even when you are initiating the treatment, take steps to increase iron-containing foods in the child's diet. Red meat is the most obvious source, but I don't recommend eating too much of that. Chicken, turkey, beans, shellfish, whole grains, and foods enriched with iron (check labels of cereals, oatmeal, and breads) are other good sources. Foods rich in vitamin C such as fruits and vegetables, when eaten along with iron-rich foods, will help iron absorption. Once the iron level has moved back up to the normal range, you can shift the child to a multivitamin with iron.

Heme vs. Non-Heme Iron

Iron found in meats, called *heme* iron, is much more efficiently absorbed than iron from non-meat sources. If your child does not eat meat often, try to maximize the ability of the child's system to absorb iron from non-heme sources (iron-fortified foods, grains, beans, tofu, spinach). Eating non-heme iron-containing foods along with vitamin C helps their absorption into the body. There are some foods that can actually *decrease* absorption of non-heme iron: tannins (found in tea), calcium, polyphenols (found in berries, tomatoes, stone fruits, artichokes, potatoes, onion, broccoli, citrus fruits, and many other vegetables and fruits) and phytates (found in legumes and whole grains). In the end, for the child who is deficient, a supplement is the least complicated route.

For more ways to optimize your child's dietary intake of iron, refer to this excellent web page from the National Institutes of Health:

dietary-supplements.info.nih.gov/factsheets/iron.asp

Potential Side Effects and Benefits from Iron Supplements

While there can be side effects with iron supplements, they are usually quite mild. A small percentage of children experience either abdominal pain or constipation from iron treatment. If abdominal pain occurs, finding a different form of iron or splitting the dose into smaller amounts may help. If your child becomes constipated, you can try the same solutions, but also take other measures to decrease constipation: increase the child's intake of water and fiber, reduce dairy products, or use a psyllium product like Citrocel or Metamucil.

You can expect iron treatment to make the child's stools look darker or even black. This is a natural result of the therapy and is nothing to worry about.

What Results Can You Expect from Iron Treatment?

If you're giving iron therapy to a child with ADHD and a measurable iron deficiency, look for an improvement in some aspect of your child's ADHD symptoms. This could include decreased hyperactivity, increased attention, better learning, or some reduction in other ADHD symptoms. Since iron stores take a while to build up, you're unlikely to see any sudden or dramatic effect.

It is not possible to predict whether and how any individual child will benefit from iron therapy. If iron therapy were the only treatment you were applying, you might expect to see steady improvement beginning after a month or two. If you're applying more than one kind of intervention, however, it can be hard to discern the effects of iron treatment in the mix.

Often, at the same time I prescribe iron therapy, I also recommend zinc, certain vitamins, and omega-3 fatty acids as well as provide guidance to the family to address the home and school environments. So unless iron is the only intervention, it may not be possible to be definitive about the exact results of the iron therapy. I would simply say that children with ADHD who are iron deficient should be treated with iron until the ferritin levels are normalized and then monitored occasionally (maybe once a year) to make sure they stay that way.

The Bottom Line. Ask your doctor to measure your child's ferritin level. If it is low, ask for a prescription for iron. Then recheck the ferritin level in two or three months to make sure it has reached the normal range.

Zinc Deficiency in ADHD

As zinc is found in many foods, true zinc deficiency is rare. Lower-than-normal amounts of zinc have been associated with ADHD symptoms, however, and small studies have shown improvement in ADHD symptoms when zinc supplements are given.

Let's look at the research. A study performed in Israel in 1996 examined blood levels of zinc in children with and without ADHD.[4] There were two major findings: first, the zinc levels of children with ADHD were significantly lower than the controls; and second, 30 percent of the children with ADHD had zinc levels below what is considered normal.

Another study, done in Turkey in 1996, measured the zinc levels of children with and without ADHD.[5] The children with ADHD had zinc levels about 50 percent lower than children without ADHD — in other words, the ADHD kids had only half as much of this mineral in their bodies as those in the non-ADHD group. (This study may not be altogether applicable to U.S children because their diets are very different.) Still another study showed that serum zinc levels were correlated with inattention, but not hyperactivity, in middle-class American children.[6]

In a different type of study, done in Iran, children with ADHD were given either methylphenidate (generic Ritalin) alone or methylphenidate along with zinc. After six weeks, the children who received the zinc scored better on ADHD rating scales than the children who received only the methylphenidate.[7] A few other similar studies point in the same direction.

Overall, this is not what we would consider a huge body of evidence. We don't have the type of study I would most like to see: where a number of American children with ADHD are given either zinc or a placebo for a few months, at which point tests are conducted to see whether their ADHD symptoms have improved. It's also true that every study that we *do* have has shown both lower levels of zinc in ADHD children and some improvement when zinc was administered.

Let's look at the plausibility question. Why should zinc be important in ADHD? Just like iron, zinc is an important cofactor in many reactions. It is, in fact, involved in the function of over 100 enzymes and has been found to be important for normal brain function. It is also crucial for normal immune function. Zinc cannot be stored in the body to any great extent, so there must be an ongoing intake of zinc from the diet.

Testing for Zinc Deficiency and Choosing a Zinc Supplement

I recommend that all children with ADHD have their zinc levels checked. If the result comes back low, or even toward the low end of normal, I recommend supplementing with zinc. A child whose zinc levels are low could reap substantial benefit, and there's no appreciable downside. Contrary to the situation with iron, a zinc supplement could be given to every ADHD child without the need for testing, since they may need it and it is unlikely to be harmful. I would not be strongly opposed to this, but as a clinician, I prefer to know what the zinc status is. Testing zinc levels is easy and fairly inexpensive.

Ask your doctor to order an RBC (red blood cell) zinc test. This measures zinc in the red blood cells, which is considered to be a better measure of zinc status than measurement of zinc levels in the plasma or serum — *the test that is typically ordered*. If the RBC zinc is low (different labs have different norms, so I can't give you a number), then I recommend that you start your child on a zinc supplement. In fact, I would supplement even if the results were at the lower end of normal.

For instance: I have a patient whose RBC zinc was measured at 10.3. The normal range for this lab is 9.0 to 14.7. I recommended a fairly low dose of zinc to keep him at the higher end of the range.

The dose of zinc given to your child should be based on the amount of elemental zinc in the preparation. Zinc comes in a number of forms, including zinc gluconate, zinc sulfate, and zinc acetate. The percentage of elemental zinc varies with the form in which it's given. For example, approximately 23 percent of zinc sulfate consists of elemental zinc; this means that 220 mg of zinc sulfate contains 50 mg of elemental zinc. (The elemental zinc content appears in the Supplement Facts panel on the supplement container.) Although you will see many claims by supplement manufacturers, there is no good research indicating any differences in how well each type of zinc is absorbed and utilized.

Zinc supplements are available in pills, lozenges that dissolve in the mouth, and liquids. Choose whichever form works best for your child. Ideally, zinc should be taken separately from meals, but if it causes stomach upset, it can be given with meals; just know that in this case, less may be absorbed into the child's body. **I usually recommend somewhere between 20 and 40 milligrams of elemental zinc per day, depending on the size of the child and the RBC zinc level.** Zinc is a pretty safe mineral, and it would be difficult to overdose provided you are in the general vicinity of these recommendations.

As you supplement, consider ways to add zinc to the child's diet. Oysters contain more zinc per serving than any other food, but I'm guessing your child doesn't eat a lot of those. Red meat and poultry provide most of the zinc in a typical American diet. Other good food sources include beans, nuts, some seafood, whole grains, fortified breakfast cereals, and dairy products.

Phytates, which are present in beans and whole grains, can decrease the absorption of zinc, just as they can decrease iron absorption. This is one of the few instances in which healthy whole grains can have a slightly negative effect. Rather than decreasing intake of whole grains to compensate for this interaction, find ways to increase zinc sources. Vegetarians may need a higher intake of zinc since they tend to eat a lot of phytate-rich foods.

Zinc in Multivitamins

Multiple vitamin/mineral supplements often contain zinc, but the amount varies greatly. They may contain as little as two milligrams or as much as

15 to 20 milligrams. This needs to be taken into account if zinc is to be added to the child's daily supplement plan. If the multivitamin supplies 15 milligrams of zinc, for example, subtract that from the overall amount to be given as a separate supplement.

Potential Benefits from Zinc Supplements

What might one expect to see as a result of zinc supplementation? The answer is similar to the one I gave about iron supplementation. If given as the only intervention, I would expect an improvement in any of the symptoms of ADHD, particularly in the area of attention.

One difference between iron and zinc supplementation: improvement with zinc, should it occur, will happen more quickly than with iron, as stores of zinc take less time to build up. Again, however, I rarely suggest zinc as a single intervention, so it can be hard to tell exactly what effect the zinc is having. For what it's worth, I have had a number of families tell me that they notice the zinc makes a big difference in their children's symptoms — more than any of the other supplements.

The Bottom Line. Measure the child's zinc level and supplement if necessary. It certainly may help, it's unlikely to harm, and it's not difficult or expensive. For more information about zinc in general, check out the NIH fact sheet at ods.od.nih.gov/FactSheets/Zinc.asp.

Magnesium

Along with iron and zinc, magnesium is a mineral important for good health and for the treatment of ADHD. This mineral is necessary for more than 300 biochemical reactions in the body. It helps maintain normal muscle and nerve function, keeps heart rhythm steady, supports a healthy immune system, and keeps bones strong. Magnesium also helps regulate blood sugar levels, promotes normal blood pressure, and is known to be involved in energy metabolism and protein synthesis. Several studies have also linked low magnesium levels to ADHD, and intuitively, when we consider the roles of magnesium in the body, this association makes perfect sense.

Magnesium is often thought of as a "calming" mineral. It can function as a relaxant, expanding blood vessels, bronchioles (the passageways that carry air in and out of the lungs), the muscles of the uterus, and the muscles that move every part of our body. Magnesium seems to have a direct effect on the nervous system: it decreases its sensitivity and excitability.

This mineral's relaxant, soothing effects have been applied to the treatment of migraines and insomnia, and some studies show magnesium supplementation can decrease anxiety. Severe magnesium deficiency, then, can lead to tension, anxiety, excitability, insomnia, high blood pressure, and seizures.

Five separate studies have shown that children with ADHD have lower levels of magnesium than children without ADHD. In every study, the difference was statistically significant — which means that the results are very unlikely to have been due to chance. Here's one example: a study in France examined red blood cell magnesium levels (the best way to measure magnesium) in 52 children with hyperactivity.[8] Of the study participants, 30 children, or more than 60 percent, had RBC magnesium below the limits of normal. It is interesting to note that not a single one of these studies was done in the United States; all of this research measuring magnesium levels in ADHD children was done in Poland and France. So there is good evidence, at least from Europe, linking low magnesium levels with ADHD in children.

Now let's consider whether further evidence demonstrates a positive effect when ADHD children are treated with magnesium.

The best study on this topic examined 75 children with ADHD and magnesium deficiency.[9] Fifty of these children were treated with magnesium for six months; 25 were not treated. The children treated with magnesium showed improvement in ADHD symptoms as compared to the control group. The problem with this study — and with two other studies showing similar results, one of which used vitamin B-6 with the magnesium — is that it was not *blinded*. Remember that the gold standard studies in nutrition are *double-blind*, meaning that neither researchers nor families knew which subjects were getting the treatment and which were getting the placebo. Here, both the families and the researchers knew who was taking magnesium and who wasn't. This can have a great influence on a study's results, as we've discussed. So far, at this writing, no double-blind studies have evaluated magnesium supplementation for children with ADHD.

Why would children be magnesium deficient? As with other minerals, it all goes back to the diet. Magnesium is found in a wide variety of foods, including beans, nuts, whole-grain cereals and breads, and green vegetables. A varied and healthy diet should supply adequate magnesium. Refining and processing of whole foods, however, all but drains them of their magnesium content, and this helps explain why some children (and adults also) have measurably lower levels of magnesium than others.

The recommended requirement for magnesium increases from 130 mg per day for children aged four to eight to 240 for those ages 9 to 13. Magnesium requirements are even higher for older teenagers. Individuals absorb and process magnesium differently; one person may need to take in more from the diet in order to maintain magnesium levels. If your child has low RBC magnesium, then magnesium intake needs to be increased even if the child seems to be eating enough of the right foods. The easiest way to accomplish this is with a supplement.

Overall, the research on magnesium and ADHD is suggestive but sparse. I find it very frustrating that this research has not been more aggressively pursued. It would certainly be easy enough to measure magnesium in children with ADHD here in the U.S. and elsewhere and to test whether treating ADHD children with low magnesium would be helpful.

Again, in situations where we don't have all the evidence we need to decide whether to recommend a particular treatment, we look at the possible benefit versus the possible risk — the upside vs. the downside. Magnesium is a great example. The benefit, as suggested by the studies we have, could be significant, and the risk of magnesium treatment is negligible as long as it's added in accordance with medical guidelines. **My recommendation is to measure red blood cell magnesium in all children with ADHD.** It is a simple test and easily accomplished with the other mineral tests already recommended.

During my years of practice, I often find abnormalities in magnesium levels but rarely the high percentage of deficiency reported in these studies. I would estimate that 25 percent or less of the children I see are magnesium deficient. Even if only five percent were deficient and could improve with treatment, it would be worth testing for levels of this mineral.

If an RBC magnesium test shows that levels are low, I recommend a magnesium supplement. The best forms are magnesium citrate, chelate, or glycinate. Avoid magnesium oxide, which is irritating to the bowel. Most magnesium supplements are powders that can be mixed with some type of drink.

How much should you give your child? The usual dose would be about two to three milligrams of magnesium for each pound of body weight. A 60-pound 8-year-old, for example, would take about 120 to 180 milligrams of magnesium per day. The most common side effect of magnesium is diarrhea or stomach cramps. If these occur, just back off on the magnesium dose and try increasing it again, slowly.

With supplementation in a child who has been deficient, I would expect some decrease in hyperactivity and impulsivity. As magnesium levels may take a while to build up, you may not see quick results. Improvement should be apparent in a month or two. As with the other minerals, it is rare for me to start magnesium as a single treatment, so neither research nor my own clinical experience helps me predict how quickly the magnesium might help your child. Consult the NIH fact sheet for magnesium online if you'd like more information: ods.od.nih.gov/factsheets/magnesium.asp.

Minerals and ADHD: Summary

So there you have it: three separate minerals crucial to normal neurological function, all of which can be deficient in ADHD, and all of which can be accurately measured in your child. Each of these minerals can be easily and economically given as a supplement, with very little risk of serious side effects.

Make sure to ask your doctor to measure serum ferritin, RBC zinc and RBC magnesium in your child — regardless of whether he or she has just been diagnosed with ADHD or has had the diagnosis for years. If levels are below normal, supplement as appropriate. This simple intervention could make a big difference in your child's life.

Chapter 9

Herbs for ADHD

A great number of our most effective modern medicines were originally derived from plant sources. Aspirin is made from willow bark. Digitalis, a life-saving heart medication, is made from foxglove. Not only have our most important medications been derived from plants, but we still look to plant sources in our search for new ones. The practice of healing with plants, known as herbalism or herbal medicine, has been a mainstay of medical treatment in all cultures.

With the recent resurgence of herbal medicine into the American mainstream, you've most likely heard of or used common herbs like chamomile, peppermint, or echinacea. Many herbs that have medicinal qualities, including garlic, ginger, turmeric, and green tea, are also a regular part of our diets. To use these herbs therapeutically, we simply ingest them in larger quantities than we would use in our meals. Garlic, for example, can lower blood pressure, but only when taken regularly and in fairly hefty doses. It won't have this same effect when used simply as a seasoning.

In this chapter, we'll discuss some of the common botanical preparations used to treat ADHD. I will use the terms *herbal* and *botanical* interchangeably to refer to products that are made directly from plants, rather than having been synthesized or produced in a laboratory.

It is important to know that herbal products, as opposed to nutritional supplements, can have hundreds of active chemicals in them. Often, we don't know which chemicals within that botanical have the healing effect we are looking for; therefore, we usually employ a whole herb rather than one or two chemical constituents extracted from that herb. Various parts of the plant may be used: root, leaf, stem, or flower. For some herbs, all of these may have an effect; for others, only one part is useful — for example, only the root of the ginger plant or the leaf of the peppermint plant.

However, safety is a crucial factor with herbal therapy, even more so than with nutritional supplements. Please always remember: **Just because something is 'natural' does not mean that it is safe!**

A Few Precautionary Words: Please Read Carefully!

Many dangerous poisons come straight from plants: *Amanita* mushrooms, water hemlock, castor beans, and oleanders are all common plants that have the capacity to be very quickly fatal to humans. The herbal products one can purchase in stores will not be quite so dangerous, but some can have serious side effects.

Even a properly prepared herb from a reputable manufacturer can be dangerous. A good example of this is ephedra, an herb that was once commonly used to treat asthma. It was removed from the market because of its toxic effects on the cardiovascular system, but not before a great many people had used it. Herbs tend not to be as well-regulated or tested as drugs, and they can interact with prescription drugs in harmful ways. Use great care, consult with your physician, and do your homework before adding any herbal medicine to your child's treatment plan.

Here are a few botanicals that you should always avoid giving to children:

Ephedra	Pennyroyal
Oil of wintergreen	Sassafras
Comfrey	Chaparral

Be aware that an inexpert botanist can pick the wrong herb due to its visual similarity to another herb. Deaths have occurred for this reason, but rarely. Make sure to choose a reputable brand to ensure that you avoid this problem. (You will find out more about how to do this in an upcoming section of this chapter.)

Another reason to pick a reputable herb supplement company: contaminants like lead and other heavy metals or traces of prescription drugs have been found in some herbal formulations. This has been especially true of Chinese herbs and Ayurvedic herbs produced in India. This contamination rarely causes acute poisoning but over long periods can definitely be detrimental to health.

Herb Risks Dwarfed by Those of Pharmaceuticals

It is not my intention to overstate the dangers of herbs. If you took all of the serious adverse reactions to herbs that have ever happened in this country, they would represent a tiny fraction of the fatal and severe reactions that come from pharmaceutical drugs we all use daily. For example: **over 7,000 deaths a year are attributable to use of over-the counter pain relievers like ibuprofen.**

For that matter, the misuse of over-the-counter cold medicines (antihistamines, decongestants, and cough suppressants) has resulted in so much toxicity that the FDA has banned them in children under two and advised caution in children under six. No herb of any kind has been responsible for as widespread a health problem as these particular drugs.

The cough and cold medication racket is a multibillion-dollar industry. Its products have been recommended routinely to children for decades, despite the dangers. And to add insult to injury, research has shown that **they don't even work** to decrease the length or severity of colds and coughs! We know this now, but it would have been good to find this out 50 years sooner.

By the way, recent research has shown that *plain honey* works better than dextromethorphan, the most commonly prescribed over-the-counter cough suppressant, to stop that annoying nighttime cough. **Exception: never give honey to infants under 1 year of age.**

It is interesting to me that these OTC (over-the-counter) pharmaceutical products, which can be truly dangerous, have been allowed to flourish and to be advertised to both doctors and the general public as effective without any good research substantiating their effectiveness. Yet it is illegal for herbal products to claim any specific therapeutic benefits at all, even for something as simple as chamomile soothing an upset stomach. I'm all for truth in advertising, but we need to level the playing field.

Overall, I believe it is quite reasonable for children and adults alike to make use of beneficial herbs, as long as two conditions are met:

1. Be sure that you are using an herb that has been shown to be safe and that has a good chance of being effective for the intended purpose. This is best accomplished by following advice from a physician or other health care provider.

2. Purchase any herbal product from a highly reputable company with high standards of quality. The FDA's new GMP (Good Manufacturing Practices) regulation is now in effect for any company with over 20 employees, so this should provide assurance of baseline reliability. (See next section, "How to Choose a Reputable Herbal Brand," for some additional tools to aid you in finding quality herbal products.)

How to Choose a Reputable Herbal Brand

Evaluating the reliability of any producer of non-pharmaceutical products, even when shopping for something as simple as a multivitamin, is not a simple task. Evaluating makers of herbal or botanical products is even harder. The right herb has to be picked at the right time; it must be stored and processed in the right way. If it is not, you may not be getting the product you think you are getting, and it won't have the desired effects. Here are some tips that might help you find good-quality brands of herbal medicine.

Two groups, the **United States Pharmacopeia (USP)** and **National Sanitation Foundation (NSF International)**, have begun dietary supplement quality verification programs. These are voluntary programs requiring manufacturers that use their quality seals on their labeling to undergo a rigorous auditing of manufacturing sites for Good Manufacturing Practices compliance, laboratory testing of product samples, label review, and periodic off-the-shelf testing of products. Unfortunately, only a small percentage of companies participate in these programs — but you can have confidence in those that do.

An organization called ConsumerLab.com performs independent testing of nutrition and herbal products. Its main role is to take samples of a product like ginkgo biloba, for example, and test to see that the product is what it claims to be — that it contains the right herb in the right amounts. ConsumerLab also tests for contaminants and evaluates products on other relevant criteria. When a company submits its product for testing and passes, consumers get some reassurance of quality. However, ConsumerLab does *not* test for effectiveness; it only looks at whether a product is what it says it is and whether it's free of dangerous contaminants. One reasonable complaint about ConsumerLab is that it is a private, for-profit company and charges a significant amount of money to test a product. For this and some other reasons, some very good companies do not participate in ConsumerLab testing. Therefore, the fact that a company is not being tested by ConsumerLab does not necessarily mean that it is not a quality company.

Few readers have the time and expertise to contact herbal companies and obtain details of their collection and manufacturing process; however, you can consult a qualified health care professional who uses botanicals frequently enough to have done this leg work for you and who is able to recommend companies he or she has already researched. *Please do not include people who work at health food stores among your list of "qualified professionals."* I see increasing numbers of people receiving their health care advice in this way, and it worries me greatly. Although mainly well-intentioned, these workers have no formal training in health or medicine, and most of the information they offer comes directly from advertising material sent to them by the companies making the products they are selling. Not only might they recommend the wrong product, but they could be completely unaware of the significance of a symptom or set of symptoms that is serious and requires medical attention. I especially urge you not to ask health food store clerks for advice about treating your children, as the risk of harm to a child's small body from a wrongly prescribed or poor-quality herbal formulation is even greater than the risk to an adult.

Herbs for ADHD

The list of herbs that have been scientifically studied for the treatment of ADHD is actually quite short. Unfortunately, we cannot look back to a long tradition of using herbs for ADHD because we only recently began to treat large numbers of children for this disorder. Additionally, there is always less research on herbs as they relate to children than to adults; the fact that ADHD has until recently been mainly a syndrome of children has not encouraged botanical research.

Here, we'll discuss three botanicals/herbs or herbal combinations that have promise for children with ADHD: Pycnogenol, valerian/lemon balm, and gingko/ginseng. I will also mention some herbs that some people use for ADHD that do **not** appear to be helpful and that I don't recommend.

Pycnogenol

Of all herbal formulations studied for ADHD treatment, Pycnogenol (pronounced *pik nógge nàwl*) shows the most promise.

Pycnogenol is the trade name for an herbal extract — meaning a product prepared by some process from a whole herb or plant — derived from the bark of the French maritime pine, *Pinus pinaster*. This extract has a high concentration of a class of naturally occurring chemicals known as *polyphenols*, which are natural components of a wide variety of plants and have significant health benefits. (Foods rich in polyphenols include onion, apple, tea, red wine, red grapes, grape juice, strawberries, raspberries, blueberries, cranberries, and certain nuts.)

Polyphenols act as powerful antioxidants, enhance immunity, have anticancer effects, repair DNA cell damage, and help prevent macular degeneration (a potentially blinding age-related eye disease). They have also been found to help the liver process toxins more effectively. I am going to delve into some of the research on Pycnogenol in somewhat more detail because it gives a fascinating window on another way to look at what is going on in children with ADHD.

In the late 1990s, a series of case reports on Pycnogenol and ADHD surfaced. A report published in 1999 in the *Journal of the American Academy of Child and Adolescent Psychiatry* was most interesting: A 10-year-old boy with ADHD who had been taking dextroamphetamine (Dexedrine) with limited success was brought to the study's author by his parents.[1] They reported to him that they had treated their son with Pycnogenol for two weeks and had noticed significant improvement during that time. As a trial, they then stopped the supplement for four weeks. After two weeks his behavior worsened as exhibited by more demerits in school and more fights on the playground. When the Pycnogenol was restarted, the boy improved again. This is only one case, but certainly was food for thought (no pun intended).

Several other case reports and a small pilot study also indicated similar success. In my own practice, one of my teenage patients who really did need to be on stimulant medications found that Pycnogenol helped significantly when it was added to his stimulant.

Here's a direct comment about Pycnogenol from the parent of one of my patients:

"From personal experience I think the supplements have been an excellent choice for my son, especially Pycnogenol and omega-3. This summer he couldn't take any antioxidants and I noticed that he had struggled more to concentrate when he was doing his daily Kumon homework. As the beginning of the school year approached, I put him back on his normal supplement regimen; I noticed a GREAT improvement! — both in the time it took him to complete his task, and also making many fewer mistakes. I am a firm believer in supplements!"

In 2006 and 2007, a group of researchers in Slovakia published several studies on Pycnogenol and ADHD.[2,3,4] They also looked at the relationship of ADHD to antioxidant status, DNA damage, and neurotransmitter levels. We've discussed antioxidants previously, and we've touched upon the possible relationship of antioxidant status and ADHD. I won't recount all the research specifics here, but the findings of these studies are worth noting:

1. Children with ADHD had more free radical damage (free radicals are chemicals produced by oxidation that damage DNA) than children without ADHD. Pycnogenol decreased the damage.

2. Children with ADHD had lower concentrations of one of the most important antioxidants, *glutathione*, in their bodies than children without ADHD. Pycnogenol increased the glutathione level.

3. Children with ADHD had higher levels of the excitatory neurotransmitters *adrenaline* and *noradrenalin* in their urine than children without ADHD. Pycnogenol normalized this in some children and decreased ADHD symptoms. (This was not a blinded study — the researchers and subjects knew that they were getting the Pycnogenol and not a placebo.)

4. Finally, the researchers performed a randomized, double-blinded, placebo-controlled study using Pycnogenol for children with ADHD. The 61 children with ADHD in the study were divided into two

groups: one received Pycnogenol while a placebo group received an inactive pill. After a month, the children who had been receiving the Pycnogenol had significant improvement in their ADHD compared to those who didn't. The researchers also did an interesting follow-up: one month after stopping the Pycnogenol, the children were reevaluated, and their ADHD symptoms had relapsed to or near where they were before the study.

While all of this information about Pycnogenol sounds promising, there are a couple of caveats to keep in mind. All of these studies were done by the same group, and their research was funded, at least partially, by a company that produces Pycnogenol. This tends to make me take these results with a grain of salt, but we should remember that much of the research *on conventional stimulant medications for ADHD is funded in the same way.* As a specific example, one of the key studies on Vyvanse, a relatively new ADHD drug, was funded by Shire Pharmaceuticals, which makes the drug. Three of the major investigators chosen to do those studies had a connection to Shire by being members of the company's speakers' bureau — a very lucrative arrangement for those doctors.

One other study of note on ADHD and Pycnogenol was conducted with adults and showed that Pycnogenol did not work better than the placebo.[5] This same study, however, also failed to show any benefit of methylphenidate (generic for Ritalin) over a placebo, a very unusual outcome. Therefore, this study cannot be used to deny the effects of Pycnogenol any more than it can be used to deny the effects of Ritalin.

Another product called grape seed extract (GSE) is a source of high concentrations of the same type of polyphenols found in Pycnogenol. Some people use this for ADHD as well. There is, however, no research supporting the use of GSE in ADHD.

Overall, the evidence for Pycnogenol is promising but not convincing. Personally, I've had a small number of patients who have found it very helpful, especially for concentration. I don't hesitate to recommend it. No significant safety issues have emerged with this supplement so far.

Valerian/Lemon Balm

Valerian and lemon balm are two separate herbs. Both have been widely used for thousands of years for their calming and sleep-inducing effects. They are both herbs that I consider completely safe, both because of the research that has been done and their long history of safe use. Both are on the Food and Drug Administration's Generally Recognized as Safe (GRAS) list.

Their use for ADHD has to do with their calming properties, not with any ability to increase concentration or performance. There has been only one study of this herbal combination for ADHD, but it was a very interesting one.

This European study involved 918 children with the diagnosis of motor restlessness (*hyperkinesis*) and sleep difficulties (*dyssomnia*).[6] When these children were treated with a combination product containing valerian and lemon balm for about one month, both hyperkinesis and dyssomnia were significantly reduced: they went from "moderate/severe" to "mild" or "absent" in most of the patients. In total, 80.9 percent of the patients who suffered from dyssomnia improved, and 70.4 percent of the patients with restlessness improved. These children had several other symptoms including lack of concentration, aggressiveness, and fatigability, but the findings only stated that these symptoms improved an average of 37 percent. Unfortunately, they did not state how many children had lack of concentration and whether the valerian/lemon balm helped. Remarkably, no adverse effects were reported related to the herbal treatment.

This study has some strong points and some weak points. The strong points: this was quite a large, multi-center study (meaning that it was performed at several clinical centers, not just in one geographic area) that showed a solid positive effect without any significant adverse effects. The weak points: there was no control group, so everyone knew these children were taking an herb to calm them down, meaning there could have been a placebo effect. And this was not a study designed to evaluate the effects of the herbs specifically on ADHD. The authors hint that many of these children had ADHD, but no measure of concentration or impulsivity was applied, so it's hard to know exactly how the findings pertain to ADHD children. It also would have been nice if they had reported on the improvement in concentration as a separate category.

Personally, I have found this herbal combination to be quite helpful in some children with ADHD. It can be used with other natural treatments, but I have found it especially helpful in children taking a psychostimulant. For example: Nick was a 9-year-old who had been taking Concerta for ADHD. The medication really helped him function at school, but when it wore off around 3:00 p.m., he would have a rebound effect and become extremely hyperactive, irritable, and argumentative. His doctor advised adding a short-acting Ritalin dose at this time of day, which worked somewhat — but ended up causing Nick to have difficulty falling asleep. Naturally, the doctor prescribed Clonidine, another drug, to help him fall asleep at night. The Clonidine helped somewhat but caused some morning grogginess.

So now, instead of one medication, Nick was on three and still not having great results. When the family came to me, I recommended that they give him a dose of the valerian/lemon balm combination at 3:00 in the afternoon rather than the short-acting Ritalin. This ended the rebound effect, and Nick was able to mellow out after the Concerta wore off. Since he stopped the Ritalin dose, he didn't need a sleep medication either, and everyone was happier.

Valerian/lemon balm is also used for anxiety and can be quite helpful for children with ADHD who have this problem. It can also be used to help children fall asleep and has fewer side effects than the pharmaceutical sleep medications. I do not believe it directly affects attention and concentration, so I would *not* use valerian/lemon balm alone for ADHD. An interesting combination would be to use lemon balm/valerian and Pycnogenol together to modify both hyperactivity and concentration.

One interesting aspect of valerian is that it seems to take a couple of weeks to reach maximum effectiveness. If you try it and there's no immediate improvement, don't give up too soon.

Ginkgo/Ginseng

At this writing, a single pilot study has used a combination of American ginseng (*Panax quinquefolium*) and ginkgo biloba for the treatment of ADHD.[7] Investigators used a combination product called AD-fx, which contains 200 mg of ginseng and 50 mg of ginkgo. Thirty-six children with ADHD between the ages of three and 17 were given this combination twice a day for four weeks. ADHD symptom rating scales were filled out by the parents before and after treatment. Children showed improvement on a number of scales, including a 74 percent reduction in the overall hyperactivity index.

This sounds pretty good — but, again, we're looking at an uncontrolled study. In addition, this time only the parents rated results of treatment. (Most ADHD studies use a teacher rating as well.) It was also a small study, and the age range was quite broad; most studies do not combine 3-year-old up to 17-year-old subjects. To be fair, the investigators noted that this was only a preliminary study, also known as a pilot study. It was published in 2000, and I know of no follow-up research that has been done as of 2009.

The idea of using ginkgo for ADHD makes some sense. Ginkgo has been used to improve cognitive function in elderly people with age-related memory problems or cognitive impairment and has also been shown to improve certain measures of cognitive function in healthy young and middle-aged people. Its method of action appears to be related to improved blood flow to the brain and decreased oxidative stress. Maybe we should all give it a try!

The theory behind using ginseng is less obvious but not illogical. Ginseng is an herb used as an adaptogen (also known as a *tonic*), and is generally used to increase the body's resistance to stress, anxiety, and fatigue. I believe that life for many children with ADHD is quite stressful; they have to put a lot of energy into accomplishing things that are pretty easy for the rest of us, and they typically get more negative feedback from people around them. (We'll talk more in depth about this very crucial topic, and how you can change this stress level, in Chapter 12.)

A few of my patients have tried this ginkgo/ginseng combination, and a few children have seemed to respond well while others did not. I have not used it in a large number of children. Still, both are well-known herbs and safe when used in correct doses. **But always remember that children who are taking pharmaceutical medications should use herbs only under the guidance of a doctor who can ensure that there won't be any harmful interactions.**

Herbs That I Do *Not* Recommend for ADHD

It is very common for parents of children with ADHD (or any other disorder or illness for that matter) to network, to read voraciously about the disorder, and to generally search for as much advice as they can that might help. I have given you an overview of several herbal products that may indeed help in your child's situation. But now we must look at a few other botanicals you might hear about that I advise against for treating ADHD.

St. John's Wort (Hypericum perforatum)

A number of people have asked me about using St. John's wort for ADHD, and I'd like to start out this discussion by clearly stating that *there is no evidence that it works* for this purpose.

For some reason, many people interested in alternative therapies have come up with the notion that St. John's wort is a good ADHD treatment. I'm not sure why this idea became popular. St. John's wort is effective for depression and has significantly fewer side effects than the usual pharmaceutical antidepressants given out far too freely by some physicians (I find the overuse of antidepressants by physicians deplorable). However, I see no good reason why anyone with an understanding of St. John's wort and its mechanisms of action in the body would consider it to be a good herb for ADHD. Not a single study has indicated that this herb is helpful in ADHD treatment.

Because it is used so often for this purpose regardless of this total lack of evidence in its favor, a colleague of mine from Bastyr University, Wendy Weber, designed an excellent randomized, placebo-controlled trial of St. John's wort with ADHD. The results came as no big surprise: it didn't help at all.[8] Children who received St. John's wort did no better than those receiving the placebo.

My advice: don't use St. John's wort for ADHD except possibly in situations I will describe next.

One such instance would be if you have a child who has ADHD and depression, and a physician or other qualified person is willing to supervise a trial of St. John's wort for your child. A child who is depressed and has ADHD might experience some relief from ADHD symptoms if the depression is lifted. Still, even if you do try St. John's wort in a child with ADHD and depression, I strongly recommend that you combine this with other interventions likely to help with the ADHD more directly.

A child with depression can get misdiagnosed with ADHD; when this happens, it's usually because he or she is too depressed to concentrate. This would be an entirely different situation where St. John's wort might be worth trying on its own, but only after determining that the ADHD diagnosis is inaccurate and the problem is actually depression.

Combination Products

If shopping for nutritional supplements for a child with ADHD, you'll find many combination products that claim to be helpful. Rather than containing one or two nutrients or herbal products, these combinations tend to contain many different ingredients, including traditional herbal remedies, vitamins, minerals, various types of fatty acids, homeopathic remedies, and traditional Chinese medicines. One such combination product has 72 different ingredients! The advertisements for these products usually claim to have helped hundreds or even thousands of children, often with very convincing testimonials. However, at this writing, *no studies have been published concerning these products in any medical journal.*

Does this mean that they don't work? No! I have had a few parents tell me that one or another of these products was very helpful for their child. Those that contain ingredients already discussed here — such as zinc, omega-3s, or ginkgo — could have some positive effect, as long as the dosage is adequate. But I've had more parents tell me that they didn't seem to do much at all.

Some of these products contain herbs that have never been tested in children, or they don't have a track record of safe use in the West, so there are safety concerns. Also, some combination formulas contain various forms of caffeine, sometimes enough to have significant side effects.

Overall, it could be that one or another of these combination products might be helpful, but I cannot generally recommend them because of a lack of good data and possible safety considerations. If you are interested in using one of them, check with a knowledgeable health care professional concerning the specific product in question.

Products with Caffeine

Tea and coffee are herbal products that contain caffeine among other active ingredients. Caffeine is a stimulant, in the same family as methylphenidate (Ritalin and derivatives) and Dextroamphetamines (Dexedrine and derivatives). The effects of caffeine are in fact quite similar to the effects of these two medications. In the 1970s and 1980s, several studies compared the effects of the psychostimulants to caffeine. Although the results varied somewhat, the medications were generally more effective and had fewer side effects. However, this was not true for everyone in these studies; for some subjects, the caffeine was actually more effective.

I do remember one teenager with ADHD who had terrible reactions to psychostimulants. They made him irritable, angry, and depressed. His solution was to sip on a large caffeine-containing soda through the school day. Unorthodox, but it helped him concentrate and had minimal side effects. I wouldn't recommend caffeine in general, especially for small children, but in certain situations it might be a possibility.

Going Deeper into Herbal Medicine for ADHD: Herbalism and Herbalists

Herbalism describes the practice of treating disease and maintaining health entirely through botanical products. Herbalism has been used for thousands of years in many healing traditions around the world. Skilled herbal practitioners often have a depth of knowledge about herbs that far surpasses that of many 'alternative doctors' who use herbs as only a small part of their treatment protocols. Herbalists rarely use one herb at a time but combine a number of herbs based on an individual's specific set of symptoms and general health. It follows that an herbalist is not likely to prescribe only the herbs covered in this chapter; he or she is likely to advise a combination of herbs that together may have a stronger impact. On the other hand, they are more likely to use botanicals that haven't been thoroughly researched in terms of their effectiveness in ADHD.

Unfortunately, no research has been published about traditional herbal treatment of ADHD (except in Chinese herbal medicine, which is covered in Chapter 11), so it is hard to know whether a more comprehensive herbal approach could be effective for your child. If you know of a well-trained herbalist with experience treating ADHD, however, and are willing to research the safety of the recommended herbs, such an approach could be beneficial.

Chapter 10
Neurofeedback and
Other Mind-Body Therapies

As discussed in Chapter 2 on neurobiology, children with ADHD tend to have some differences in brain wave patterns and neurotransmitter function when compared to children without ADHD. However, these factors can be modified in a number of ways, many of which I have discussed already in the chapters on nutrition and supplements.

One particularly interesting set of techniques involves using the power of the mind to improve its own function. These are generally known as "mind-body" methods and include neurofeedback, hypnosis, Yoga, and meditation. Let's start with the most high-tech of these methods, EEG neurofeedback.

What Is EEG Neurofeedback?

EEG neurofeedback is a fascinating and unique approach to the treatment of ADHD. Basically, it is a type of biofeedback that allows a child to alter the pattern of his or her own brain waves...by playing video games! It's hard to imagine a treatment more agreeable to the average child.

These aren't just any video games, however. You can't plant your child in front of a home video game console to achieve the kind of results seen with EEG neurofeedback. The games employed are highly specific and have to be played under controlled conditions. To understand why something like this could be effective, you might want to review the material on brain waves and ADHD that was covered in Chapter 2.

In that chapter, you learned that that most kids with ADHD have somewhat different brain wave patterns than do kids without ADHD — that, in general, children with ADHD have fewer beta waves and more theta waves when they are in a normal waking state than do children without ADHD. In fact, the ratio of theta to beta waves is probably the most accurate measurement of the brain wave difference between ADHD and non-ADHD kids; and **a child who has this particular difference from normal children on the EEG stands an 80 to 90 percent likelihood of being diagnosed with ADHD** through common methods of diagnosis.

This suggests that most children with ADHD are in a chronic state of under arousal, at least as far as brain waves go. Their brains essentially under-react to stimuli when compared with the brains of 'normal' children. When little Melissa is sitting in class, her beta waves are reduced relative to most of the other kids sitting there with her; at the same time, her theta waves are increased.

A small proportion of ADHD children have higher-than-average beta wave activity, which is called *over arousal*. This can also cause problems with attention and learning and can be treated with EEG neurofeedback as well. Although the research on the relationship between the different types of ADHD and brain wave patterns is not definitive, it may be that kids with the *inattentive* subtype of ADHD — those who don't experience hyperactivity — have yet another brain wave pattern. Their pattern may be a predominance of alpha waves, which are associated with relaxation and daydreaming. This is different from the brain waves of ADHD kids with hyperactivity or children without ADHD (and would require a different emphasis when using neurofeedback therapy).

How Neurofeedback Works

It turns out that you can teach children to alter their brain wave patterns by measuring their brain waves patterns and giving them positive feedback for changing them. It is a remarkable fact that **most children can quite easily learn to alter their own brain wave patterns!**

Here's how it works. The child sits in a comfortable chair and has two or three small electrodes clipped to his or her scalp. These electrodes just sense electricity, they don't deliver it — so there's no discomfort at all. The sensors are fed into a computer that measures brain wave patterns. Then, through the wonders of computer technology, the whole thing can be transformed into a video game on the screen in which the child succeeds at the game by increasing his or her beta waves. The child's experience is one of trying to pilot a spaceship or knock off a bunch of enemies — but he has to do it by increasing his beta waves and decreasing his theta waves. Amazingly enough, children learn to do this quite easily, often getting the idea in a single 20- or 30-minute session.

For those who are familiar with biofeedback in general, this is not at all surprising. People can use biofeedback to raise or lower blood pressure or heart rate, change the temperature of their hands (useful in treating migraines), and regulate many bodily functions that typically occur at the subconscious level. Neurofeedback is simply a more specialized type of biofeedback that focuses on the brain.

One way to think of neurofeedback is that it is basically a structured learning opportunity for the brain that also happens to make use of some pretty sophisticated computer technology. This technique is not new: it has been used for ADHD since the 1970s. EEG neurofeedback has also been used extensively for brain trauma, alcoholism, and seizures. So far, this sounds good, doesn't it? A non-drug therapy for ADHD that causes change at the very place the problem seems to exist: the actual function of the brain. If it works, why aren't more doctors recommending it?

Beyond the fact that it is simply not a mainstream pharmaceutical, there is also considerable controversy about EEG neurofeedback research: many ADHD experts would argue that the research doesn't demonstrate enough of a benefit to justify its widespread use.

The Roots of the Neurofeedback Controversy

Let's take a look at what the research shows us. I'll summarize the evidence from both sides as objectively as possible.

The first and most basic research question is whether this technique can teach children to alter their brain waves in the desired way **while they are in the session.** I believe there is no doubt about this. Multiple research studies have consistently demonstrated that this happens readily.

The second question is whether neurofeedback training actually improves ADHD symptoms. This question is a bit more complicated. If, indeed, an EEG neurofeedback course teaches children to alter their brain waves, does this translate to more "normal" results on tests that measure symptoms of ADHD (namely attention, concentration, and impulsivity)? And equally important, does this improvement occur only during the EEG sessions — or **does it persist after each session or group of sessions?** Does this benefit last for some number of months or even years?

These are essential questions in deciding whether a therapy is of value. Neurofeedback-induced changes in an ADHD child's readouts on a high-tech EEG test are meaningless unless those changes actually *improve the life of the child.*

So the most relevant question is: Can we expect to see, as a result of neurofeedback treatment, a partial or complete decrease in ADHD symptoms that have caused difficulty at school and home? And how long does this improvement last — if it occurs at all?

Even proponents of neurofeedback have to admit that the answers to these questions are debatable. This is because of two major shortcomings inherent in research on neurofeedback:

1. In a neurofeedback study, it's difficult to create that all-important control group because the kids (and their parents) are going to know whether they're getting neurofeedback or not. It's kind of hard to

disguise. So if a child improves after a set of neurofeedback sessions, is it because of the neurofeedback itself or a placebo effect? Even the simple fact of receiving so much individual attention from an adult could have a positive effect on a child that is unrelated to the neurofeedback itself. Researchers have developed a few creative ways to get around this, but the issue still comes up in most discussions about the validity of EEG neurofeedback research.

2. It is difficult to randomize study subjects when configuring the neurofeedback and placebo groups. Randomization entails random assignment of children to one or the other group. But since neurofeedback involves a significant time commitment, many parents will not consent to a random assignment in which all their time will have been "wasted" with a placebo treatment.

Even taking these points taken into consideration, my overall assessment is that **researchers *have* shown that EEG neurofeedback is probably, although not certainly, effective in improving ADHD symptoms during and immediately after treatment.** Children who receive EEG neurofeedback *do* show improvements on computerized tests of attention and on parent and teacher rating scales. Let's examine a few studies that led me to my conclusion.

One study compared neurofeedback to methylphenidate (Ritalin) among children with ADHD.[1] This investigation enrolled 35 children with ADHD, 23 of whom were given three months of EEG neurofeedback while the remaining 12 were given methylphenidate for three months. At the end, their performance was measured via two methods: the TOVA (a computerized test of attention) and ADHD rating scales by both teachers and parents. The result? Both groups improved on all measures, and there were no significant differences between the two groups. In other words, for these children, neurofeedback worked as well as methylphenidate.

This study had one of the weaknesses mentioned earlier, however: it wasn't randomized. The parents decided which children received neurofeedback and which received methylphenidate. Another point to note is that testing was done only once, immediately after the three-month treatment protocol. No later follow-up was performed. The question of whether EEG neurofeedback has long-term benefit wasn't answered by this study.

Another interesting study — this one by German researchers — involved 38 children with ADHD between the ages of eight and 13. All of the children received a six-month course of one of two different types of neurofeedback treatment.[2] Nineteen of these children received theta/beta training, where feedback was used to increase their beta rhythms and decrease theta (in other words, to alter the lower beta and higher theta waves inherent in most ADHD cases). The other 19 children received a different type of EEG neurofeedback for the training of slow cortical potentials. (Rather than go into this form of neurofeedback training, which is not easy to describe, let's just say that slow cortical potentials are a different type of brain wave pattern that can be described as shifts from a positive to a negative current. Like beta and theta waves, they are associated with attention and concentration and can be trained with neurofeedback.)

Both groups had significant improvements in scores on computerized tests of attention and parent and teacher symptom evaluations. No difference was found between the groups; both neurofeedback methods were effective.

Unlike the first study described here, this one was followed up: the children were re-tested six months after the study was completed and had maintained the improvements seen in the study on almost all of the measurements used. *This is very important.* Previous studies had been criticized due to the possibility that any positive effect of the EEG neurofeedback could have been attributable to the interaction between the child and the trainer and not specifically to brain wave changes. In this study, the researchers were able to report actual changes in the children's EEG patterns — an indication that the desired changes came from the EEG training itself, not from any other influence. The one weakness of the study was the lack of a control group.

In recent years, many variations of basic EEG neurofeedback have popped up. There is an almost bewildering list of techniques from which one can choose: very low frequency wave biofeedback, interhemispheric EEG biofeedback, low energy neurofeedback, hemoencephalography, and others. Although they may claim to be more effective than the standard EEG therapies used in the studies described above, there is either no research support, or less support, for these newer methods than for the standard method of basic EEG neurofeedback.

Neurofeedback Risks and Side Effects

Few neurofeedback studies have reported any side effects. Occasionally, patients report transitory headaches, tiredness, and/or dizziness after treatment. However, it does seem to me that if altering brain waves can produce positive changes in mental states, it could produce negative changes as well. I wonder whether some children might become more irritable, develop a greater tendency to hyperfocus, or become more obsessive or rigid in response to EEG neurofeedback therapy. I have not seen any evidence of this in the research and am not sure whether anyone has looked carefully for these types of changes yet. If such changes have been seen in any study, they haven't been reported as of this writing.

Neurofeedback has also been used for the treatment of seizure disorders, including epilepsy. While it can be helpful, some work has shown that neurofeedback has the potential to decrease the seizure threshold: that is, make seizures more frequent in those who already have a seizure disorder. If your child has seizures and ADHD, be sure to seek an EEG therapist who is experienced in neurofeedback in patients with seizure disorders. If your child does not have a seizure disorder to begin with, you need not be concerned that neurofeedback will cause them.

Also, if your child is already on stimulant medication for ADHD, neurofeedback could still be helpful; however, there is potential for an additive effect between the neurofeedback and the medication. An additive effect means that the effects add to each other; it would be like taking two medications that do the same thing. In certain situations, this might be detrimental. For instance, if medication tended to make your child over focus and the neurofeedback did the same thing, one might need to decrease the medication dose. Therapist and parents should stay aware of this and be prepared to decrease medication dosage if needed.

Overall Recommendations on Neurofeedback

In general, I view neurofeedback as an appealing, potentially effective tool when used as part of an integrative treatment program for ADHD. If it works as claimed, it has the advantage of teaching a child to take control of his own brain — correcting or improving his function in the brain regions that seem to be most affected in ADHD. So if he has too little beta wave activity and too little theta when concentration is called for, the feedback allows him to selectively and intentionally increase the beta activity to increase concentration. Presumably, and this is not entirely proven, learning this skill will carry over to school and life in general, rather than just in the EEG lab, and will last well beyond the treatment period.

EEG neurofeedback requires significant time and money to be effective, which is a real disadvantage of this treatment method (and also one reason do-it-yourself programs are becoming popular). The average number of sessions required is 40 or 50, although some practitioners claim that they can produce results in as little as 20 sessions. The average cost ranges from $80 to $150 per session, with a typical overall cost of between $3,000 and $5,000.

This may seem quite expensive, but perhaps not if we put it in perspective. Compared to many medical procedures, EEG neurofeedback isn't such a bad deal. I received a $2,500 emergency room charge for a one-hour visit for a bad case of poison oak! A 20-minute endoscopy, a test where a tube is introduced into the body to enable an examination with a special camera, costs up to a thousand dollars. Six months of weekly psychotherapy with a psychologist averages around $3,600. Of course, these expenses are generally covered by insurance, while insurance companies tend to deny payment for neurofeedback treatment (although I have known parents who did receive some reimbursement).

Viewed in this light, the payment neurofeedback practitioners receive for their time and effort is really not out of line. The difficulty lies more in paying for this therapy given the vagaries of our current health care system, which rewards procedures more than time spent with patients and arbitrarily picks and chooses what it pays for.

Still, this is a considerable amount of money and time for a treatment that does not have the full research base of many conventional treatments...one that comes without a guarantee, so to speak. It's understandable that many parents are reluctant to begin such an undertaking.

This is where the question of the duration of any gains made through neurofeedback becomes so important. Evidence about how long or whether the gains made by EEG neurofeedback last is still, at this writing, pretty thin. I, for one, would be an unhappy camper if I invested a significant amount of time and money for a treatment that at first seemed effective but six months later left no trace of benefit. One possibility is that ADHD children may need brief "tune-ups" — one or two sessions every so often to remind them how to do it. But there is no research as to whether this technique might make neurofeedback a more trustworthy intervention.

Neurofeedback also requires commitment from the children themselves. Although most kids seem to enjoy the sessions, many ADHD kids have limited tolerance and bore quickly. The child may get tired of showing up every week and doing neurofeedback instead of playing with friends. If you're considering this therapy, it's important to first assess your child's commitment level, with or without appropriate rewards.

Do-It-Yourself Neurofeedback

What about home-based "do-it-yourself" methods of neurofeedback (some of which are advertised and you therefore may have heard of)? Equipment and software is sold directly to parents for use in training their own child on the home computer. Theoretically, this could be effective, but I worry about this type of treatment being carried out by parents who do not have any expertise. I think it is entirely possible that adverse effects could occur and not be recognized. There is no published research on the effectiveness of these home training systems. I am very reluctant to recommend them at this point in time.

Selecting a Neurofeedback Practitioner

Should you decide to proceed with EEG neurofeedback, you now face the weighty task of choosing a practitioner. Many practitioners advertise neurofeedback, but how do you find the right one?

Start by looking at the practitioner's training and experience. Look for (preferably, but not necessarily) a clinical psychologist or medical doctor (MD) who has been certified by an appropriate body like the Biofeedback Certification Institute of America. Call the office and ask about the practitioner's experience in treating children with ADHD — it should be extensive. Ask friends or parents of other ADHD children (listserves or online support groups could be helpful here) if there is anyone they would recommend.

The Bottom Line. In my view, neurofeedback is a reasonable approach for ADHD. The rationale is appealing, the benefits may be significant and long-lasting, and the side effects and risks are minimal under appropriate guidance. Before trying neurofeedback, however, make sure you have tried all the recommendations made in this book regarding nutrition, food sensitivities, and vitamin and mineral levels, along with implementing an effective behavioral approach (see Chapter 12). If all of this isn't working and medication is looking like the only answer, neurofeedback might be a worthwhile alternative to explore.

Other Mind-Body Methods: Hypnotherapy and Guided Imagery

The word *hypnosis* might produce thoughts of stage hypnotists making people cluck like chickens or do other things that make them look ridiculous. It might remind you of some thriller novel or movie featuring a nefarious political group that uses hypnosis to exact mind control over others. These uses of hypnosis are mostly the stuff of myth and fantasy. In reality, **hypnotherapy, or the use of hypnosis to treat a medical or psychological problem, is a well-respected, thoroughly researched technique that has long been accepted in conventional medicine.**

What *is* hypnosis, exactly? If you asked 10 respected practitioners, you'd probably get at least 10 different answers, maybe more. Most generally, it can be described as a technique that helps a person's subconscious mind make positive changes for the mind and the body. For kids, I'd make it even simpler: hypnosis teaches children to use their own imagination and creativity to make positive changes in their health and well-being. The way I apply it, the more apt term would be self-hypnosis whereby children learn to do this for themselves rather than relying on a practitioner.

Children, in general, are very responsive to hypnotherapy; they learn self-hypnosis more quickly and easily than do adults. In fact, the peak of a person's ability to make use of hypnosis (hypnotizability) usually occurs around early adolescence. I use hypnosis frequently for children from the age of six or seven through the college years.

When I use hypnosis, I don't put children to "sleep" or in a deep trance state. I just help them reach a state of mind where they can relax and easily use their own creative imaginations to focus on whatever problem area needs addressing.

Here is a simple example. One of my patients was a 9-year-old girl who had been suffering from stomach aches almost on a daily basis for over a year, which was causing her to miss school and many of her favorite activities. A medical exam showed no identifiable problems and I believed it was stress-related, so self-hypnosis seemed likely to bring her some relief. In the self-hypnosis session, I encouraged her to relax, which she did easily, and go to a favorite place in her thoughts. Then I asked her to make an image of her pain, and another image to get rid of it. "I imagine the pain as a big red softball," she said (she was a softball player), "and I'm imagining hitting it out of the park." I made her an audiotape of the session and asked her to practice with it daily simply by listening to it. *Within two weeks, her pain was entirely gone…and it didn't come back!*

This is not an unusual case. In fact, a well-designed research study showed that one variation of hypnosis, called *guided imagery*, is a very effective treatment for abdominal pain in children.[3]

What does this all have to do with ADHD? I have found that, in certain circumstances, hypnosis can be a helpful treatment for ADHD. I'd love to cite some research to back up my point, but I am unable to do that because there is none. A few individual cases have been mentioned in books and articles, but not one good study exists showing that hypnosis is effective in ADHD. No studies show it to be *in*effective, either. The research hasn't been done because most practitioners believe that the very nature of ADHD would make it difficult to treat with hypnosis. They believe that these kids are too hyper to relax, or too lacking in attention span to respond to the suggestions.

My own experience has not borne this out because I have had some success using hypnotherapy/self-hypnosis training for children with ADHD. I don't think I have ever cured or completely resolved symptoms in a child with ADHD via hypnosis alone; however, I have found that it can be a helpful adjunct with certain children. It helps increase their confidence and improve their ability to control their behavior and to pay attention when circumstances demand.

Let me tell you about Joey, a 16-year-old junior in high school who had severe ADHD. He really did need medication, and despite taking the maximum dose he could tolerate, was still only performing marginally at school. While he could get his regular school work done, he would become anxious and distracted when tests began, often failing or getting poorer marks than he otherwise would have.

It turned out that Joey was a major fan of the *Lord of the Rings* fantasy novels by J.R.R. Tolkien. He read them repeatedly and watched the movies often. To try self-hypnosis with him, I began by teaching Joey some relaxation techniques, and he responded beautifully — it was amazing to see how easily this very hyperactive young man could achieve a deep state of relaxation. Then he imagined himself as Aragorn, one of the heroes of the *Lord of the Rings*, encountering and overcoming the various perils and threats that take place in the novel. I interjected some positive suggestions about his own ability to overcome difficulties and reminded him how using self-hypnosis would help him at school.

After three or four sessions, Joey reported that his test-taking anxiety was greatly reduced and he had achieved the best grades ever on his finals! Joey also happened to be a serious gymnast, and a side benefit of self-hypnosis emerged in his gymnastics practices because he was able to overcome an anxiety reaction related to a particular move that had been causing him much difficulty. Overall, there was a huge improvement in Joey's quality of life from just a few hypnosis sessions.

Was Joey "cured?" No. Was he able to use this technique to improve his ability to function successfully despite his ADHD? Yes. And how much time and expense did these improvements require? Very little.

I do not think every child with ADHD will respond to self-hypnosis training, guided imagery, or similar techniques. However, I think these are underused methods that can be quite helpful for certain children.

Adverse Effects of Hypnotherapy

When it's employed by a responsible, certified practitioner, hypnosis has few if any adverse effects. In older people or in those who have been abused, it could bring up previously repressed or hidden memories — a circumstance that the practitioner must be able to deal with. This has never happened to me in my practice and rarely happens with the type of hypnosis training we are discussing here. If a child has serious psychiatric issues in addition to ADHD, I would be careful about using hypnosis except with a very experienced psychologist.

Selecting a Good Hypnotherapist

I strongly recommend working with a hypnotherapist who has been certified by the American Society of Clinical Hypnosis. This is the only certification that has standards rigorous enough to be reliable. To achieve and maintain this certification, a practitioner must already be licensed and must substantiate many hours of approved training and continuing practice and education. This means that ASCH-certified practitioners are generally MDs, psychologists, social workers, or other well-trained professionals. Another reliable certification program is the one conducted by the Academy of Guided Imagery.

There are many lay hypnotists — individuals not in any medical or counseling field who have learned to practice hypnosis on their own, often with less formal training. They could be quite skilled in the art of hypnosis, but it is hard to evaluate their qualifications for working with any particular condition.

A general rule of thumb: **Practitioners should not treat a condition *with* hypnotherapy unless they are comfortable treating that condition *without* hypnotherapy.** I do not treat children with schizophrenia or victims of sexual abuse; therefore, I would not use hypnosis to treat any child suffering from either of these two conditions. But I do treat many children with ADHD, and hypnotherapy is only one tool in my toolbox, so I am confident in treating ADHD with hypnosis. Be sure that the hypnotherapist you select to treat your child has substantial experience with children with ADHD. If you can get a personal recommendation from someone you know, so much the better.

Yoga and Meditation

Two other modalities that could loosely be termed mind-body methods are Yoga and meditation. They have the common purpose of teaching children to be able to achieve a relaxed and quiet state of mind while performing certain mental and/or physical exercises. The hope is that mastering these skills will generalize to other aspects of their life.

There is some very preliminary research indicating that these two techniques might be helpful in some children with ADHD. One particular meditation technique, termed "mindfulness based stress-reduction," has been shown to be effective in a number of medical conditions. A recent but as yet unpublished study trained 72 families in this technique.[4] Compared to controls (who received no training), the children in these families showed a significant increase in attention skills and a decrease in their baseline anxiety.

Using these techniques makes intuitive sense, since both Yoga and meditation are designed to calm and relax, certainly useful skills for children with ADHD. I have had some parents tell me that either Yoga or meditation was quite helpful for their child as part of an integrative treatment program. I myself teach a simple "relaxation breath" to many children with either ADHD or anxiety, and it can be quite helpful for the child to develop a sense of a calm center. All of these approaches are quite safe, pose almost no risk, and are relatively inexpensive. I encourage exploring these methods if they are of interest to you and your child.

A Final Word on Mind-Body Techniques

It really isn't a surprise that these types of interventions can be helpful for children with ADHD. As we emphasized very early in this book: *the messages children get from their environment, and especially from their parents, are crucial in helping them modify their behavior — for better or for worse.*

Even though we know there may be brain wave differences, neurotransmitter imbalances, and other 'physical' dimensions of ADHD, it is clear that these children's attitudes, beliefs, and expectations can have very significant effects on their behavior and achievement. The mind-body techniques are simply a different approach to helping children modify their own behavior. They enable the child, with the assistance of a skilled teacher or therapist, to use his or her own creative energy and imagination to make desired changes wherever they are needed.

Chapter 11
The Alternative Therapies: Traditional Chinese Medicine, Homeopathy, and Energy Medicine

While one might consider the approaches we have already discussed — nutritional approaches, biofeedback, hypnosis, and herbal medicines — to be in the realm of alternative medicine, most of what we've looked at so far turns out to have foundations in the usual theories and principles of Western medicine. After all, does the measurement of iron and zinc levels qualify as a true alternative to Western medicine if scientific studies show that these minerals might be important for children with ADHD?

Similarly, the idea that food sensitivities or allergies might cause behavioral reactions is well known in conventional medicine, even if this notion is not usually applied to ADHD; and, again, studies in well-respected medical journals support the validity of this. Omega-3 fatty acids have been so extensively researched in recent years that it would be hard to describe their use as 'alternative' in any sense of the word. And finally, although the herbs discussed in Chapter 9 might be viewed with suspicion by many physicians, the fact is that the majority of our medications are derived from plants, and the methods used to study herbs and their effects are very similar to those used to study medications.

In this chapter, we'll look at some healing systems that are *truly* alternative — meaning that they have a completely different theoretical basis and approach from that of conventional Western medicine. We'll look at *traditional Chinese medicine* (TCM), *homeopathy*, *manipulative therapies*, and *energy medicine*.

TCM (which includes acupuncture) and homeopathy are what I would describe as *whole systems*: they involve complete systems of theory and practice that have evolved independently from, or parallel to, systems of conventional medicine. The manipulative therapies rely on a traditional Western understanding of anatomy and physiology but tend to take an alternative approach to the understanding of disease and treatment. Energy medicine is not really a single system; it's a term that describes a number of types of healing, all of which are based on the use of some type of non-physical energy to produce healing effects.

There is some research supporting acupuncture and homeopathy as therapies for ADHD. While manipulative therapies and energy medicine do not enjoy support in the form of medical research as direct treatments for children with ADHD, they have a good amount of anecdotal support — this means that while research hasn't been published on their efficacy for ADHD, many parents who have tried these therapies report positive, helpful outcomes for their children. Some of these outcomes seem to bring some level of relief from ADHD symptoms while others promote the child's ability to relax and be calm or promote the healing of other symptoms that may or may not be related directly to the child's ADHD.

Even if you are skeptical about these alternative practices, I ask that you keep an open mind. Consider that people have been using these methods successfully for hundreds or even thousands of years. We should not be too quick to dismiss a method of healing simply because it is not in line with current dogma.

Traditional Chinese Medicine: An Overview

Traditional Chinese medicine is one of the oldest complete medical systems on earth. People have been developing and using this system for over 2,000 years. In many parts of the world throughout this period, it was the only health care available. Even now, TCM is used on a daily basis as a basic form of medicine for hundreds of millions of people in China and other parts of Asia.

TCM is often mistakenly believed to consist exclusively of acupuncture. However, it also incorporates a sophisticated, complex approach to herbal medical treatment, as well as bodywork, movement therapy (*t'ai chi* and *qi gong* — the latter is pronounced "chee kung"), and dietary prescriptions.

TCM is based on theoretical principles that differ dramatically from those of Western medicine. Describing TCM in these few paragraphs here will give you only an inkling of its complexity and can hardly do it justice. My intention is merely to give you the information you need to decide whether or not you'd like to check into it further and consider it as a possible treatment modality for your child.

In TCM, there are two fundamental concepts: *qi* or *chi* (pronounced "chee") and yin/yang. Qi is the vital energy or force that permeates the entire body and mind, and yin/yang refers to the two major principles of the universe whose interaction creates qi and thus all life. In the most simplistic sense, yin refers to female or receptive energy and yang refers to active or male energy.

Disease, according to TCM, has one very basic cause: the disruption of qi energy. If qi is disrupted, disease of some kind occurs. This disruption has three major causes: internal (emotions), external (outside factors such as infection or cold wind), or lifestyle (factors such as poor diet, stress, and lack of sleep). These disruptions create problems in the flow of qi, which in turn throws the opposing yin/yang energies out of balance. All of TCM medical practice is based on restoring the flow of qi and righting these imbalances through acupuncture, herbs, movement, and/or diet.

Acupuncture is the best known of the TCM therapies and the most researched. It restores the flow of qi through energy channels called *meridians*, which are the means by which qi circulates throughout the entire body to nourish, warm, and protect all cells, organs, and tissues. Energy, or qi, flows up and down these meridians. This energy can be blocked, deficient, or excessive. In acupuncture, very thin needles are inserted into the skin at specific points along these meridians. The purpose of this is to restore the correct flow of energy and the return of balance and good health.

These notions of health and healing may sound somewhat foreign to you if not downright strange. Whether or not you accept the theory behind a healing modality, the most important consideration is whether it works. And, as it turns out, there is a sizeable body of research demonstrating that TCM is effective for many conditions.

An Even Older Traditional Medical System

There is another complete medical system known as *Ayurveda,* the traditional medical system of India, which is much older than TCM, predating it by 3,000 years or more. Loosely translated as "the science of long life," Ayurveda incorporates dietary, herbal, and life-style therapies in an elegant and complex system that millions of people have used effectively as their single source of medical care for centuries. I have chosen to leave Ayurvedic medicine out of this discussion — not because it isn't effective (it is) for many medical conditions or because it isn't fascinating and full of useful wisdom, but because it is a very complex system with relatively few well-trained Ayurvedic practitioners in this country.

TCM Research

It's not easy to perform research studies on acupuncture. As with neurofeedback or hypnosis, it's not possible to do a traditional double-blind study as with a medication. People know when they've had needles stuck into their bodies or not! Also, since TCM practitioners don't use the same diagnostic system used in Western medicine — 'yin deficiency' just doesn't translate well into "medicalese" — it is hard to replicate traditional acupuncture practice in a Western study. Despite these obstacles, enough research has been done to show that TCM is effective for a number of medical conditions.

Since 1996, over 7,000 articles have been published about TCM, and most (over 5,000) were published in English. Much of this research was performed in conventional research settings.

For example, a medical group called The Cochrane Review had this to say about acupuncture for chronic tension headache, a medical condition that is very difficult to treat: *"The authors conclude that acupuncture could be a valuable non-pharmacological tool in patients with frequent episodic or chronic tension-type headaches."*[1] While this may not sound like an unequivocal endorsement of acupuncture, it is actually a very strong statement given that the Cochrane group requires any treatment to meet *very* demanding standards before stating that it is effective.

Here is a short list of diseases, symptoms, or conditions for which acupuncture has been shown to be effective in at least some controlled clinical trials, as compiled by the World Health Organization (WHO):[2]

- Adverse reactions to radiation therapy and/or chemotherapy
- Biliary colic (cramping caused by gallstones)
- Correction of malposition of fetus (for example, a baby that is breech, or upside-down, in the mother's uterus) or for induction of labor
- Dental pain
- Depression
- Dysentery (diarrheal disease caused by the *shigella* bacterium)
- Facial pain (including pain caused by temporomandibular joint dysfunction, or TMJ)
- Headache
- Hypertension (high blood pressure)
- Hypotension (low blood pressure)
- Knee pain
- Leukopenia (abnormally low white blood cell count)
- Low back pain
- Menstrual pain
- Morning sickness
- Nausea and vomiting
- Neck pain
- Postoperative pain

- Renal colic (kidney pain)
- Rheumatoid arthritis
- Runny nose caused by allergy (including hay fever)
- Sciatica
- Shoulder pain caused by arthritis
- Sprain
- Stomach pain (in peptic ulcer, acute and chronic gastritis, and spasm of the stomach wall)
- Stroke
- Tennis elbow

Thus there is little doubt that acupuncture can be an effective treatment modality for many conditions. You may have noticed that ADHD is missing from this list, however.

Unfortunately, not much research has been done in English or in other Western languages about TCM for treatment of ADHD. At this writing, a search of the U.S. National Library of Medicine's database reveals only seven studies on acupuncture for ADHD. Of those, only one was an actual research study that used acupuncture for the condition.

According to Dr. Bob Flaws, a leading Western expert on TCM, ADHD has only recently been recognized in China. Dr. Flaws notes that interest and research in ADHD surged in China in 2003 — perhaps, he speculated, due to the adoption of Western food and lifestyle. There could have been a true increase in the number of children developing ADHD or just an increased focus on previously unrecognized children who exhibited symptoms of ADHD.

In translations of seven recent articles on the treatment of ADHD with acupuncture or herbal medicine, Dr. Flaws reports consistently positive results.[3] However, the studies have a number of limitations. None of them had an adequate control group, there is no randomization, and some of the results are so dramatically positive as to defy belief. I think all one could reasonably say is that these studies indicate that TCM *could* be an effective treatment method for ADHD but higher quality research needs to be done to prove it.

Here is an interesting story from one of my patients. Her son had Asperger's syndrome as well as attention issues and had developed disturbing involuntary, obsessive movements of his fingers.

"You saw my son G who was diagnosed with Asperger's syndrome. I wanted to report the positive results we received from acupuncture with Dr. C.

G had involuntary movement of his fingers. He touched his fingers to each other over 100 times a minute. He did this almost non-stop. He had this involuntary movement for almost 6 months before the acupuncture started. G did not experience any involuntary movement while he was actually receiving acupuncture. After each visit, it took longer and longer for him to revert back into the involuntary movement. His frequency became less and less after each visit.

After 4 weeks, there was no involuntary movement at all. Nothing else changed for G during this time he received acupuncture. He had been on fish oil and zinc for 6 months when he started acupuncture. He was not on any medications and was not receiving any other treatments. G had the acupuncture with Dr. C twice a week for 6 weeks. Then, G received follow up acupuncture once a week for almost a year. The involuntary movement has not returned. I accredit the involuntary movement cure to acupuncture. G also reports feelings of calm and well being from acupuncture.

The Chinese Medicine Perspective on ADHD

Although this particular information is not necessary to know to receive treatment, you might share my fascination with the way in which Chinese medicine looks at this disorder. According to the TCM perspective, the main symptoms of attention deficit hyperactivity disorder correspond to the traditional Chinese disease categories of irritability (*yi nu, duo nu*), insomnia (*bu mian*), profuse dreams (*duo meng*), oppressive ghost dreams (*meng yan*), vexation and agitation (*fan zao*), and impaired memory (*jian wang*). According to Flaws' translation of a Chinese medical text on the subject, "The main disease mechanism of ADHD is the presence of some sort of heat evils which harass and stir (*dong*) the heart spirit."[4] I imagine the part about vexation, agitation, and harassment rings a bell with some of you!

Is TCM Safe?

Acupuncture is very safe. Any responsible practitioner uses new, sterile needles each time, eliminating danger of contamination. The incidence of complications from acupuncture is extremely low. For smaller children who don't like needles, acupressure or other non-needle methods can be used.

Chinese *herbal* medicine may not be as safe. As mentioned in Chapter 9, contamination has been an issue with a number of Chinese herbal preparations. Some were found to contain lead; others, pharmaceutical additives that would produce the effects the herb was supposed to produce. Some Chinese herbal creams for eczema, for example, have been found to contain steroids — the pharmaceutical treatment for eczema. Sticking with the most reliable Chinese herbal companies — those that observe strict standards of safety —

is the best way to avoid this problem.

The other problem with Chinese herbal medicines is less easily solved: the fact that each preparation usually contains a number of different herbs, often 10 or 20 of them, most of which have never been tested for safety in children, either alone or in combination with other herbs. The herbs' long tradition of use is a good indicator of safety, but there is at present some unavoidable risk involved.

The Bottom Line on Traditional Chinese Medicine for ADHD

Overall, I would recommend the use of acupuncture for any child with ADHD if previous interventions have not solved the problem, especially when the only other choice appears to be pharmaceutical medication. The risks are low, it is not overly expensive — some insurance plans even cover it — and a few sessions should be enough to indicate whether continuing the treatment is worthwhile. On the other hand, I cannot recommend Chinese herbal medicine across the board for children with ADHD because of safety issues. It could be used on an individual basis with the guidance of a trusted practitioner, especially if treatment was confined to herbs with known safety profiles.

Finding a Good TCM Practitioner

Acupuncture has become an extremely popular treatment modality in the United States. It is practiced by two main groups: (1) acupuncturists whose medical training has been entirely devoted to traditional Chinese medicine, either in China or in the United States; or (2) Western medical doctors who have added acupuncture to their qualifications through coursework and practical training. The most respected courses require over 300 hours of the trainee's time.

I suggest looking for someone whose full training and work is in traditional Chinese medicine. Make sure the practitioner is certified by the National Certification Commission for Acupuncture and Oriental Medicine, which is the main certifying body in the United States for traditional Chinese medicine (the commission's web site is www.nccaom.org). Ask practitioners about their experience in treating children in general and children with ADHD in particular. Of course, a recommendation from someone whose own child has been successfully treated for ADHD is always helpful.

Homeopathy

While TCM operates on a set of assumptions foreign to Western medicine, homeopathic theory turns Western medical assumptions completely backward and upside down. If traditional Chinese medicine is viewed with suspicion and skepticism by many conventional doctors, the idea of homeopathy drives them completely bonkers!

Before going into this theory, let's take a look at the history of homeopathy. Unlike TCM or Ayurveda, which have thousands of years of history behind them, homeopathy was established by a single man, Samuel Hahnemann, around 1790. Hahnemann was a dedicated medical doctor who became disillusioned by the harsh and essentially useless medical procedures of his time.

The established, conventional medicine of Hahnemann's time was truly horrendous. The main treatments were bloodletting (often with leeches); administering substances that led to purging (severe diarrhea) or vomiting; blistering the skin; and the use of toxic doses of sulfur and mercury. The latter type of treatment is widely assumed to have caused the death of George Washington and probably killed thousands of others. It's no wonder that Hahnemann was moved to look for something better. His efforts to find more humane and effective methods of treatment led him and his followers to develop the gentle therapy now known as homeopathy.

Homeopathic medicine became widely popular in Europe, the United States, and many parts of the rest of the world, especially India. It was as popular as conventional medicine in the United States until driven out of business by the American Medical Association in what was basically a turf war. (Ironically, until recently, the name of one of the most prestigious medical schools in Philadelphia was the Samuel Hahnemann School of Medicine.)

The Principles of Homeopathy

Homeopathy is based on three main principles: the Law of Similarities, the Principle of Individualization, and the Principle of Minimal Dose.

The Law of Similarities

This law, also known as the Law of Similars, can be boiled down to the concept of *like cures like*. To treat a person with any set of symptoms, the homeopath uses a medicine that would *cause* those symptoms in a healthy person. (In allopathic Western medicine, we take the opposite tack, using drugs to *oppose* the action of the disease.)

To use a simple example: Onions cause watery discharge from the eyes and nose of a healthy person. Therefore, one would use a preparation made from an onion to treat a person who has watery discharge from the eyes and nose, such as hay fever.

To the uninitiated, this might sound strange...and it gets stranger.

Principle of Individualization

A homeopath finds a remedy by looking not just at the main complaints of the patient, but at every aspect of the patient's health. Homeopathic diagnosis requires a thorough evaluation of the individual's entire mental, emotional, and physical state.

The homeopath asks detailed questions to find out how well the patient sleeps, eats, and reacts to various stimuli. Remedies are prescribed according to these in-depth evaluations. For each disease or disorder — high blood pressure or depression, for example — one or more of many remedies might be prescribed, depending upon all of the above factors. This is also a difficult concept for conventional doctors to accept, since allopathy (Western medicine) relies on finding specific remedies for specific symptoms or pathologies.

Principle of Minimal Dose

Once the proper remedy is found, it is diluted in water until the original substance is barely present. Typical dilutions of remedy substance to water are from 1:10,000 to less than 1:1 trillion! **In homeopathy, the more dilute the substance, the more powerful it is.** A substance diluted to a ratio of one part substance to one million parts water is considered to be a stronger medicine than the same substance with a dilution of one part substance to ten thousand parts water! Some homeopathic remedies are so dilute that no trace of the original molecule remains in the medicine! According to homeopathic theory, the medicine leaves an "impression" — an energy or some other type of information — in the water in which it is diluted. The water thereby takes on the original healing properties of the substance in question.

This, more than any other factor, is what makes most Western doctors dismiss homeopathy as complete nonsense, and in a way one cannot blame them. I am not going to try convincing the scientifically minded that this makes sense. It's a hopeless task. For our purposes here, it is more important that I talk about the evidence as to whether homeopathy works regardless of the theory behind it.

However: I *will* point out one scientific fact that you may not know. It is actually true that water has a complicated structure (not just random hydrogen and oxygen, as in H_2O) that can be 'seen' by sophisticated scientific instruments. We know that this structure can be changed or affected by various types of energy. It is also true that the structural effect of some types of energy interacting with water will persist after the energy is removed.

Therefore, it is not completely implausible that a homeopathic substance will have an effect on water and that this effect could remain when the substance is diluted out of that water.

You also may not know that vaccination, which has saved the lives of countless millions of people all over the world, works more along homeopathic principles than allopathic theory. We inject very small amounts or fragments of viruses or bacteria (for example, influenza virus or diphtheria) into the body to cause the immune system to have a reaction. This reaction is not a full-blown disease, but it's adequate to protect the body against the disease in the future. I would not want to carry this analogy too far, but it is food for thought when skepticism arises about the value of homeopathy.

Does Homeopathy Work?

Although much less ancient than traditional Chinese medicine, homeopathy has been used by millions of people worldwide in its 200 years of existence. It is widely accepted in England and Europe, where homeopathic medications are available in traditional pharmacies. It is even more popular in India, where homeopathic practitioners, colleges, and hospitals abound. The royal family of England has had its own homeopathic practitioner since the 1830s. More than 1,000 homeopathic practitioners work in the U.S. — although we're lagging behind the rest of the Western world in embracing this alternative therapy as we have most others.

Does widespread use of homeopathy prove that it works? Of course not. Only research can 'prove' that a treatment works. However, it is hard for me to believe that so many millions of people around the world are being so fooled by a treatment that has no efficacy whatsoever.

It is true that the mechanisms by which homeopathy works are not well understood, and ideally, we would know exactly how a treatment works before using it. However, this is not always practical or even necessary. In conventional medicine, we used aspirin for many years before anyone figured out how it worked. We still don't know exactly how some of our most effective seizure medicines work. There is a long tradition in conventional medicine of using treatments before understanding their exact mechanism of action. We shouldn't hold alternative medicines to a higher standard.

Homeopathic Research

Unlike some other alternative treatments, homeopathy lends itself fairly well to traditional scientific research, at least in a basic way. Homeopathic treatments come in the form of little white pills or clear liquids, so it's easy to create a placebo that looks just like the real medicine. Overall, I believe the research indicates that homeopathy is effective in at least some situations.

A number of research studies have looked at the effectiveness of homeopathy for a wide variety of conditions. Some of these studies have shown homeopathy to be effective; some have not. *Meta-analyses*, which combine and evaluate the results of a number of different studies, have been mostly positive. In other words, they generally support the theory that homeopathy works. Two of the meta-analyses that showed homeopathy to be effective were published in the *Lancet* and the *British Medical Journal*, two of the world's most respected medical journals.[5,6]

When these studies were published, some physicians wrote letters to the editor in which they essentially said, "Homeopathy can't work because its principles make no sense. Therefore, it doesn't matter how good the research is; it can't be right, and you shouldn't publish it." Talk about wearing blinders....

Research concerning the use of homeopathy for ADHD is limited. Although there are a number of studies, only three have used the kind of randomized study design we discussed previously.[7,8,9] Two of these showed that homeopathy was effective, while one showed it was not. At this point I would have to say the scientific research on homeopathy and ADHD is inconclusive.

Is Homeopathy Safe?

From a conventional scientific point of view, homeopathic remedies are completely safe because the medicines used are so dilute that they could not possibly cause any harm. This is reassuring. On the other hand, it makes no sense to me to believe that a substance can have the power to heal but not have the power to cause a negative effect. In fact, homeopaths often warn that there can be a temporary worsening of symptoms after taking the remedy.

Overall, however, I believe that homeopathy is quite safe, and I personally have not seen any negative effects that persist after the remedy is stopped.

Finding a Homeopathic Practitioner

Finding a good homeopathic practitioner can be a challenge. Many kinds of alternative practitioners use homeopathy to some extent in their practices, including naturopaths, chiropractors, nutritionists, and even a few medical doctors. These providers have varying degrees of training, from one or two courses to quite extensive study. They use homeopathy as part of their holistic medical toolkit — and some may use it quite well.

On the other hand, there are homeopaths who have gone to a four-year homeopathic college, and they practice homeopathy exclusively and on a daily basis. In general, these well-qualified practitioners would be more likely to have the skills and experience to treat children with ADHD successfully. For homeopathic treatment of ADHD, I would strongly recommend a homeopath who has been to a four-year homeopathic school for training in classical homeopathy and who does homeopathy as a full-time specialty.

Constitutional vs. Acute Homeopathy

The true classical homeopathic practitioner practices *constitutional* homeopathy in which the Principle of Individualization is upheld. The homeopath would not just use a treatment or two for ADHD but would individualize his remedies to take into account the patient as a unique person based on that patient's extensive history.

On the other hand, you can go the health food store to buy homeopathic remedies for many different ailments: colds, stomach aches, sleep problems, and even ADHD. I'm calling this *acute* homeopathy; it is not true homeopathy. Samuel Hahnemann would probably turn over in his grave if he saw people purchasing homeopathic remedies in a health food store to treat a particular symptom. With apologies to the good Doctor Hahnemann, I believe that these preparations *can* be effective, especially for simple, acute problems. For more chronic or deep-seated problems like ADHD, the constitutional approach would be best.

The Bottom Line on Homeopathy for ADHD

I believe homeopathy is a reasonable treatment alternative for ADHD. I have met a number of families who believe it was helpful, but also many who said it was not. The risk is very minimal and it does not require frequent visits or a big time commitment. Most insurance does not cover homeopathy, so paying for the visits can be expensive, although the cost of the remedies is quite reasonable. In my opinion, those of you who feel drawn to this type of treatment should go for it.

The Manipulative Therapies

Manipulative therapies are modalities that employ physical manipulation of various parts of the body in order to prevent or treat disease. The two most well-known manipulative therapies are *chiropractic* and *osteopathy*. Less well-known modalities include *craniosacral therapy*, the *Alexander technique*, and *Feldenkrais*. The Alexander and Feldenkrais techniques are actually movement-based therapies where the patient manipulates his or her own body; I won't go into these two therapies here.

Manipulative therapies have been employed by physicians since the dawn of medicine. They were used in our most ancient traditions. Manipulative therapies have gained tremendous popularity in the United States and the West in the last 100 years. Chiropractic especially is extremely popular; yearly, there are more patient visits to chiropractors in this country than to any other practitioner of alternative therapy. At least part of the reason for this statistic is that insurers usually cover chiropractic treatment; in some states, insurers are required by law to provide coverage for chiropractic.

In chiropractic, osteopathy, and craniosacral therapy, the emphasis is on the optimal positioning of the vertebral column, which houses the spinal cord and the roots of all the nerves that come out of the spinal cord. By far, the most common use of these therapies is for painful musculoskeletal problems — especially for back pain. You probably know at least one person who has gotten tremendous relief from chronic pain through chiropractic or another manipulative therapy. Overall, research has confirmed that these therapies are effective means of treatment for various musculoskeletal problems. Often, such treatments prove more effective than conventional approaches.

Many but not all practitioners of manipulative therapy believe that adjustment of the vertebral column and other musculoskeletal structures has a significant effect on systemic diseases, which are diseases not confined to the musculoskeletal tract. In children, for example, some practitioners feel that they can cure or improve such diseases as asthma, gastroesophageal reflux, colic, constipation, and various other childhood problems through manipulation. Not much research exists to support such claims aside from several studies that demonstrate the possible effectiveness of chiropractic manipulation for colic in infants.

Personally, I have seen some types of manipulative therapy result in very significant improvement in a wide variety of pediatric diseases. I have worked closely with a craniosacral therapist who has produced remarkable results in a number of children referred from my practice. Here's one striking example: Robert was a 5-year-old who had a very serious congenital liver disease. Because of this disease, he had high bilirubin levels in his blood, which caused chronic, serious itching. He also had painful gastroesophageal reflux. As a result, he awoke from sleep three times every night, which meant his parents also had to awaken to help him get back to sleep. After a single visit to the craniosacral therapist, Robert went home and slept 11 hours in a row. He slept through the night every night from then on! I have no idea how this happened, but it did. I've seen similarly impressive results with this same therapist's treatment of a number of different medical problems.

These experiences have convinced me that manipulation of the musculoskeletal system *can*, most definitely, have effects on systemic health and disease.

Strain-Counterstrain

Strain-counterstrain is a type of manipulation generally performed by osteopathic physicians. It is one of my two favorite manipulative therapies (the other is craniosacral therapy, which is mentioned above). In strain-counterstrain, pain or disease is ascribed to tender musculoskeletal "knots" or tender points that resolve with astonishing quickness when the muscle involved is held in a position of maximum relaxation for some period of time.

I have personally witnessed a few amazing cures with strain-counterstrain therapy. One teenager who had debilitating neck pain and tics for three years — and had been placed on every psychiatric medicine known to man — was completely cured in two sessions. I also remember an adult who had suffered from gastrointestinal problems for years and was similarly cured.

The only problem with this technique is the difficulty finding a good practitioner. Osteopathic physicians, chiropractors, physical therapists, and even massage therapists can undergo training in strain-counterstrain. The best you can do at this point is to ask the practitioner in question whether he or she has had training in this form of manipulative therapy and discuss with him or her whether it might be helpful for your child.

Safety of Manipulative Therapies

All of the manipulative therapies appear to be quite safe for children. Research shows the incidence of serious side effects to be extremely low. Some parents worry about the somewhat abrupt neck movements (high-velocity adjustments) used by some therapists, especially chiropractors. If this is a concern, you could ask the therapist to avoid high-velocity adjustments with your child, or you could seek out a craniosacral therapist, who will perform extremely gentle hands-on adjustments.

The Bottom Line on Manipulative Therapies and ADHD

Although I have been unable to find any research whatsoever concerning use of any of the manipulative therapies for ADHD — it just hasn't been done — I have met a number of families who have used these therapies for their children with ADHD. While the results haven't been dramatic, many of these parents felt that some type of manipulation really did help keep their child's ADHD symptoms in check.

This is rarely a permanent effect; the therapies usually need to be repeated periodically. Personally, I have never come across a family who credited a manipulative therapy with curing or resolving a child's ADHD. The most common result didn't involve great improvements in concentration and attention; rather, the therapy seems to help the child better attain a state of calm relaxation.

If you are inclined to try these therapies, seek out a licensed practitioner who is experienced with children — particularly children with ADHD. My first recommendation would be craniosacral therapy, but the other disciplines could be of value as well.

Energy Medicine

Energy medicine is based on the theory that human beings are infused with a subtle form of energy — a vital energy or life force. In this form of medicine, imbalances or blockages of this vital energy are believed to be a cause of disease. Treatment modalities of energy medicine have the common aim of healing people by affecting, enhancing, manipulating, or adjusting these energy fields.

This energy has different names in different healing traditions. It is called qi in traditional Chinese medicine; other traditions and fields of study have given it other names: *prana, doshas, ki, biofield energy, electromagnetic energy*. Whatever name is used, the fundamental premise is the same: that energy blockages or imbalances in the body are either a cause or an effect of disease and that by re-balancing or unblocking that energy, we can bring about healing.

Within the broad category of energy healing are many different modalities or specific types of energy healing, including:

- Qi gong, a Chinese practice
- Healing touch
- Therapeutic touch
- Polarity therapy
- Shamanic healing
- Jin shin jitsu
- Reiki (see below)

What all of these methods (and the many others that exist) have in common is that a practitioner is working with the energy fields of the patient and/or his or her own energy field to bring about some desired change in the flow or state of that patient's energy. Some energy healers use the Indian idea of *chakras*, which are energy centers along the spinal column that can provide a focus for balancing, strengthening, or otherwise modifying vital energy in the body.

Usually, energy healers work without touching the patient at all or use only a very light touch. Many energy healers often state they can see or feel the patient's energy in some way and are thus able to determine whether the intervention has been successful.

This is, of course, a highly controversial set of healing methods. Energy medicine is spurned and sometimes ridiculed by most physicians, and it's not difficult to see why. No one has really found a way to measure these energy fields (although various measurable forms of electromagnetic energy are indeed emitted from human bodies). The few attempts made so far to measure the human *biofield* (energy field) have not been convincing, so there is really no way to measure whether these energy fields are affected by any particular intervention. We can't measure changes in something we can't measure yet in the first place! Doctors are extremely uncomfortable with things that aren't measurable or detectable by at least one of the five senses.

What can be measured, however, are the *results* of energy therapy. Do patients get better as a result of treatment? This is where the discussion on energy medicine gets really interesting.

Therapeutic touch is the most researched of these modalities, probably because it has close ties to the nursing profession. According to the National Institutes of Health's NCCAM (National Center for Complementary and Alternative Medicine) web site, many small studies have been performed to evaluate therapeutic touch.[10] Out of 11 identified well-controlled studies — studies where a control group was used to weed out the placebo effect — seven had positive outcomes. This research suggests that energy healing may be effective. A number of studies have found benefits from qi gong, but few of those studies met the criteria for good science that we have here in the West. The other energy modalities have less research support than therapeutic touch or qi gong.

While the science is still young on energy healing, I've been told by many people of their intense, amazing personal experiences with these practices. Here is a personal story of my own experience with this modality. During my fellowship in Integrative Medicine at the University of Arizona — a program directed by Dr. Andrew Weil — I had the good fortune of spending two days with Rosalyn Bruyere, a well-known energy healer. At one point she demonstrated to me how, as a healer, she "moves energy" from herself to the patient. She gripped one of my hands in her hands and said she was sending light energy. I had to admit I didn't feel anything. Then she said she would send sound energy. I immediately felt strong, clear, separate, pulsing vibrations going up my arm and into my chest, as if I were attached to some kind of machine. I opened my eyes while this was happening and both her hand and mine were absolutely motionless!

One experience can be worth a thousand studies, and this experience convinced me that some healers *are* able to direct the flow of energy in a conscious way. I believe that many of these healers can facilitate healing. How often and consistently this happens is probably a function of the talent and gifts of the individual healer.

A Few Words about Reiki

Although often thought of as energy medicine, many Reiki practitioners consider it a healing practice that promotes overall balance, in some ways more similar to meditation or yoga than to something like healing touch, for example. It is a hands-on practice in which a practitioner places his or her hands lightly on a patient's body for some period of time for the purpose of balancing the energy fields throughout and surrounding the body. Reiki practitioners also commonly treat themselves on a regular basis, again similar to a yoga or meditation practice. Although there is no research concerning Reiki and ADHD, some studies in other medical situations indicate a positive effect on stress and anxiety. Reiki practitioners are permitted to practice in a number of hospitals around the country.

One mother I knew had learned Reiki and used it with her son before bedtime, usually calming him quickly and easily. First-level training takes about eight to 12 hours, and even children can be taught Reiki, so it is a very accessible practice for those who would like a hands-on way of helping their children. I know of no dangers or adverse effects from this modality, so I encourage those who are interested to explore further.

The Bottom Line on Energy Medicine and ADHD

Unfortunately, there is no research concerning energy medicine and ADHD. I have heard anecdotes from families about their children feeling calmer and quieter when treated, but I have never heard that any of these modalities had any lasting effect on ADHD. Any parent of an ADHD child knows, however, that even temporary calming and quieting can be a big relief.

Energy medicine is never paid for by insurance so the cost of regular treatment could become significant. If a parent could learn to use one of these methods so that it could be done regularly, I can see that it could become a useful part of an integrative approach.

All in all, energy medicine could be a useful adjunct to an integrative ADHD treatment program for some children. There is little chance of harm if a practitioner is carefully chosen, and positive results can come from it. So if you feel drawn to one of the energy modalities, and the expense is not too great, I would encourage giving it a try.

Surrendering Skepticism

Much of what we thought to be correct in conventional medicine as little as 50 years ago now seems horribly misguided to current practitioners. At one time, mainstream medicine put neurotoxic mercury in children's vaccines, treated simple tonsillitis with cancer-causing radiation therapy, advised mothers that formula feeding was much healthier than breastfeeding, and said that smoking was good for one's health. There is little doubt that much of what we view now as correct will similarly turn out to be completely mistaken.

Many of the theories and practices discussed in this chapter may be new or seem quite strange to some of you, especially if you hold a somewhat scientific point of view. But keep in mind that these therapies all have a longer track record of safety and efficacy than many of the therapies considered mainstream in the West today.

These therapies might not be for your child; or they might make a big difference. The only way to know for sure is to find a practitioner you can trust and see how the child responds. Hopefully, research will continue to be done on these therapies. Maybe in a decade's time I'll be able to give more solid recommendations on these alternative practices. Maybe, by then, some will even be considered mainstream therapy.

Chapter 12

Behavioral Interventions: Supporting Your Child at Home

It is my belief that the type of parenting a child receives at home is as important as any supplements, herbs, dietary changes, or medications that I could recommend. A child's sense of identity and worth comes directly from his or her parents. A strong foundation of self-worth is absolutely crucial for any child's happiness and continued success, no matter what their ADHD symptoms are — or whether they have ADHD at all. Therefore, no program designed to help ADHD children is complete without specific, intentionally applied strategies for parenting. Without such strategies in place, parents of ADHD children often find themselves floundering in an inconsistent, reactive approach that consists largely of trying every way they can think of to keep the child under control. The child's self-esteem and self-worth end up being adversely affected. It's a lose-lose situation.

Is there one single parenting approach that will succeed with all ADHD children? Likely not, but any well-thought-out approach is probably better than none for parents who are dealing with a difficult or intense child. There is one parenting strategy that I highly recommend, but before we get to that, let's discuss some general principles.

Parenting Does Not *Cause* ADHD

Let's be clear about one thing: nothing you have or haven't done as a parent caused your child's ADHD. As you know by this point in the book, ADHD is a syndrome with a strong genetic component that is influenced by a complex set of environmental factors that include diet, nutritional deficiencies, chemical toxicities, and a host of other factors. Parenting and behavioral management are among those factors, and by implementing an optimal approach to parenting, you are taking advantage of another set of tools that can significantly improve the life of your child with ADHD.

Except in more extreme cases, it is very important to work at parenting and behavioral management before placing a child on medication. I say this for several reasons. First, studies show that parents who use medication rarely follow through with behavioral programs, unless and until the

164

medication stops working. Second, giving medication does not teach the child anything about how to manage ADHD without it. If a child was on medication for five years and then stopped, there may be no difference from five years ago because it is far from clear whether the long-term effects of medication are positive or permanent. Finally, I have seen many children for whom a change in parenting strategy (along with some good nutrition and supplements) made the use of medication completely unnecessary.

General Principles for Parenting the ADHD Child

The problem with finding parenting solutions for children with ADHD is that kids with this diagnosis can differ so dramatically from one another.

On one end of the continuum is the somewhat classic ADHD child. Imagine 7-year-old Lance, who is hyperactive and impulsive. He is constantly in trouble at school and at home. His attention span is short. He is oppositional and argumentative, often throwing temper tantrums when he doesn't get what he wants. He frequently acts the role of the class clown. He can make friends but loses them easily and is starting to receive fewer social invitations than he once did. His parents are frustrated and exhausted from trying to deal with his behavior.

On the other end of the spectrum is the inattentive child. Picture 9-year-old Jenny, who is quiet and dreamy. She is loving and cooperative and not at all hyperactive or impulsive. She has never been any trouble at home, but at school she is unable to concentrate for more than a few minutes on academics, although she is talented artistically. Despite making a good effort, she is falling behind in her school work. Socially she does well and has lots of friends. Her teachers love her.

Can there be one strategy that is optimal for working with these very different types of children?

Perhaps not entirely, but one overriding principle has to be the basis of any successful approach for any child with ADHD: **Every effort and priority must be aimed toward promoting and maintaining the child's sense of self-esteem, self-confidence, and self-worth.**

Although this is true to some extent for all children, it is absolutely essential for children with ADHD. These kids are often subject to a steady barrage of criticism and negative feedback from everyone around them. They end up being nearly constantly corrected by their parents, their teachers, their coaches — even by random strangers in the grocery store! During the school years, most of their waking hours are spent focused on things they don't do easily or as well as the people around them. All of this can result in a relentless assault on the child's sense of competency and self-worth.

A thought exercise: Imagine you are a very bright and competent second grader who is pretty good at reading and math and generally does well socially. The only thing you are really bad at is the arts. Your right brain skills are really poor. Your drawing is terrible, you have no ear for music, and anything involving spatial relationships is agonizingly difficult. But that hasn't been much of a problem so far. There are only a couple of art periods all week.

Your parents, both of whom are artists, decide to send you to a school completely devoted to the arts. Every day is one class period after another of drawing, painting, sculpture, singing, and learning to play an instrument. All week long, you have only one class of English and one of math. No matter how hard you try, each thing you produce is clearly near or at the bottom of the class in quality. Kids either tease you or try to ignore your off-pitch singing, the screeching of your musical instruments, and your uninspired artwork. When the report card comes, you barely manage to get Cs and Ds. You get remedial tutoring, but it is only minimally helpful.

How do you think you would feel about yourself? How long would you keep trying? How long do you think it would be before you would start acting out in some way or become depressed?

This may seem like an exaggerated or artificial situation, but in a very real sense, this is what happens to many children with ADHD. The one thing that is hardest for them is academics — perhaps because of their difficulties with focus and distractibility or perhaps because they are among the 40 percent of ADHD children with a learning disability.

So what do we ask them to do for most of the day? Academics. And what do we let them know is the most important thing for us and for their future? Academics. A child could be good at sports, art, social networking, building or computers, but we put our emphasis on reading, writing, and math — precisely the areas that present the most problems for the ADHD child.

Your response might be: "But reading and writing *are* crucial for our child's future. Being good at sports or the arts is unlikely to help him attend a good college or get a good job. Like it or not, we have to make sure our child does well at school and learns what is necessary." This is certainly true. The percentage of people who can make a successful living from sports or the arts is pretty small. It *is* hard to be very successful in this world without reasonable academic skills.

I am not suggesting that we stop trying to help our kids succeed academically. I *am* suggesting that we need to pay as much attention as possible to what our kids are good at and what makes them feel successful. We need to make sure they spend time doing things at which they excel and, even more importantly, make sure we appreciate every accomplishment. There is probably no child who does not have *some* strength or area of interest that can be used to bolster that child's sense of worth and value.

The irony is that ***by reaffirming children's sense of competence, value, and worth, we give them the psychological and emotional wherewithal to put in the extra effort needed to succeed academically.***

When we reinforce children for the things for which they have a natural facility, it's a win-win situation. We are helping them have fun and feel good about what they can do well and at the same time we are increasing their chances of academic success.

In practical terms, what do we need to do to accomplish this goal of continuing to improve on the child's academic abilities while not making them the only focus of the child's life?

- **Make sure your child is doing something beyond school work that is rewarding.** Zack should not have to go straight from school to tutoring and then do homework until dinner. ADHD children need to spend time doing something they are good at daily and on weekends. This could be sports, the arts, interacting with nature, or just being outside with friends. (And I am *not* referring to electronic media.)

- **Make sure your child knows that you value what he or she is good at.** If Jenny is good at art, take her to a museum, watch a TV show on art together, and give her lots of opportunity to participate in it. Let her know you think art is important and valuable. If George likes collecting stamps above all else, get involved. See if there is a stamp club he can join, and come home with neat new stamps once in a while. You might think stamp collecting is the most boring and useless thing in the world, but what's important is what *he* thinks about it and the recognition he gets from you about it.

I am reminded of a 7-year-old patient of mine who had ADHD, wasn't doing well in school, and had some behavioral issues. While her mom and I were talking, the girl quietly drew this incredible picture, which showed a great deal of talent. I said, "Wow, she's a really good artist!" Mom looked a little surprised, kind of shrugged, and said something like, "Yes, I guess she is pretty good at that kind of thing." How much positive feedback for her talents do you think this girl gets at home?

Of course, not every interest is created equal. For example, I don't think watching television is an interest you would be wise to reinforce. We've already discussed in an earlier chapter how detrimental the fast-moving images can be, especially for the ADHD child; plus there is just not a sense of accomplishment involved in TV watching that a parent can capitalize on for positive feedback. The same is true about video games in general, although with certain kids that may be the only thing you can start with, and it might be okay *if it is a constructive game* rather than one of mindless violence.

If your child is like Lance, whom we talked about at the beginning of the chapter, home life may be a series of frustrations and difficulties. His constant oppositional behavior may make it seem quite difficult to find things to value. You might find yourself almost constantly embroiled in arguing, yelling, or correcting him just to keep the daily routine on track. (We will talk soon about a specific approach to reverse this type of interaction that benefits no one.) Nonetheless, you still need to find things he is good at and help him see these, and himself, as valuable. If building with Legos is all that makes him happy, find a way to value that and get him to feel good about it.

- **Don't let homework occupy every waking hour!** This is cruel and unusual punishment for everyone, including you. An elementary school child should not be doing hours of homework each night! Although there is some disagreement about how long homework assignments should be expected to take, I think a good guideline is no more than 20 minutes a night in the first three years of school and no more than one hour per night by fifth grade. If your child's ADHD issues are causing a 20-minute assignment to take forever, this is when you need to work closely with his teacher and/or school counselor to come up with a reasonable solution.

- **Control the electronics.** Although it is difficult in our society to completely eliminate TV, video games, and computer games, they can have a very negative effect on some children with ADHD. The following is a direct quote from a parent whose son had greatly improved his ADHD symptoms through diet and supplements:

"I must also mention that computer games negate whatever we can do with diet. If he has been engaged in any type of game that elicits even the slightest adrenaline response, he will lose emotional control for at least an hour after being off the computer — which can lead to no eating — which can lead to an entire day lost in a myriad of depression, fighting, and crying."

Admittedly this is an unusually strong reaction, but I would advise paying close attention to the effect of electronic media on your child's behavior and setting firm limits on the content and time spent using them.

- **If necessary, help your ADHD child make and keep friends.** For some children with ADHD, making and keeping friends is easy; but for many others, it is an ongoing problem. Their impulsivity and restlessness may be off-putting to other children, and their social skills are often significantly below age level. **It is important to remember that ADHD children tend to have a delay in emotional maturity and often act three-fourths their chronological age.**

As a parent, it can be sad and frustrating to see your child rejected by his or her peers. If this is an issue for your child, be proactive. Try to determine with whom your child does get along well and make opportunities for them to be together. See if there is some after-school club or group that includes children with similar interests. Initially, you might have to be the one to go the extra mile to invite kids over for play dates and overnights. If your child does better with neighborhood children who are a year or two younger, don't worry about it. Emotional maturity will come eventually.

When I was young, the kids in my Queens neighborhood ran around in a group that included a fairly broad age range; the oldest was three or four years older than the youngest. We had a great time and didn't much worry about the age difference. The same was probably true in rural areas, where the number of kids was limited. It didn't seem to bother anyone back then, and I don't think having a friend who is a couple of years younger has to be a problem now.

It is not an easy job to play social secretary to an ADHD child, but if your child has real difficulty maintaining friendships, your help in this area is just as important as your academic help. For more difficult situations, some counselors or psychologists have social skills groups that can be helpful.

■ **Make sure your child gets adequate sleep.** For any child, getting adequate high quality sleep is very important for good health and optimal functioning. For children with ADHD, who often face increased stress and challenges in their lives, it is even more vital for their overall functioning. Unfortunately, many children with ADHD have difficulty with sleep. Most often they are so mentally and physically active that it is hard for them to wind down and fall asleep easily at night; this situation becomes even worse if they are taking psychostimulants. If they need to wake up early for school or because of parental work schedules, they may start the day tired, stressed, and grouchy. Fortunately, there are some simple measures that often solve this problem.

Avoid Caffeine. First, it is important to make sure that the child is not ingesting anything, especially caffeine, that is keeping him or her from sleeping. I recall recently evaluating a teenager with sleep problems; it turned out he was drinking ice tea all evening right up until bedtime. He changed to decaffeinated ice tea; problem solved. Second, it is important to establish a definite bedtime and be as consistent with it as possible. During the 30 minutes before bedtime, there should be no high activity, bright lights, TV, or computer games. A predictable bedtime ritual with reading, music, or storytelling is a great transition to sleep.

Herbal Remedies. There are some natural remedies that can be quite effective if your child still has difficulty falling asleep. Here are two. We already discussed a **valerian and lemon balm combination,** which can be used for sleep as well as calming. Obtain liquid tinctures for small children or capsules for older ones and adjust the dose based on how well it is working. Valerian can take a week or two before having maximum effect, so don't give up too soon. Valerian is generally recognized as a safe herb in reasonable doses. Some products add other calming herbs such as Hops, Melissa and skullcap. These are also generally safe for children. **Melatonin** is the hormone that is responsible for the day/night sleep cycle in all of us. During the day, light coming through the eyes reaches the pineal gland and melatonin production is shut off. When it gets dark, the pineal gland begins to produce melatonin, leading to sleep. Before electricity, the onset of darkness was a gradual progression beginning at sunset and by dark we were ready to sleep. Now we are exposed to bright lights until the minute we decide to go to sleep, so our melatonin may not kick in correctly. Taking a supplemental dose of melatonin 30 to 60 minutes before bed can be helpful. I advise starting with one milligram and increasing it gradually if needed. Doses up to 5 milligrams are safe in older children. Melatonin has been proven safe for as long as several months in a row. Longer term use has not been well researched so you should consult a health care professional.

I strongly advise against pharmaceutical products like antidepressants, benzodiazepines, and Clonidine unless they are absolutely necessary. They can be habit forming and often have significant side effects.

Self-hypnosis. Also, self-hypnosis training is an excellent way to teach children to fall asleep more easily. Many children in my practice have responded well to listening to "Dr. Sandy's" sleep tape made just for them. Audio tapes are also available online. (See the hypnosis section in Chapter 10 for more about this modality.)

■ **Get your child involved in a sport if he/she has natural ability and enjoys athletics.** Sports are important, valued, and prestigious in our country. If your child happens to be good at them, which some ADHD children are, you have a big advantage regarding the self-esteem issue. Sports success is a boost to a child's own self-esteem, and peers will forgive a lot of annoying behavior if Johnny or Jill can hit a ball over the fence or score a winning soccer goal.

Choosing a Sport for Your Child

Unfortunately, many children with ADHD are not very good at sports. They may be clumsy, follow instructions poorly, or have difficulty keeping their focus during team sports. The classic example is that 9-year-old out-fielder with ADHD, standing around and picking grass or looking at the clouds until the rare ball that actually comes his way hits him on the head. (Baseball is usually not a great sport for the ADHD child!) If your child's problem is not one of coordination, but of attention, individual sports like tennis, where the action is pretty much non-stop, can bring more success.

Martial arts can be a positive and confidence-building activity for many children with ADHD. The repetition, the discipline, and the overall atmosphere can be engaging and supportive. Regular reinforcement comes in the form of new and varied colored belts, which is often affirming for ADHD children. Martial arts have the advantage of being considered cool by other children, which can be an important social aspect for ADHD kids. Even kids who are somewhat clumsy at other sports can often master the limited series of moves necessary for karate, kung fu, jujitsu, or other forms.

Regardless of the type of martial arts, the most important element is the teacher — who sets the tone and attitude of the class and is crucial to whether the whole thing can be a successful experience for all involved. Remember *The Karate Kid?* You want Mr. Miyagi, not the other guy.

Recommended Behavioral Approach

For the remainder of this chapter, I will present the most successful and powerful approach I have found for working with the child with ADHD and with difficult children in general. It is called the **Nurtured Heart Approach** and was developed by Howard Glasser, a Family Therapist from Tucson, Arizona. I have been using it for many years, and the vast majority of families who have made a serious effort to apply it have had excellent results.

Before I proceed, I want to address, right up front, what might appear to be a conflict of interest in my recommendation of this particular approach. You may have already noticed that Howard Glasser is the publisher of this book. It would be quite reasonable to suspect that I am championing his method because he is the publisher rather than for any objective reason. The reverse is actually true. We both lived in Tucson, and I met Howard long before this book was written. Many of the families he was working with came to my pediatrics practice over the years, and long ago I became aware of the amazing results his approach was achieving with individual families, in schools, and even in Head Start programs. Since about 2003, I have been recommending and teaching this approach to almost all the families with

ADHD children that have come to my pediatrics practice.

In fact, I was about to sign a contract with another publisher when I ran into Howard and began discussing this book with him. In the course of our conversation, we both realized how similar our perspectives were and discovered a unique fit with the work we were each doing. I feel fortunate to have Howard publish my book. After you read about his approach, I am quite confident you will understand why I use it in my own practice and recommend it here.

The Nurtured Heart Approach: Transforming the Difficult Child

The Nurtured Heart Approach is a method of parenting children with ADHD and others who are highly intense or difficult by transforming the focus of their intensity and energy from one of ongoing opposition, negativity, and failure into one of success and achievement.[1] It is extremely simple in its theoretical framework and straightforward in its execution. Here are its basic principles.

ADHD children are more intense and have a far higher need for attention, energy, and interaction than do children without ADHD.

If they do not receive the needed energy and intensity through positive behaviors (like following rules, cooperating, behaving well), they will quickly find ways to receive it for negative behavior. To them, this is far better than receiving no energy at all.

Another way of looking at this is that ADHD children, because of what are very natural behaviors for them, receive huge amounts of attention, energy, and intensity from their parents for everything they do wrong, even as they receive little to none when they do things right. They learn, and very early on, that the way to get what they need is to break rules or threaten to break rules. This then becomes a primary way in which they seek reinforcement. A cycle ensues in which parents unwittingly continue to feed into these children's inner sense that they get more from the adults in their lives when they create problems than they do when they are "good."

The Nurtured Heart Approach provides tools for consciously increasing the levels of attention and energy given to positive behaviors while drastically decreasing the attention and energy given to negative behaviors.

Parents learn a few simple techniques for giving their energy to the child when he's following rules or reflecting desirable values or failing to break rules. As the child begins receiving all of his parents' attention/energy for what he does right and well, he begins to do more and more to get this energy and thereby begins to succeed more and more often. The flow of energy is reversed; the pattern of reward for negativity is flipped upside down, leading to a remarkable transformation in the child's behavior and self-esteem.

Consistent discipline is crucial: rules are strictly and consistently enforced through brief, un-energized "time-outs" or other interventions.

Don't think that this is a parenting method that ignores or lets children get away with rule-breaking or negative behavior. On the contrary; in this system, discipline must be enforced in a very consistent and predictable manner. The difference from more traditional parenting approaches is that the consequences are applied calmly, with as little 'fan fare' or emotional energy as possible, the goal being to remove all of the excitement that the child gets from breaking the rules.

The Usual Approach: Take One

Let's see how the typical interaction might play out between child and parent. Jesse is a relatively typical 8-year-old with ADHD. He is oppositional, tends toward temper tantrums, and is often disruptive. One day, at 5:30 in the afternoon, Jesse and his sister Carol arrive home from aftercare. They decide to play a board game while Mom makes dinner. After about 15 minutes, something goes wrong. Jesse throws the board at his sister and starts yelling at her. She runs into the kitchen crying. Mom, in an angry, loud, and intense voice, says something like: "Why can't you ever play with your sister quietly? Look at her! You just made her cry. What is the matter with you? Don't you know how bad you make her feel? Go to your room and don't come out until dinner. I'm just sick of this!"

Sound familiar? I doubt there's an ADHD family in the world where this has never happened, and in most, this kind of exchange sadly happens on a fairly regular basis.

Now let's examine the interaction from another point of view. What happened during the first 10 minutes of this scene? *Jesse played quietly with his sister, behaving exactly as his mother wanted. What feedback, energy, or attention did he get for this? Nothing! Zero! Zilch! He did not get one single ounce of attention, approval, or praise.* What happened next? Jesse had a mini-fit, hurting his sister and breaking several household rules in the process. *Now* he immediately got lots of attention, emotional intensity, and interaction with his mother. It didn't matter that he was then sent off to his room, the damage was done in the form of energizing negative behavior.

So what does Jesse learn, subconsciously or consciously, from this interaction? *Be good and you get ignored. Be bad and you get lots of juice from Mom.* Simple, isn't it?

From Jesse's perspective, it doesn't matter that he received a punishment (sent to his room), nor that the attention he received was negative. ***The over-riding factor is that he received so much emotional charge or energy from his Mom.*** Knowing he's misbehaved, and even feeling bad about it, just adds to his confusion. Howard Glasser refers to this as giving "$100 bills for negativity" — basically, where we tell the child *not* to do what he's been doing but at the same time ***hand him a hundred dollars worth of our energy!***

At this point, many parents are saying to themselves something like, "Shouldn't you be able to expect your son or daughter to play quietly or obey a few simple rules without having to make a big deal of it?" (I said this to myself many times while raising my own difficult child.) Well, maybe they *should* act like that without extra praise, and actually, most children do. For many kids with normal intensity and normal attention needs, just the fun of playing with a sibling and the tacit approval of their parents is plenty of re-inforcement. They don't need to act out to get that extra juice. But for the difficult, oppositional, or ADHD child, *it is just not enough.* If normal parenting worked for them, you wouldn't need to be reading this book!

Applying a New Approach: Take Two

Now let's replay the scene, with a mom who is just beginning to use the Nurtured Heart Approach. It's after school and, again, Jesse begins to play the board game with Carol. Three minutes later, Mom pokes her head in and says, "Hey, I notice you're playing Monopoly. That's great! I used to love playing Monopoly when I was a kid!" Then she goes back to cooking. If nothing goes wrong, Mom checks again in about three minutes and says enthusiastically, "Wow, I really like it when you guys play well together. Thanks, Jesse, for being such a fine big brother." Then back to cooking. (By the way, total time for those two positive interactions: less than one minute, perhaps less than 30 seconds depending on their proximity to the kitchen.) With this kind of support focused around making good choices, Jesse and Carol may play well until dinner.

But imagine instead that things go differently and Jesse gets mad and throws the board at his sister, who comes into the kitchen screaming. Now Mom says, *in a completely calm and neutral tone*, "That's a reset Jesse. Carol, you stay here and help me." A minute or less later, you can then welcome Jesse back with words of encouragement that reflect the truth of the current moments: "Jesse, I appreciate that you chose to calm down and get yourself reset. Even though you may still be mad, you are handling your strong feelings well and using your control to not argue and fuss. You are showing great control."

That's the whole interaction. No yelling. No lecturing. No warnings. No

bargaining. No emotional energy at all from Mom except to applaud the fact of his having calmed down. No more discussion, except for Mom saying, "I like the way you are back to getting along with your sister. Excellent cooperation. I know you like to peel potatoes — want to peel these for me?" He's back to what is called *time-in,* that experience of being appreciated for making good choices and following the rules.

So what did Jesse learn from this interaction, subconsciously or consciously? *Play nicely with your sister, and you get some nice connection and energy from your mom. Have a temper tantrum and you get no energy or connection at all.* And in this particular story, Jesse also benefits from seeing Carol get more attention for following the rules.

A reset is a time-out with an emphasis on moving forward to the new moments after the problem is over — when the child is restored to a place of not breaking rules. It's a reset to time-in. This approach to consequences gives parents the advantage of creating more momentum in the desired new direction of success. There may be times when a longer reset/time-out is merited or even some additional consequence, but it is still always given without the energy and relationship that so many conventional consequences carry, and it's always right back to recognizing and appreciating good choices.

It is not the purpose of this book to go into detail about the various subtleties of this approach or the various obstacles that can arise (like Jesse refusing to reset) or how it applies to the teenage years. These are all carefully spelled out in Howard Glasser's books and videos, referenced in Appendix B.

When this scenario happens on a daily and regular basis — when Jesse or Julie or Sam start to get more and more attentive relationship for everything they are doing right and little or no attention for what they are doing wrong — their behavior just naturally changes. They begin to see that their positive behaviors produce the intensity and relational connection they crave, while their negative behaviors don't produce much of anything. They are no longer getting those $100 bills (in the form of energy) for acting out, but for acting appropriately. Their self-esteem also improves as the proportion of positive to negative feedback in their lives soars higher and higher.

This Simple Approach Simply Works!

I know this sounds way too simple, perhaps too good to be true, but I will tell you from personal experience that I have seen the Nurtured Heart Approach result in significant and often dramatic changes in many, many families. To emphasize even more: I do not think I have worked with a single family who wholeheartedly applied this program without seeing significant results. It just flat-out works!

From a scientific point of view, this approach makes perfect sense. In behavioral psychology, positive reinforcement is accepted as the most powerful way to modify behavior; punishment is the least effective.

Video Game Parenting

As most of you know, even the most hyperactive child with the shortest attention span can usually focus on playing video games for hours. Why is that? Think of what transpires during a video game: almost constant energy and intensity; colors, lights, and sounds; and more importantly, *constant positive reinforcement*. During nearly every second of the game, the player is accumulating some kind of reward — points, swords, lights, treasures — as she plays. There may be an ultimate big prize at the end, but there is no time period during which some positive feedback is not occurring. What about the negative? That's also the genius of it. If the player makes a mistake, the consequence is quick and simple: either no sought-after reward, or the game ends. The video game doesn't get mad, yell, lecture, or punish. You can't argue with it either. You lose. Game over. On to the next one. It's a perfectly designed reinforcement system.[2]

While I don't recommend video games, aside from those with a really positive or learning-based foundation, this is the kind of reinforcement that kids crave and that can be applied to your parenting strategies with the Nurtured Heart Approach.

I recall my very first exposure to the Nurtured Heart Approach, which came by way of a parent of a patient. One of the most difficult children I had ever seen had become my patient. He was about four years old, extremely hyperactive, oppositional, and had already been diagnosed with ADHD and bipolar disease. He was on several medications, none of which fully controlled the symptoms. When his mom began using the Nurtured Heart Approach, she told me the results were incredible. She called it the most powerful positive intervention she had instituted, exceeding the results of any of the psychotropic medications. Her son's behavior improved almost overnight, changing him from an almost unmanageable terror into a child who still had significant problems but could be parented and enjoyed.

Sheri, a 12-year-old who had both high-functioning autism and ADHD, was another patient whose parents implemented the Nurtured Heart Approach. I knew the family well; they were wonderful, concerned parents. Mom described every school morning as a nightmare. Sheri hated to get up, couldn't get started, and had to be dragged through every step of getting ready. Showering, dressing, and eating breakfast required constant attention and usually ended up with tempers flaring and everyone miserable. Her 4-year-old sister was beginning to react with her own negative behaviors in response to this constant drama. Within a week or two of implementing the new approach, the entire situation improved dramatically. Sheri happily went about her morning routine with minimal attention, and the tantrums and anger resolved. Mom said, with all sincerity: "This changed our lives."

Nurturing the Inattentive Child

If you have a dreamy, inattentive child like Jenny, who was described earlier in this chapter, you might think much of this method would not apply. She may rarely break rules; she's likely to be so sweet that she gets little criticism. For such a girl (or boy), aspects of this approach will still apply and you can modify what you use from it accordingly. As well as needing positive feedback for what she does well, it is important to contain your emotional response to her shortcomings; do not let them become the focus of her life. As long as her self-esteem is maintained, you may be able to apply the program in a less intense and focused way than you would if your child were more invested in pushing limits.

The Nurtured Heart Approach in Schools and Foster Care: Stories of Success

The Nurtured Heart Approach is not just for families. It has been applied in schools, foster care programs, and even juvenile court, all with instances of great success.

The most dramatic story involves Tolson Elementary School in Tucson, Arizona. Tolson's 500-plus students live in an area on the lower end of the socioeconomic spectrum. In 1999, the school had eight times the average amount of school suspensions, many children on Ritalin, 15 percent of its students in special education, and a teacher attrition rate above 50 percent per year. A far-sighted principal then adopted the Nurtured Heart Approach as the behavioral program for the entire school. Within a short time, *special education utilization had dropped from 15 percent to one percent; no new children had been diagnosed with ADHD and placed on medication; only one child was suspended; and teacher attrition went to almost zero.* **The school also went from having the worst standardized test scores in the district to "excelling" (defined as having dramatic and continuing positive progress).**

I spoke to the school's principal recently, 10 years after she initiated the program. It is still the behavioral program used school-wide, and still just as successful. She told me that there are families moving into the area from the more affluent districts, and even from out of state, simply to have their children be in this environment. Teacher satisfaction is very high because the method is effective, not just for kids who are difficult, but for everyone. This is a very impressive and hopeful success story.

Amazingly, these results were achieved with no extra expense and no extra personnel. In fact, reduction in special education utilization represents a significant cost savings to the school district.

The Nurtured Heart Approach has also been used in Head Start programs around the country. In Tucson, Head Start serves 3,000 underprivileged children each year. From 1998 to 2006, the program did not need to send a single child for a diagnostic assessment or medication services. Head Start used the approach with all children; it helped all of them flourish even as it promoted improved behavior and classroom performance for the at-risk children without the need for outside services.

The Drenk Center in New Jersey is a foster home placement agency. Before 2007, which was when the Nurtured Heart Approach was adopted and taught to foster parents, the "broken placement" rate was 25 percent. Between 2007 and 2009, the rate dropped to *zero*. This represented not only a great reduction in financial cost but also in the human cost to children and foster parents, all of whom suffer greatly when placements fail.

Would Other Programs Work as Well?

I have studied, read about and heard parents report on many behavioral methods, formal or informal, for the treatment of ADHD. Most parents I meet in my practice report limited success, but in all fairness, this could be because the families who have had great success don't end up coming to see me.

As long as these methods have a strong emphasis on accentuating the positive and giving limited energy to negatives, they are likely to have a significant positive effect for some children. In fact, any consistent and behaviorally sound approach will probably be better than the somewhat random, reactive approach so many parents employ in response to their difficult or intense child.

A Short Primer on Nurtured Heart Approach Techniques

Here is a brief description of the basic steps of the Nurtured Heart Approach so that you can begin implementing it immediately, even before you acquire the book or tape covering the complete approach.

Step One: Increase Positive Feedback Dramatically

This can be in the form of simply noticing things a child is doing ("I see you are coloring the elephant red") to enthusiastic praise ("Thank you so much for taking your dish to the sink! I appreciate that you took the time and made the effort to be so helpful."). This feedback needs to occur as frequently as possible.

If your child doesn't seem to do much that's 'right' or praiseworthy to start with, you'll have to not only "catch him doing something right" but maybe even create it.

Howard Glasser tells a story about a dad who made this happen one day with his difficult child. (This is a man who initially saw no chance he could ever find his son doing something praiseworthy.) Just as his son was closing the car door, he quickly said, "Thanks for closing that door! I was just thinking I'd ask you to help me out by doing that — you must have read my mind!" You might be thinking that a child shouldn't have to be praised for closing a car door, but just remember the enormous amount of negative feedback these children get every day. It takes some extra effort and awareness by the parent to make up for that. In this case, it was the very first step to both the father's and the son's transformation.

One surefire method for finding ways to appreciate your child: consider, at any point in time, what rules the child is *not* breaking. It may seem radical to appreciate your child for not hitting, for not being rude, or for not talking out of turn — and it *is* radical! But it's certainly not harmful, and it gives you a lot of fodder for positive reinforcement. And if you're concerned that noticing the child for not breaking a rule will then drive the child to break it, be assured that this rarely happens. If it does, you know what to do: give an un-energized time-out or reset. Children will break the rules no matter what, and this is a good thing — because it gives you a chance to show them that you are not emotionally triggered by rule-breaking. You're like a referee in a sporting event: *out of bounds, penalty, then back in the game.*

Know that as your child becomes more successful and self-confident, she will do more and more things right, and you'll be praising her more for things that are really meaningful.

By the way, when you first start this, most children will know something is up. Some may even act a little miffed at the change. Don't worry; they actually like the positive attention — they just don't know how to handle it at first and may be untrusting of it. If asked, you can say something like, "I don't think I've been letting you know how many good things you do every day, and it makes me feel good to tell you."

Step Two: Once an Environment of Positivity Is Established, Withdraw Energy for Negative Behavior

As I mentioned earlier, rules still exist and consequences are applied consistently *but with the least amount of energy possible*. That means no yelling, no lecturing, no emotion, and no arguing.

I must warn you: **this is *really* difficult!** Almost every parent really struggles with this element of the approach. We are so accustomed to being reactive to misbehavior and so convinced that our words or emotions will convince a child to behave that it's very difficult to give up this aspect of parenting. No one does this perfectly, especially at first, but as long as you keep at it, good things will happen. Time-outs or "resets" are the most common consequences used in this approach; how you configure yours will vary by the age and type of child. The cardinal rules are to accord the consequence as little energy as possible and to get the child right back to 'time-in' as soon as possible.

Step Three: As Soon as the Child Successfully Performs a Time-Out or Reset, Jump Right Back into Positive Recognitions

Remember the video game analogy. Create a situation where the child gets to simply start over, accruing virtual 'points' in the form of positive reinforcement for good choices he or she makes. While this sounds simple, it may not be. Everyone slips and accidentally energizes negative behavior; everyone forgets to give adequate positive reinforcement. When this happens, just give *yourself* a little reset/time-out, jump back into applying the approach as best you can, and recognize yourself for the ways *you* are being successful in doing so!

Step Four: Apply a Credit System if the First Three Steps Don't Have the Desired Effect

For children who are more resistant to the basic application of the approach, Howard suggests a credit system. Children earn points for good behavior and get to spend them on specified privileges.

I know many of you have used star charts or other reward systems in the past, with varying degrees of success, but this is somewhat different. In this system, children are not saving up for some future "treat," but actually earn and use their rewards on a daily basis. For example: Tony would like to play a half-hour of an approved video game or watch a DVD for an hour, but he will need to have 50 points to spend to do so. He might have earned those points by handing in his homework, getting ready for school without fuss, or doing his chores without being asked. Parents should be extremely generous with points, giving them at every opportunity as a form of energizing success. Points are never taken away but can be 'frozen' when a child refuses a consequence for breaking a rule.

In essence, the credit system is a device that enables the parent to give a consistent and frequent flow of appreciation and recognition to the child. The child experiences watching points accrue as a reflection of his or her own growing sense of accomplishment.

If you do decide to use the credit system, know that the details will vary greatly depending on your particular child's needs. It does require more of a time investment than the previous steps, but the reward may be quite substantial and will save time in the end. This credit system may need to be adapted somewhat for very young children to make it understandable for them. Most children don't need it at all once the approach is in full swing.

This is the Nurtured Heart Approach in a very small nutshell. But even a general sense of how this approach works can give you enough knowledge to begin applying its principles. It requires a major change in parenting style for most people, but the rewards for the whole family make it well worth the time and effort.

One parent of a teenager was heard to say this after only two weeks of using the approach: "I always loved my daughter, but I never really liked being with her. Now, I actually like her and am surprised at how much I enjoy spending time with her." The fact that two weeks of this parenting technique could overcome the negative patterns of 15 years of unsuccessful interaction is truly amazing and heart warming.

The Bottom Line

Optimal parenting can have a tremendous effect on your child's eventual success in life. You can not only help your child handle the difficulties caused by ADHD, but you can also furnish the self-esteem and confidence required for using his or her unique gifts to their fullest potential. I urge you to help your child and whole family by starting to use the principles described in this chapter; and, if you are so inclined, consider the Nurtured Heart Approach.

Chapter 13
Working with Schools and Teachers

During the elementary school years, most children spend more waking hours in school than with their parents. Therefore, providing an optimal school environment is an essential part of helping a child thrive, especially for children with ADHD.

Providing that optimal environment isn't easy. Many school systems are under-funded and overcrowded. You may be lucky enough to live in a wonderful school district with adequate resources, but the recent recession is taking a toll on schools across the country. Even the best public schools are at risk from massive funding cuts.

Unfortunately, these cuts have the greatest impact on kids with ADHD or those with even mild attention and focus difficulties. When class size increases, there is less opportunity for individual attention. Music and art classes, where some of these kids shine the most, are eliminated. Physical education, which gives children time to use up extra energy, is also cut back or eliminated. Even lunch periods are shortened, making it harder for children to take the time to eat a healthy meal and get ready for the afternoon.

What's worse, eight years of 'No Child Left Behind' has created tremendous pressure in classrooms to 'teach for the test.' Grading of schools and children based solely on test performance has forced teachers to abandon creativity and individuality in favor of producing higher standardized test scores. In this context, the ADHD or other learning-challenged child may be seen not as an individual with a unique set of strengths and challenges, but as a downward pull on school test performance.

On the other hand, **I am constantly amazed at the wonderful teachers, principals, and staffs across the country who are doing great things for children even in the face of all of these pressures.** I see teachers taking their own personal time to communicate daily with parents and spend that extra few minutes with students who need help. There are principals setting up special classes or after-school homework clubs and counselors going the extra mile to support kids in trouble. It is the parents' task to find these resources or even help create them when possible.

Finding the Best-Fit Teacher

Judy, 10 years old, was having a terrible fourth-grade year. She couldn't pay attention or finish her work; she was falling behind academically and even becoming disruptive in class. Her parents brought her to me for a medical evaluation for ADHD.

I asked how the previous years in school were. Mom told me, "It's really funny how things have gone. She had some problems in kindergarten, but muddled through okay. First grade was great, no problems at all. Second grade was terrible — she had problems the entire year. Judy didn't want to work, got into trouble for her behavior, and fell behind academically." Mom explained that third grade was wonderful; while Judy had some focusing issues, the teacher was able to handle her without difficulty and Judy caught up academically. Just as her parents thought everything was settled and on track, fourth grade had been a nightmare since day one.

What was going on? Same school, same parents, same child. Why was each year so different? It turns out that *the difference was the fit between the child and the teacher.*

We all know that some teachers (like some doctors, some plumbers, and some lawyers) are better than others. Despite the fact that each one of Judy's teachers was competent and qualified, certain teachers work or 'fit' better with ADHD children. If your child is lucky enough to get one of them, things can go very well. If the child isn't that lucky, it may be time to intervene.

One of your most important jobs as a parent is to do your best to make sure your child has a teacher who is a good fit. To be proactive on this front, learn about the strengths and weaknesses of every teacher in the upcoming grade and try to make sure your child gets the one that is best for him. If your choice doesn't turn out to be a good fit, achieving this end may mean a middle-of-the-year switch. You may need to become a very squeaky wheel and administrators may come to dread the sight of you. Just bake them some healthy cookies and they'll feel better! But don't worry about this kind of reaction because finding the right classroom for your child is worth it. Pat yourself on the back for being a good advocate for your child!

Because every child with ADHD is different, I cannot say that there is a teaching style suitable for all of them. However, I consider the following three teacher qualities to be the most important. The ideal teacher of a child with ADHD must be able to combine a strong sense of **structure**, reasonable **flexibility**, and a **positive, loving attitude**. If those attributes are present, other characteristics are not as significant.

Structure. ADHD kids have difficulty staying organized, and having a teacher who is not structured will only exacerbate the situation. If the home-work assignment is written down clearly in the same place on the board and homework is collected at the same time every day, the ADHD child benefits. He or she will perform best when the classroom routines and rules are pre-dictable and the consequences for breaking rules are consistent.

Flexibility. Structure without flexibility, on the other hand, can impede the ADHD child's chances of succeeding in school. A suitable teacher needs to be flexible enough to accommodate the child's needs and abilities, which often differ from what the teacher expects or is used to with other children. Later in this chapter, we will discuss specific and formal accommodation plans such as the 504 and IEPs, as well as just general accommodations or modifications needed in the ADHD child's school environment regardless of whether they are defined in a formal plan. If your child's school uses one of these plans and your child is eligible, then the teacher has to be flexible enough to implement and modify it based on the child's needs.

A Positive, Loving Attitude. Chapter 12 discussed how crucial positive feedback, along with greatly limiting criticism and correction, are for the child with ADHD. This applies just as much to school as it does to the home environment.

If a child is only noticed by the teacher when doing something wrong, *she will continue to behave just that way to gain the energy and attention.* But if that same child receives even a short word of encouragement for the little things she does well — particularly for choices that are taken for granted in other children — she will do more and more things well. This is simply human nature, and ADHD children are particularly sensitive to criticism and open to praise.

I realize that the *ideal* teacher may not be available, but it's your job to find the teacher who is the best fit possible and then to work closely with that teacher to help your child succeed.

What Is the Best Type of School for Children with ADHD?

Your choice of school can make all the difference for your child, particu-larly when that child has been diagnosed with ADHD and is facing the pos-sibility of being medicated.

Catherine was a delightful 11-year-old. She was very bright, friendly, and had a great sense of humor, but was also quite impulsive. Often she would blurt out answers in class, talk out of turn, and generally disturb the teacher's equilibrium. Her academic progress was excellent and she was talented ar-tistically. Her parents had no problem with her behavior at home. Still, because of her classroom difficulties, her family consulted with me about the possible need for ADHD treatment. My conclusion was that she was simply a bright and creative child who needed a more adaptable and less restrictive school environment. Catherine's family enrolled her in a school that specialized in children who were gifted in one way or another, and almost immediately, the problem was solved. They loved her there! Her creativity and talents were valued, and no one seemed to mind the extra talking and speaking out of turn. There was no more speculation about ADHD. The thought that she might have been given pharmaceutical treatment instead of a better placement still makes me shudder.

Here's the ideal school, in my view, for the child who actually does have ADHD or who is challenged with even mild attention or focusing difficulties:

The children arrive and begin the day with about 20 minutes of unstructured play. Then they go into a classroom of no more than about 20 students to begin work. Every 50 minutes, they have a 10-minute break in which they can go outside, run around the yard, or do some other non-academic, non-sitting activity. Lunch is a full 45 minutes, giving them time to eat and take a reasonable break from focused activity. The school lunch is healthful and delicious. Physical education classes with organized sports and exercise happen every day. Art, music, and gardening are integral parts of the curriculum, as are science and ecology classes that involve hands-on exploration of the natural environment.

After school, there is a one-hour homework club enabling children to finish their homework in a quiet environment. During this time, those who have disabilities requiring specialized instruction can meet in small groups with the appropriate teachers. On most days, the children, especially the younger ones, are able to arrive home finished with their work so they can enjoy unstructured time to play and be kids.

This may sound like an impractical dream, but I have seen schools that fit this description. I am a physician and not an educator, so I readily admit that many would have sound arguments about the details; still, I think that most children, especially those with ADHD, would learn very well in this environment. I also think that increased efficiency of learning would outweigh time lost during frequent 10-minute breaks. And we would be training a generation of well-rounded and healthy children.

Schools differ a great deal from one another, as do children with ADHD. But below are some basic principles that I recommend for schools you are considering for your child with ADHD or similar issues.

First, it's very important that the school provide structure, routine, and a quiet classroom. Children with ADHD are not able to provide this structure from within themselves, so it helps if schools provide it for them. Although some children thrive in environments where they can move freely around the room and work in groups on different projects, this sort of classroom may be too distracting for most children with ADHD. They do better when they have their own space in which to remain seated during work periods — as long as they have the occasional 10-minute break to move around. For this reason, I generally do not recommend Montessori schools. Although I have seen some ADHD kids do well in them, more often they end up wandering around and getting little done.

Second is the question of how challenging the school should be. Although choices are fewer in small towns, most cities have certain schools known for their academic rigor — where children are challenged to attain higher academic standards than normal. To many parents, these are the "good schools" that attract the brightest kids and the best teachers. However, these are not necessarily the best schools for children with ADHD. They may be for a child who is extremely bright and is having attention issues or doing poorly due to boredom, but for a child with ADHD of average intelligence for whom school is difficult at best, this type of school environment can create even more pressure and frustration.

Think of it this way: if your child were great in math and terrible at music, would you place him or her in a school that taught music five hours a day and little math? What would happen to that child's self-esteem? The same is true for kids for whom academics are difficult and whose talents are in other areas, whether it is arts, sports, or even being a great 'people person.' Of course, a certain level of academic achievement is necessary (we all need to learn to read!), but why put that child in a place where academics are overemphasized and more difficult than they have to be? I have treated a number of children with ADHD whose academic problems resolved when they moved from the "best" school to one with normal academic standards.

A third consideration, and one that parents often ask me, is whether to choose a public, private, or charter school (in states where they are allowed). I won't delve into the political aspects of the debate (for example, whether charter or private schools negatively affect public schools and the community at large by removing resources, or whether these schools end up removing the brightest kids from the public school system). This is not because I don't have an opinion (as you've come to realize, I have plenty of those), but because it is not my area of expertise.

For the parents of a child with ADHD, however, the decision really should depend on their particular child. If the public school has the quality, resources, and the desired attributes I've already described, then that's where your child should go, which provides the added advantage of keeping him in the neighborhood where his friends and activities are. On the other hand, if the public school is inadequate in some way and there is another school that will serve the child's needs much better, you should consider it seriously. It's a decision you and your child (if he or she is old enough) will need to make together, taking all factors into account.

Home Schooling

Many parents whose children have ADHD and who have limited school choices ask me about home schooling. I believe this is a viable alternative for some families, given the right circumstances. Many kids who have severe problems with distractibility and focus in a classroom environment learn very well in a one-on-one situation with one of their parents (usually it's the mom; I don't recall meeting a home schooling dad, although I am sure they are out there).

Parents who home school often tell me that they can finish all academic work in the morning, leaving time for field trips and other reinforcing activities in the afternoon. Think of all the time that's consumed just in getting to school, in getting classrooms organized and settled, and in fulfilling school district requirements for incessant testing. How much of a typical public school day is spent actually learning? In a home schooling situation, time can be used more efficiently and the academic day shortened significantly, to everyone's benefit.

Critics of home schooling often raise the issue of social isolation. This has not been a problem for the home schooling families I've known. For starters, most larger communities have strong home school networks that form a very viable social community. And most home schooling parents are very aware of the child's social growth needs and do all they can to provide for them via after-school sports, church or club activities, etc.

The decision to home school is a major commitment for the family and should be made only after careful evaluation — hopefully with some objective help — of the designated home schooler's willingness and ability to undertake this effort. If the designated parent has difficulty organizing or focusing, as is sometimes the case, or if the child is particularly oppositional, home schooling may not be wise.

School Modifications for the ADHD Child: The 504 Plan

Every child with ADHD has the right to reasonable classroom modifications to ensure success. If it is a public school, this will likely involve a formal 504 plan in which the teacher, school, and parents agree upon a certain set of modifications. (The term 504 plan refers to Section 504 of the

Americans with Disabilities Act, which is discussed shortly.)

Although one could make the argument that ADHD is a type of learning disability, it is not classified as such for the purposes of public education. This is important because classifications such as these determine any child's eligibility for specific services.

If your child has a specific learning disability as determined by psychoeducational testing, he or she is eligible for an Individual Education Plan (IEP), which describes the type of services the child can receive and lists specific goals the child is expected to achieve. These services can include special education such as individual or small group tutoring outside the normal classroom.

Although ADHD is not classified as a specific learning disability, children with ADHD are generally accepted as having a disability under Section 504 of the Americans with Disabilities Act. This act mandates that all children with disabilities be provided a free, appropriate public education in the least restrictive environment. A person with a disability under Section 504 is defined as "any person who (i) has a physical or mental impairment which substantially limits one or more major life activities, (ii) has a record of such an impairment, or (iii) is regarded as having such an impairment."

Most children with ADHD are eligible for a 504 plan, which legally requires public school systems to make accommodations to meet the needs of students with disabilities. For the most part, these will occur in the regular classroom with what are termed "reasonable accommodations" — although in extreme cases, other placements may be necessary. If you have a child who does not qualify for special education under the Individuals with Disabilities Education Act (IDEA) but has a mental or physical impairment that substantially limits one or more major life activities, including learning, your child may qualify for special help in a regular classroom setting under Section 504.

For more information on 504 plans, check out the following websites:

www.greatschools.net/LD/school-learning/
section-504.gs?content=868&page=all

www.slc.sevier.org/iepv504.htm

504 Accommodation Checklist

Here is a fairly complete list of possible accommodations that may be helpful for the child with ADHD.

PHYSICAL ARRANGEMENT OF ROOM:
Seat student near the teacher
Seat student near a positive role model
Stand near the student when giving directions or presenting lessons
Avoid distracting stimuli (air conditioner, high traffic area, etc.)
Increase distance between desks

LESSON PRESENTATION:
Pair students to check work
Write key points on the board
Provide peer tutoring
Provide visual aids, large print, films
Provide peer note taker
Make sure directions are understood
Include a variety of activities during each lesson
Repeat directions to the student after they have been given to the class, then have him/her repeat and explain directions back to teacher
Provide written outline
Allow student to tape record lessons
Have child review key points orally
Teach through multi-sensory modes – visual, auditory, kinesthetic, olfactory
Use computer-assisted instruction
Combine oral directions with written directions for child to refer to on blackboard or paper
Provide a model to help students, post the model and refer to it often
Provide cross age peer tutoring
Assist the student in finding the main idea via underlying, highlighting, cue cards, etc.
Break longer presentations into shorter segments

ASSIGNMENTS/WORK SHEETS:
Give extra time to complete tasks
Simplify complex directions
Hand worksheets out one at a time
Reduce the reading level of the assignments
Require fewer correct responses to achieve grade (quality vs. quantity)
Allow student to tape record assignments/homework
Provide a structured routine in written form
Provide study skills training/learning strategies
Give frequent short quizzes and avoid long tests
Shorten assignments; break work into smaller segments
Allow typewritten or computer printed assignments prepared by the student or dictated by the student and recorded by someone else if needed
Use self-monitoring devices
Reduce homework assignments
No grading of handwriting

No marking wrong of reversals and transpositions of letters and numbers, just point out for correction

No lengthy outside reading assignments

Arrange for homework assignments to reach home with clear, concise directions

Recognize and give credit for student's oral participation in class

TEST TAKING:

Allow open book exams

Give exam orally

Give take home tests

Use more objective items (fewer essay responses)

Allow student to give test answers on tape recorder

Give frequent short quizzes, not long exams

Allow extra time for exam

Read test items to student

Avoid placing student under pressure of time or competition

ORGANIZATION:

Provide peer assistance with organizational skills

Assign volunteer homework buddy

Allow student to have an extra set of books at home

Send daily/weekly progress reports home

Develop a reward system for in-school work and homework completion

Provide student with a homework assignment notebook

BEHAVIORS:

Use timers to facilitate task completion

Structure transitional and unstructured times (recess, hallways, lunchroom, locker room, library, assembly, field trips, etc.)

Praise specific behaviors

Use self-monitoring strategies

Give extra privileges and rewards

Keep classroom rules simple and clear

Making "prudent use" of negative consequences

Allow for short breaks between assignments

Cue student to stay on task (nonverbal signal)

Mark student's correct answers, not his mistakes

Implement a classroom behavior management system

Allow student time out of seat to run errands, etc.

Ignore inappropriate behaviors not drastically outside classroom limits

Allow legitimate movement

Contract with the student

Increase the immediacy of rewards

Implement time-out procedures   (Source: *Nebraska Department of Education*)

Obviously, no one student would receive all of these accommodations, but at least it gives an idea of what is possible. This is important because many parents have no idea that their child deserves these types of accommodations, or even any extra help, because of ADHD.

The Most Helpful Accommodations for ADHD

The following accommodations in the school environment can be particularly beneficial for children with ADHD:

Requiring fewer correct responses for multiple-item work (quality vs. quantity). There is nothing more frustrating for a child with ADHD than to be given a paper with 50 math problems, all pretty much the same. If a child can add three two-column numbers correctly five times, why should she have to do it 50 times? Children with ADHD should not be expected to do such repetitive work in one sitting. If they know the work, they know the work and should receive a grade/mark that takes this into account (and not be penalized for it compared with other students). When I was in school, assignments such as this used to frustrate me to no end; I can only imagine what it is like for someone who has difficulty remaining focused.

Not grading handwriting. Many children with ADHD have great trouble with handwriting, sometimes because fine motor skills are lacking or sometimes because their thoughts are too fast for their pens. Whatever its root, difficulty with handwriting is very common in ADHD children. In this day and age, the quality of one's handwriting should really take a back seat in the teacher's or school's priorities. Let's be real: by fifth or sixth grade, most schools require all papers to be typed on a computer, and in the real world very few people write down much more than their signature and a shopping list. It would be nice if everyone wrote well, but handwriting improvement is not where to expend precious time and energy. Another accommodation that should be made is allowing students to produce their work on a keyboard if that is easier for them.

Adjusting the seating arrangement. Often, but not always, children with ADHD do best at the front of the room where distractions from other kids are not in their visual field. This also allows them to be a little closer to the teacher for that extra bit of eye contact. You and the teacher may need to experiment with the optimal arrangement, but it can make all the difference for your child's behavior and learning. However, please *do not allow your child to be placed in a far corner facing the wall as a way to decrease distractibility*. This is not only humiliating but rarely produces positive results.

Allowing extra time to complete tasks and for exams. What is important is determining if a child knows the work, not how fast he can do it. If it takes a little extra time, so be it. I realize that a child will eventually have to cope with time constraints when taking the SATs and on the job, but younger children need to get the basics down first. The child, teacher, and parents all need to know what the child is capable of doing and understanding; speed can come later. I am even aware of a high-achieving high school student who was given a special accommodation of a quiet room and twice as much time for each SAT section as other children due to her diagnosis of ADD with learning disabilities.

Cueing student to stay on task (nonverbal signal). It is not uncommon for parents to tell me about that great teacher who would just quietly touch their child on the shoulder while walking by when she noticed his attention faltering. Nonverbal cues such as this can be very effective for some children. There is something so respectful and caring about this kind of gentle, helpful reminder to a student to refocus. Not all teachers are able to do this, especially those who tend to stay at their desks, but there are other similar cues that a teacher can use to help the ADHD child.

Arranging for homework assignments to reach home with clear, concise directions. This is major. How can a child do homework if she doesn't know what it is? Children with ADHD often have great difficulty correctly copying assignments from the board or from oral directions. The frustrated parents and child end up wasting the limited time available for homework with the quest to figure out what the assignment actually is! The teacher should take whatever steps are necessary to make sure the child is well aware of the assignment and can convey it accurately to her parents. This dovetails with allowing a student to have an extra set of books at home — the child can't do assignments at home if the books are still in the desk at school.

Developing a reward system for completing in-school work and homework. This fits into the broader category of mounting *any intervention that increases the positive feedback a child receives*. From reading Chapter 12, you know how essential I believe this is. Most human beings — and *especially* children with ADHD — are motivated much more by positive feedback than by criticism. If you are using the credit system at home as described in Chapter 12, you can introduce it to the teacher and ask that he adapt it for use with your child in the classroom or come up with a similar system that rewards your child for both the work performed in school and completed homework assignments.

There are many other interventions that might help your child, but this gives you a good start. Give careful thought to the types of interventions you feel would be important and advocate for them at the school. I strongly urge you to have your list ready before meeting with the school personnel and to know in advance which interventions are most important to you; otherwise, you may leave without obtaining what your child needs.

If a 504 plan is in force for your child, you'll need to balance what you request in the form of accommodations against the realities of the situation. Every parent wants what is best for their child, but sometimes the more you ask for, the less likely it is to all get done. Remember that most often teachers do not have extra time or resources to implement these plans. Remember also that he or she might have three or four children in class with differing special needs — along with an overcrowded classroom and a principal pressuring teachers to raise test scores.

In general, I recommend starting with a few important accommodations — the ones you think are most necessary for your child's success. Try to focus on accommodations that don't take extra time from the teacher's already tight classroom schedule. If you need regular feedback, give the teacher a form to use that can be filled out quickly and easily.

Should Every Child with ADHD Have a Formal 504 Plan?

A formal 504 plan may not be necessary if your child's teacher understands ADHD and is willing to make the accommodations you seek without a specific plan. Remember, however, that teachers and administrators can leave or be replaced, and if they are not all on board, a good (if informal) plan can quickly go awry. Some children just need a little help to shift things into a much more positive gear. For the child who needs more, a formal 504 plan is usually wise. Whether or not a formal plan exists, parents need to monitor the plan's execution and continue to do so over time.

The Accommodation Meeting — How to Prepare

The parent-school meetings to determine placement and accommodations are vital for your child's educational success. They can also be intimidating and overwhelming for parents. Sometimes one parent is in a room with one or more teachers, a psychologist, a special-ed teacher, and various other administrators. Although everyone may want what is best for the student, it is also true that the school district has some legitimate financial and personnel concerns that may work against what is ideal for your child. Your job in that meeting is to be a strong advocate, which can be a tough job.

I tell you this from personal experience. My daughter had a formal Individualized Education Plan (IEP) every single year, and even as a physician I felt outgunned and outnumbered — I generally dreaded the whole thing. My wife, a psychologist herself, would get so frustrated at these meetings that she stopped going after our daughter reached high school (although she still helped me make the all-important list to take to the meeting).

I want to offer some ideas on how you can best handle these potentially difficult meetings. Keep in mind that they apply to either a true IEP

193

meeting or to a more complex accommodation plan such as a 504. A simple meeting to outline some basic accommodations would be much less intense but it won't hurt to be similarly prepared.

- **Be prepared.** Know what you want and write it down. Get a copy in advance of any testing that has been done.

- **Have a positive attitude.** Begin by assuming that everyone wants what is best for your child. Approaching the meeting angry or with a "chip on your shoulder" is not helpful.

- **Both parents should attend if possible.** If there is only one parent, have a relative or friend join you.

- **Don't be afraid to ask questions, clarify, or even challenge.** No one else will do it for you.

- **Don't sign anything unless you are satisfied.** If you need to go home and think about it, then do so.

- **Hire an advocate.** These are people who make a profession of supporting parents at these meetings. I can guarantee that they are not going to be intimidated.

Two Common Questions about Accommodations

During conversations about accommodations for ADHD children, these questions often arise.

Q. *Won't giving my child accommodations make adaptation to the 'real world' more difficult?*

A. This is a legitimate question. It is true that, at some point, children have to begin taking responsibility for things like bringing their books home or knowing what the assignment is. However, it is also true that, all through college and graduate school, children with learning issues can receive extra time for tests or quiet rooms to take them in.

I recently signed a disability form for a 22-year-old young man with ADHD who was preparing to take his final exam to become a licensed stockbroker at one of the giant financial companies. One unusual accommodation he needed pertained to the color of the paper on which the test was printed. On this colored paper, he had a hard time maintaining focus due to the lack of contrast between foreground and background. The company complied, and the young man did very well. So it is not true that our world makes *no* accommodation for people with learning issues. Still, it *is* true that in many situations, accommodations may be difficult to obtain.

In my view, the answer to the question really rests with the age of the child. Elementary school is where a child's lifelong feelings about school and education will be formed. It is where children learn the basic academic skills they will need for the rest of their lives. Therefore, it is best to give them all the help we possibly can in these years and then gradually help move them to self-sufficiency. If the child can develop a positive attitude about learning early on, the rest of his or her educational life will be much easier.

Q. *Won't an accommodation plan make my child feel "different" or diminish self-esteem?*

A. This is also a reasonable question. The right answer has to do with balancing the serious negative effects of chronic school failure against the possible negative effects of the accommodations. Many accommodations are not noticed by most other kids, although some may be. For example, if your child has such difficulty with handwriting that he or she needs to use a keyboard instead, the other kids may comment or even tease about it (although envy is a more likely reaction from kids forced to write longhand). However, that type of reaction has to be weighed against the feeling of success a child will have when the teacher reads, out loud, the wonderful story that he's always had in his head but could never get onto paper. Overall, I believe that appropriate accommodations do much more good than harm to children's self-esteem.

Remember Roger Pensrose

Roger Penrose is one of the great theoretical physicists of our time. His name is mentioned in the same breath as Albert Einstein and Stephen Hawking. He was the physicist able to prove that "black holes" come from dying stars. Yet as a child, he could not finish his math tests on time! These are his own words:

"I was unbelievably slow.... When I was 8, sitting in class, we had to do this mental arithmetic very fast, or what seemed to me very fast. I always got lost. And the teacher, who didn't like me very much, moved me down a class. There was one rather insightful teacher who decided, after I'd done so badly on these tests, that we would have timeless tests.... I was allowed to take the entire next period to continue and even then sometimes it would stretch into the period beyond that. Eventually I would do very well. You see, if I could do it that way, I would get very high marks."[1]

Imagine what would have happened if that insightful teacher had not come along with an "accommodation." Roger might have given up on math and we would have forgone one of the premier physicists of our time. And what if he had been placed on medication? Perhaps he would have done just as well, but perhaps medication would have so altered his brain chemistry that he would have lost the creativity and brilliance that made him so great. I'm glad we didn't have to find out. And the next time you might wonder if an accommodation will be beneficial, remember Roger Penrose.

Following Up on the Accommodation Plan

Even with the best of intentions, elements of the accommodation plan will likely be forgotten, omitted, or just ignored due to time pressures or other priorities. It's just entropy — the natural tendency of things to fall apart if energy is not added to the system.

A great many parents have told me that many of the carefully considered accommodations they worked out with their child's teachers were not being implemented, even just a few months after the initial meeting. My daughter had a formal IEP every year of school, and I am sure there wasn't a single year when the entire list of interventions was carried out; sometimes very few were. We tried to pay attention and pick our battles, but nothing about it was easy.

Post your accommodations in a prominent place in your house (a manila folder in the desk drawer does not count as prominent) and regularly make sure that they are being followed. If they are not, ask why. Sometimes the reason is very legitimate; or it might be just a matter of adding energy into the system to get things back on track.

No one else is going to stay on top of this. Teachers may just have too much to do and too many individuals to monitor to reliably supervise these plans. **The bottom line is:** *it's up to you.*

ADHD and Middle School

Many parents who have helped their ADHD child successfully through elementary school are seized with dread at the thought of middle school. This is understandable. Instead of one teacher to communicate with, there may be six or seven. Instead of one desk to keep organized, the student has to figure out how to have the right books and papers at hand in seven different classrooms. In general, teachers don't know your child well and have less ability to make specific accommodations. It certainly is a challenge.

All is not lost, however. Middle-school age usually brings welcome changes for the ADHD child:

- If hyperactivity has been a problem, your child may naturally transition from hyperactive to fidgety. This is the natural evolution of ADHD. Instead of needing to run around the room, the child might just fidget in his or her seat. The ADHD child may also benefit from being able to walk around for a few minutes between each class period compared to sitting in the same room nearly all day.

- ADHD kids need variety to keep motivated, so having six or so different teachers may actually make it easier for them to stay focused.
- If the middle school has classes like music and art or makes the effort to incorporate hands-on activities into each school day, your child may get a chance to shine there.
- With a variety of teachers, some may bring out the best in your child. Others may not, but they also will be spending much less time with your child than was the case in elementary school.

Many of the interventions I discussed earlier in the chapter will still apply, but here a few suggestions specific to the middle school years:

- Establish a relationship early on with the school counselor, who can be your contact point for all of the teachers. Try to get your child to establish a relationship with the counselor as well. A good counselor can make the difference between success and failure in middle school.
- Key in on organization methods early. Make sure the child has a specific folder or loose-leaf section for each class, that papers are where they need to be before the school day starts, and so on.
- Try to arrange a class period that can be used as a study hall where your child can complete homework in school.
- Find out if the school has an online homework site where all assignments and grades are posted. These are becoming increasingly common and make parents' lives much easier. If the school does not have an online site like this, arrange some type of weekly report so you can closely monitor how things are going. Often, the counselor will help you with this. Staying on top of things can be a much bigger challenge for middle school parents than was the case in elementary school because no one person is responsible for giving you the news when things are not going well.
- Try to stay relaxed. Middle-school grades are not going to appear on your child's transcript when he or she applies to college or medical or law school. Help the child get through with self-esteem intact, and don't worry if there are a few C grades that should have been B grades.

A Final Thought

Yes, school is often difficult for children with ADHD; and yes, school success is important, both for self-esteem and for future academic progress. On the other hand: *there is more to life than school.* Make sure that your child gets to spend a substantial amount of time doing things that he or she is good at — activities that make him or her feel successful and happy. If your child is spending almost every waking hour either at school or doing homework, something's wrong.

Praise your child for achievements in what he or she enjoys and is good at — whether sports, dance, being out in nature, or just hanging with friends, even if school isn't going all that well. This will go a long way to counter any difficulties presented at school.

Children only get to be children once. Let's not sacrifice their childhood on the altar of educational achievement.

Chapter 14

Medications for ADHD: When Are They Necessary and How Should They Be Used?

If you have a child with ADHD, you've probably had many well-intentioned people tell you, in no uncertain terms, that *"you ought to medicate your child."*

"It'll calm him down."

"She'll get better grades."

"You'll ruin your child's self-esteem if you don't."

Such advice has caused many parents to feel obligated to start the child in question on some kind of ADHD medication, which is unfortunate because this a serious decision, and these recommendations are often based on incorrect assumptions and unreliable information. Just because an ADHD medication helped someone's second cousin does not mean that it is the right thing for your child.

Sometimes ADHD medications are necessary; more often, they are not. Sometimes they work and sometimes they don't. It is my experience that there is more myth and misinformation about the risks and benefits of ADHD medications (and about the risks and benefits of *not* taking these medications) than on any other ADHD topic.

On one hand, the medical establishment — and sometimes the educational establishment — champions these medications as highly effective interventions with minimal side effects. They imply that, if your child has the 'diagnosis' of ADHD and is not taking medication, then you must be a neglectful or uncaring parent. I've actually had parents tell me that a principal or teacher has responded to their reluctance to medicate by threatening to call Child Protective Services!

On the other hand, there's the equally fanatic anti-medication crowd whose mantra is that Ritalin and other stimulants are "narcotics just like cocaine" and that giving your child these drugs will doom him or her to a life of horrible drug abuse and crime — that is, if the child's liver or kidneys don't fail first.

In this chapter, I'm going to studiously avoid both of these extremes to take a frank, objective look at the pros and cons of medications. This is what any parent of an ADHD child needs: not polemics, but clear, well-supported facts with which a careful determination of potential risks and benefits can be made.

First the Assumptions

There are certain factors that should exist before anyone would need to consider medication. So let's assume that your child:

- Has undergone a comprehensive evaluation for ADHD and had a trustworthy diagnosis.
- Is having significant difficulties at home and at school.
- Is having a serious problem with focus and attention — serious enough to cause him or her to fall significantly behind in learning.
- Exhibits hyperactivity at home that creates true difficulties in family life; pandemonium reigns, and the other kids are getting less attention than they deserve.
- Is showing signs that his or her self-esteem is beginning to suffer.
- Has been evaluated adequately to rule out other conditions like learning disability or depression.
- Has not responded to non-medical modifications in the classroom and at home.

From earlier chapters, you already know my opinion that children who meet all these criteria represent a *minority* of kids who are said to have ADHD. More often, evaluations are shoddy, other conditions have not been ruled out, and little effort has been made to institute even simple corrective measures in terms of dietary or behavioral interventions. If your child does not fall into this minority, you don't need to consider medications until appropriate evaluations have been performed and all appropriate non-pharmacological approaches have been tried.

We therefore assume that the diagnosis is accurate and the situation is serious. Now we can move on to an intelligent discussion of the risks and benefits of these medications for the child who may really need them.

ADHD Medicines: What Are They and Do They Actually Work?

The most common ADHD medications by far belong to a class of drugs known as *psychostimulants*. These medications increase the brain's supply of the neurotransmitters *dopamine* and *norepinephrine* — especially in the frontal lobe, where much of the problem in ADHD seems to reside.

Within this single class of drugs, there are two main categories:

methylphenidate (Ritalin) and its derivatives, and *dextroamphetamine* (Dexedrine) and its derivatives. Methylphenidate and dextroamphetamine are generic names for these drugs, while Ritalin and Dexedrine are brands. By 'derivatives' I mean medications that have been produced by making small modifications to these chemicals that allow them to have a longer period of effectiveness.

Another medication called atomoxetine (Strattera) is sometimes used in ADHD. Strattera is not a stimulant, and in my experience it seems to be less effective and often has worse side effects than the stimulant drugs. We'll address Strattera in more detail later in this chapter.

How do stimulants help children with ADHD? Aren't these kids already hyperactive and over-stimulated? Although this would be a natural conclusion to draw, recall from the neurofeedback chapter that these children tend to be *under-aroused* in their ability to focus, plan, and control impulses. This tends to manifest as hyperactivity, and using these medicines to stimulate the parts of the brain that control arousal and focus produces some degree of normalization — a better balance of activity in these under-activated areas. The outward effect reduces hyperactive behavior.

Do these medications work? Yes, in the short-term, *about 70 percent of the time*. That is, for 70 percent of the people who take them, they produce a significant decrease in hyperactivity and impulsivity, along with an increased ability to concentrate and focus.

These drugs would produce the same effect in just about anyone. If you were to take some Ritalin before heading to work, you would very likely notice some improvement in your ability to focus and a decrease in distractibility. College kids have caught on to this in a big way, and Ritalin, Dexedrine, and its derivatives have become some of the most sought-after illicit drugs on campuses to enhance the ability to study longer. Previous generations used caffeine in the form of coffee, No-Doz, or even diet pills to achieve the same effect. All of this tells us that the fact that a child can focus more easily when taking these medications does *not* mean that he or she has ADHD.

Why not use these wonderful medications whenever possible if they work so well? Three very significant reasons: first, there are short-term side effects; second, there are long-term side effects; and third, *we have no good studies that conclusively demonstrate a benefit to children* in the long run.

Myth-Busting: Exposing Some Myths about the Dangers of ADHD Drugs

Before we look at the actual risks of ADHD drugs, I will address a few of the more extreme, fear-mongering arguments you might hear against these medications.

Myth: *Psychostimulants are just like cocaine, and if you give them to your child, he or she will be doomed to drug addiction later in life.*

This is a deceptive partial truth. Yes, Ritalin and Dexedrine are psychostimulants, and cocaine is a stimulant, but this does *not* mean they are the same drug. In fact, in children, Ritalin is not addicting at all in the way that cocaine can be. In my observation, the biggest problem for kids who have taken one of these medications for years is that they don't want to take the drug anymore once they reach high school! What kind of addicting medicine produces a reaction like that?

People who take the most addictive prescription meds, such as painkillers or other types of amphetamines, often try to obtain extra prescriptions. In all my years of practice, I can count on one hand the number of families who tried to get extra prescriptions for Ritalin or related drugs (usually because a parent or a sibling was taking it without a prescription). Some studies indicate that ADHD drugs have more potential for addiction in adults, but that's a topic for another book

Myth: *ADHD medications lead to drug addiction later on.*

It is a hotly debated topic as to whether these drugs might turn a child into an addict later in life or whether they might actually protect children against addiction in adulthood. Does it condition them to think of drugs as an answer to their problems — perhaps 'wiring' their brains in some way that increases their vulnerability to other agents of addiction? Or does it correct their course in ways that increase self-esteem and promote achievement, thus giving them greater ability to 'just say no' and to avoid addiction even if they do experiment with drugs? Much of what is said in these debates consists of little more than hot air. Let's look at the real facts on this matter.

Several studies have examined the influence of stimulant treatment on later substance abuse. Most of these studies and one meta-analysis (a study pooling the results of the other studies) indicate that children who took stimulants were, overall, at *less* risk of substance abuse in adolescence, although those benefits appeared to diminish substantially by adulthood.[1] At this writing, one study showed the opposite: that kids who took Ritalin were *more* likely to end up abusing drugs or alcohol later on.[2]

Unfortunately, none of these studies addressed some key factors that might have affected the outcomes. Were the kids who took Ritalin in the studies more or less severe cases? Did they have less caring parents? Did the ones who did *not* take stimulants also receive less classroom help? Was there any difference in their nutritional status? Without this type of information, it's difficult to draw a conclusion either way because all of these elements affect a child's risk of later drug addiction.

I would say that the research we have so far indicates that stimulants *may* reduce — and probably do *not* increase — later drug abuse, but the evidence is not strong enough to draw a firm conclusion. My personal opinion: I think it is true that children who have significant ADHD and receive no intervention or inadequate intervention are much more likely to develop poor self-esteem and a sense of chronic failure, which could lead to a higher incidence of drug abuse. If you are reading this book, however, you are clearly a caring parent who will be employing a wide range of beneficial options to help your child. You'll be promoting her self-esteem and encouraging her strengths and talents. I believe that, in this situation, use of psychostimulants is unlikely to increase the risk of later substance abuse.

Myth: *Ritalin is a narcotic.*

This is just nonsense. Narcotics are "downers" that slow down the central nervous system; stimulants are "uppers" that have the opposite effect. This confusion probably stems from the fact that Ritalin is — as it should be — a controlled substance. This means that strict limits govern the prescription of stimulants. Narcotics are controlled, as are various other medications, but this does not mean that all controlled drugs are narcotics.

Along with the totally mistaken idea that stimulants are narcotics comes the fear that these medications may turn children into zombies who become so sedated that they are unable to function. I *have* seen children become too sedated on these medications, but this is usually when the dose is too high. It's a problem that is generally easily remedied.

Myth: *These are new, untried drugs that could cause liver failure, kidney failure or other severe physical side effects.*

Ritalin and Dexedrine have been used since the 1950s. People have taken some drug belonging to this class for decades. Not a single case of liver or kidney failure has ever been ascribed to these medications. Although several newer variations on these medications have recently been developed, they are minor variations and not likely to cause completely new side effects.

The Real Side Effects of ADHD Medications

Having discounted some of the myths, it is also important to recognize that psychostimulants *do* have definite side effects. Some are minor and some are not. Most of them go away once the medication is discontinued. Some of the side effects below are quite common and others are less common.

1. **Loss of appetite.** This side effect is extremely common; in fact, some experts view the absence of this side effect as an indication that the dose is too low for maximum effect. This reduction in appetite often persists as long as the child is on the medication. It may not be a problem when the appetite loss is mild, but if weight loss or lack of weight gain occurs, it can be a serious issue.

2. **Stomach issues.** These medications often cause stomachache, nausea, or other abdominal complaints. Such issues usually resolve after the child has been taking the medication awhile, but this is not always the case.

3. **Tics.** Some controversy exists about what percentage of children develop tics — involuntary movements of the face or body — while taking psychostimulants, but the most common estimate from experts is five to seven percent. It's unclear whether these would have developed without the medication; childhood tics are common, and some ADHD children have associated tics even without taking medication. Mostly, these disappear once the medication is stopped; in a small percentage of cases, however, the tics are permanent and continue even after the child is no longer exposed to the medication.

4. **Headaches.** This common side effect can sometimes be mild and transitory; for some children, they are a real problem. In my patients, I've found headaches to be much more common with the drug Strattera.

5. **Sleep problems.** Many children have difficulty falling asleep when they take ADHD medications, especially if they take an afternoon dose. Sometimes this can be resolved by changing the type of medication or the time it is taken. All too often, doctors respond to this side effect by prescribing another medication such as Clonidine to help with sleep. Now you have a child on two psychotropic medications instead of one, each with their own side effects. *I would recommend avoiding this "polypharmacy" whenever possible.* (Other sections of the book describe safer ways of promoting good sleep.)

6. **Hallucinations.** This is rarely mentioned by doctors who prescribe these drugs, but an FDA (Food and Drug Administration) advisory panel noted that **two to five percent of children suffered hallucinations when taking these drugs.**[3] Usually, the hallucinations were of worms, snakes, and insects — obviously very frightening. This kind of experience would be termed a psychotic episode. Fortunately, these episodes resolve when the drugs are discontinued, but it would be

presumptuous and unjustified to conclude that these episodes could not have any long-term effects on children's psyches.

7. **Cardiovascular effects.** This is an area of significant controversy. In a five-year period, 19 children (of 2.5 million children taking stimulants) suffered sudden death from a heart-related incident.[4] The first thing to note is that *this is no higher than the rate of heart-related deaths in children not taking stimulants*. I think the most accurate statement that could be made so far is that there *may* be a very small but real increased risk of sudden death associated with stimulants, even in children with perfectly healthy hearts. You should be aware of this possible risk before placing a child on stimulant medication. The American Heart Association recommends an electrocardiogram (ECG) before starting children on stimulants; the American Academy of Pediatrics disagrees with this recommendation, judging the evidence for this recommendation to be insufficient. We do know that stimulants cause slight increases in heart rate and blood pressure, but they are insignificant for most children. Any individual could have a more severe than average increase in these two measurements, so they should be checked regularly.

My personal belief is that children should have a good exam by a qualified pediatrician before starting these medications but an ECG is not necessary. However, *any child with a history of any heart problem should be cleared by a cardiologist before beginning these medications*. In children with normal hearts, I believe these medications are reasonably safe if blood pressure and pulse are monitored regularly.

8. **Decreased growth.** Children who take these medications over a long time tend to experience a slowing in their growth rate. They don't stop growing, but they grow at a slower pace than they probably would otherwise. It is not clear quite how much height these children will lose — probably less than one-half an inch on average. Height and weight should be continuously monitored during stimulant treatment.

These are the eight most well-known and well-defined side effects of Ritalin and related drugs. However, I frequently see a few other side effects that I find very worrisome — effects that are rarely mentioned and have to do with changes in personality, mood, and the general well-being of the child.

The Medication Works, But...

I regularly talk to parents who say something like this after varying lengths of time after starting their child on ADHD medication: "Yes, the medication works. My child is less hyper, more able to focus, and less impulsive, but…

"She is just not herself."

"He's lost his spark."

"She is always irritable."

"He just doesn't seem like my Joey."

"She seems a little sad, a little depressed."

"He just doesn't seem happy."

The kids themselves sometimes say similar things, especially if they're older, but they are often less specific. Here is what I typically hear from kids:

"…makes things less fun."

"…is boring."

"I don't like how it makes me feel."

"I hate taking it!"

When I hear comments like these, and I do on a regular basis, I always take them seriously. A negative change in what I would call the 'essence' of a child is always of concern, even if it can be difficult to pin down exactly what change is occurring. I don't view this as just a short-term concern. If a medication is having a noticeable negative impact on a child now, what effect might these more subtle changes have in the long term?

I don't want to imply that these side effects occur in a majority of children. I see it quite often, but I know I'm dealing with a skewed sample. By this I mean that, as an integrative pediatrician, my patients' families tend to be those who have had negative experiences with ADHD medications; they're ready to explore a different approach. Children who started Ritalin for ADHD, immediately improved, and had no negative side effects are not usually the ones visiting my clinic.

There is really not much research on this important issue. These subtle, medication-induced changes in personality are rarely investigated in the studies that focus on side effects. Even if they were, many parents would not volunteer this type of information.

However, one interesting study did examine social interactions in children with ADHD, both on and off medication. Children in the study were shown pictures of social interactions between children and asked to interpret the interactions and say what they would do in the same situation. The study showed that children taking a stimulant medication had more hostile, aggressive responses to a perceived provocation than children taking a placebo (no medication).[5] Increased hostility and aggressiveness when taking ADHD medications has been shown in a couple of other small studies as well. Therefore, an increase in hostility or aggressiveness should be monitored as another possible side effect of ADHD medication.

The Long-Term Effects of ADHD Medications: What Do We Really Know?

Many children who are placed on ADHD medication at ages five to 10 — or, as is often the case these days, even earlier — will be taking these medications for 10 or more years of childhood and possibly into adulthood.

This is a time of ongoing brain growth and development for children. Until the end of adolescence, the brain is continually growing, producing new neural connections, re-routing old connections, and generally adapting itself to the influences and demands of external stimuli. In fact, the adolescent brain purposely *overproduces* synapses (connections between neurons) and then prunes them by about 40 percent, all in response to external influences. If one changes the 'bath' of neurotransmitters to which the brain is exposed during this critical period of development, we must expect that this will have some kind of influence over the long term. And this is exactly what psychostimulants do: *they alter the neurotransmitter environment in the brain.*

Often, the effect of a drug outlasts the exposure. Giving a child a medication when he or she is between five and eight years of age could have significant effects for years afterward. This after-effect of psychotropic medications is known as *neuronal imprinting*. **There can be little argument, then, against the hard truth that ADHD medications *will* affect brain development.** The big question is: will this effect be good or bad? The honest answer is: **we don't know.**

No long-term chronic exposure studies have been conducted on brain function to determine the effects of drug imprinting on the immature human brain. To have a totally accurate answer to this question, scientists would have to take a few thousand children with ADHD and randomly assign them to take psychostimulants or not take psychostimulants for 10 years. They would also need to do thorough neuropsychological testing and brain imaging (MRIs, EEGs) before, during, and after treatment. Then we might find an answer.

This is not going to happen. Such a study would be completely unethical. There's no way a researcher could deprive a child of treatment that might be necessary for 10 years just for research purposes, or keep a child on a medication for a predetermined period of time when he or she may not need it. Still, more limited studies could be designed, and hopefully they will be as our research tools become more sophisticated.

As in other areas of medicine, when we can't design adequate research studies with humans due to ethical concerns, we sometimes look to animal studies. Since rats grow from childhood to adulthood relatively quickly, they are much easier to study than human beings. Indeed, a few studies have involved giving psychostimulants to rats in early life and then evaluating them when they reach adulthood. Here are a few things that have been found in adult rats thus exposed.[6]

A long-lasting aversion to cocaine (this is good)

Increased depressive symptoms (this is not good)

Increased anxiety (this is not good either)

Humans are not rats, so these studies only give us hints of what the long-term effects might be. But if hints are all we have, we need to include them in this discussion.

Do we have *any* studies about long-term outcomes in children who take stimulants for ADHD? There have been a few, although none are ideal. The largest and most complete study was called the MTA (Multimodal Treatment Study of Children with ADHD).[7] In this carefully designed study, 579 children were randomized to receive one of four treatment protocols: 1) medication, 2) behavioral treatment, 3) a combination of medication and behavioral treatment, or 4) community care. When a study is randomized, there are no initial differences between the groups, and each subject is assigned to treatment by number only. Randomization is very important — one of the hallmarks of a quality study.

At 14 months, medication treatment, both with and without behavioral care, was superior to non-medication treatments. This study was hailed as the first solid proof that ADHD medication had relatively long-lasting positive effects. But that's not the end of the story.

The randomized part of the study ended, and the patients were then followed for 22 more months (a total of 36 months from the start of treatment). At 24 months, the positive outcomes were still there, but had decreased by 50 percent. At 36 months, *there was no difference between the groups on any measure, whether the children had been kept on the medication or not.*

This was quite a blow to the strong advocates of medication since it seemed to show a complete lack of long-term benefit. We need to be careful how we interpret this, however. Since the study was no longer randomized during the follow-up phase when the benefit of medication seemed to evaporate, the families could have decided to give or not give the kids medication for any number of reasons. Other types of random factors could have intervened. However, try as they might — and the authors certainly did — they could find no explanation for this lack of long-term effect. So the largest study performed so far shows *no long-term benefit of medication.*

A later study, published in July 2009, looked at the risk of "comorbid conditions" like depression, conduct disorder, bipolar disorder, and anxiety disorder in a group that had been diagnosed with ADHD as children and had either been treated or not treated with stimulants.[8] The study, which evaluated the subjects 10 years after their diagnosis, showed that stimulant treatment had significant protective effects against the development of these disorders. But again, this doesn't tell the whole story.

Because these children were *not* randomized into different groups, we know nothing about what factors in the child or family resulted in the decision to treat or not treat with medications. It's entirely possible that those who were untreated had less parental supervision, less school help, or poorer nutrition; other meaningful differences might have existed between the medicated and non-medicated children. Again, we just don't know.

In any case, any parent reading this book is likely to be doing everything possible for his or her child in every aspect of the child's life. You are likely to be paying careful attention to the effect of any intervention and taking appropriate action if it is not successful. In my view, families who place less effort and attention on finding non-drug solutions probably see a greater benefit from medication, almost by default.

At any rate, from the research so far, it seems that long-term use of psychostimulants in children could produce the following: (1) It could result in improved development and a better balance of neurotransmitters in the brain, even as it reduces ADHD symptoms without major side effects. (2) Or, conversely, it could worsen neurotransmitter balance and produce more persistent ADHD symptoms, with or without other undesirable side effects. (3) It could lead to increased anxiety or depression, but that may be worth the price in terms of good outcomes with ADHD symptoms and an overall better balance of neurotransmitters. *In other words: we just don't know.*

The Bottom Line is that we still do not have any solid evidence that the use of stimulants will improve the long-term outcome of ADHD.

ADHD Medications and the Placebo Effect

We have talked about the placebo effect previously. Could much of the benefit of ADHD medication be attributed to the placebo effect? Researchers explored this question, and the answer is very interesting. Studies indicate that the behavior of children themselves is not highly influenced by their expectation concerning the effects of medication. However, the opposite is true for parents and teachers. According to a 2009 study:

"*Evidence suggests that parents and teachers tend to evaluate children with ADHD more positively when they believe the child has been administered stimulant medication and they tend to attribute positive changes to medication even when medication has not actually been administered.*"[9]

So when parents and teachers know a child is taking medication for ADHD, they see that child's behavior in a better light and presumably ignore more negative behaviors. This is something we need to keep in mind when trying to determine if a medication is working for a child.

When Should a Physician Recommend Pharmaceutical Treatment?

This is really the million-dollar question. Given all of the information presented here so far, at what point or in what circumstances is stimulant treatment necessary or warranted? There is certainly room for honest disagreement on this point, not to mention the fact that every individual is different, so no strict rules can be applied to all children. The best I can do is give you a set of guidelines based on my extensive experience.

First, let's remember the assumption with which I began this chapter: that any child for whom medication is being considered has had a thorough and careful evaluation resulting in a correct diagnosis of ADHD. If so, I offer the following criteria for seriously considering the need for medication.

1. *The child is unable to learn at school.* This means he or she is unable to focus well enough to keep up academically, clearly a serious issue that needs to be addressed. I am not referring to the child who actually can grasp the material and can keep up academically but gets poor grades for not finishing homework or for losing it in the ether (sound familiar?). That's a different, less worrisome problem that can be corrected without medication. I'm talking about the second grader who can't focus for five minutes and is still at a kindergarten reading level.

2. *The child's behavior is so difficult that it is causing very serious problems at home and at school — enough so that the child suffers highly negative effects that may extend to the entire family.* Sometimes the child becomes such a focus of attention that other siblings are neglected, marriages are strained, and the family is on the verge of collapse. This requires intervention. (A specific intervention called Nurtured Heart Approach and described in Chapter 12 may help a family in this predicament move the child toward improved behavior without medications.)

3. *The child is suffering socially and is unable to form friendships, which in turn is negatively affecting the child's self-image and self-esteem.* Severe ADHD can often cause this problem. The child may be so hyperactive,

lacking in impulse control, and unable to focus on social cues that he or she becomes, essentially, an outcast. On the other hand, many children with the same degree of ADHD are the most popular kids in the class. It's hard to figure. Medications, in my experience, can sometimes be very effective for children for whom self-esteem, self-image, and friendships are suffering due to ADHD symptoms.

Given these three main criteria, this is where I *seriously consider* medication — *not* where I automatically prescribe it. Even in the above circumstances, a parent should take the time to apply the interventions presented throughout this book before resorting to medication. What a shame it would be to place a child on stimulants for years when a simple dietary change, a combination of supplements, or a new behavioral modification approach would have made all the difference.

The Rare Child Who Needs Medication Now

Most often, I recommend giving non-pharmaceutical solutions at least a reasonable chance before resorting to medication. There are exceptions, however. Let me tell you about Danny.

Danny was an 8-year-old whose Mom brought him in for an integrative medicine consult for ADHD. She had been told her child needed medication but was very reluctant about it.

Danny was about to be kicked out of school. Teachers had to physically tackle him to bring him in from recess. He wasn't learning anything and had few friends. Home life wasn't much better. In my office, he was a total ball of fire. He was hyperactive and uncooperative. He never stopped moving. In the midst of the visit, he ran into the reception area, grabbed the receptionist's cell phone from her purse, and went charging out into the parking lot and toward the street. Luckily, Mom was able to chase him down before he reached the main road.

There was no doubt in my mind that this child was a candidate for a prescription for long-acting Ritalin. He was not only failing academically and out of control behaviorally, but he was a danger to himself and possibly to others.

In this case, the medicine worked wonders and without significant side effects. He immediately calmed down, began to work well at school, and over time developed new friendships. Everyone was happier, especially Danny. Once things were stable, I attempted to institute some more natural treatments, but by that point the medication was so successful that the family was not very receptive. That's one of the drawbacks of starting medication too soon: if it works, families are reluctant to try anything else. Overall, however, I believe immediate medication was the right choice for this particular child.

How to Use Medications When They Are Necessary

It is not my purpose to recommend a specific medication or dose of medication for your child. That is up to your doctor. However, I have seen too many instances where children are taking these medications in a suboptimal way — a way that minimizes benefit and maximizes side effects. Therefore, I am providing some general principles concerning the intelligent use of medications for the treatment of ADHD.

If you only remember one thing from this chapter, please remember this:

> **The key to successful medication treatment of ADHD is regular and thorough follow-ups.**

ADHD medications are not like penicillin. We can't just say, "Take 500 milligrams three times a day for 10 days and you'll be fine." Every child is different and reacts differently to ADHD medications. For one 60-pound 7-year-old, 18 milligrams of Concerta may be perfect; for another child the same age and size, 54 milligrams may be necessary. It can't be predicted so there has to be excellent communication and follow-up among the child, the family, and the prescribing physician.

Here's another important principle:

The best dose of any ADHD medicine is the dose that will give the most beneficial effect with the least side effects.

It is frightening how many children I have seen who were placed on an 'average' dose of some psychostimulant and left there for years with only minor benefit and significant side effects. The family then gives up on the medication (not always a bad idea) or figures that's the best they can do (always a bad idea).

It is most preferable to start with a low dose and increase gradually if needed. So I might start a 7-year-old on five milligrams of Adderall (long-acting Dexedrine) and give it to her for three to five days. One good thing about stimulants is that they begin to work within a couple of hours, they are in and out of the system quickly, and by the next morning, the effects are mainly gone. The family knows fairly quickly how well it's working and what the side effects are going to be like. After that time and depending on results, I might increase the dose to 7.5 milligrams or 10 milligrams, each time getting feedback from the family (who should be talking to the teacher as well) about how it's going.

Some families elect not to mention anything to the teacher at first to preclude any bias the teacher might form. Some wait a week and then ask the teacher if he or she has noticed anything different. Others might try a few different doses and check with the teacher with each change to see how it's going in the classroom. This is fine, assuming the teacher will remember how Brian's day went last Tuesday compared with last Thursday.

I usually begin by prescribing a long-acting methylphenidate (Ritalin) preparation, but one can just as easily begin with a long-acting Dexedrine. Interestingly, although the drugs are similar, research and my own experience show that sometimes children do much better on one drug than another. I have seen children who experience terrible side effects from Adderall but do great on Concerta, or vice-versa.

The important thing is that *you don't need to continue a medication if it is not effective or if the side effects are not acceptable.* Sometimes there is just no dose of one particular medication that fulfills these criteria so we try another one. In some cases, unfortunately, none of the available drugs works well, but the proper dose of the drug with the most benefit and least side effects usually can be found.

What about Medication Breaks on Weekends and Vacations?

Many people ask me if their child needs to take medication on weekends and during vacations. My answer is that it totally depends on the individual child.

Susan, for example, takes Adderall because she really can't focus in school. The rest of her life goes well. She does well in sports, has a good social life, and has no behavior problems at home. She rarely has weekend homework. I see no reason for her to take the medication on weekends or vacation. Her parents could give her breaks from the medication during these times, observing to ensure that she is able to move smoothly into the swing of things on Mondays or at the end of vacation.

Todd, on the other hand, is extremely hyperactive and oppositional, tends to fight with his friends, and throws terrible tantrums at home. Combined with some good nutrition and behavioral interventions, Concerta is very helpful for him. I suspect that Todd would have significant trouble on weekends and might alienate new friends as well as ruin everyone's weekend if he were to be given a medication break. Todd probably needs to continue his medication on weekends and during the summer until he has matured somewhat.

Strattera (Atomoxetine)

Strattera is a relatively new medication for ADHD. It is not a stimulant, so it's assumed by many people to be a safer choice. It also produces 24-hour coverage with one dose per day. Often, people elect to try it before the psychostimulants because of their general fears about the stimulant class of medications.

What is Strattera, exactly? It is a *selective norepinephrine reuptake inhibitor*, which means that it increases the amount of the neurotransmitter norepinephrine in the nerve synapses — the miniscule spaces between nerve cells. (The amount of a neurotransmitter in the synapses is the amount said to be "active.") Strattera was originally designed as an antidepressant; most antidepressant drugs work this same way by tweaking the amount of active neurotransmitter in the synapses. While Strattera didn't prove effective for treating depression, it has shown effectiveness in the treatment of ADHD.

I am not a fan of Strattera. Of the kids I've worked with who have tried it, many report significant side effects: headaches, stomachaches, depression, fatigue, general irritability. From my admittedly limited sample, it seems to me that only one or two of every 10 children can tolerate the medication. Strattera is also more difficult to adjust in terms of dosage than the psychostimulants because it takes much longer to get in and out of the system. It takes several weeks to achieve maximum effect. When a dosage change seems necessary, it takes weeks to fully see the effect of that change.

With Strattera, children who don't need the medication over the weekend or during a vacation would not be able to skip doses. And, finally, **like all of the newer antidepressants, Strattera carries a warning on the container stating that it is associated with an increased risk of suicide.**

The Bottom Line. I would not advise anyone to try Strattera unless the psychostimulant medications proved ineffective. There are some children who do benefit from Strattera in that situation.

Other Medications Used in ADHD Treatment

A number of other medications are used in ADHD: some for primary treatment, others to treat specific behaviors associated with ADHD, and still others to deal with the side effects of ADHD medications themselves. This won't be an in-depth examination of such drugs, but I'll touch on a few (on my way into a rant about the ill-advised polypharmacy going on in psychiatry where children are being put on two, three, or more medications at a time without appropriate evidence of safety or effectiveness).

One example is Clonidine, or a similar medication named Guanfacine, which can be used to decrease temper tantrums and explosiveness or to counter sleep problems associated with the psychostimulants. Wellbutrin is sometimes used as a primary ADHD treatment, although in my experience, it is rarely effective. A whole range of antipsychotics, mood stabilizers, and antidepressants are sometimes added to ADHD medications to deal with some other presumed "comorbid diagnosis" — which is some other psychological disorder that is determined to exist along with the child's ADHD.

I find the willingness of some physicians to treat ADHD children with two, three, or more psychotropic medications truly frightening. Here's a good example. James is brought to a child psychiatrist for ADHD treatment and is started on Ritalin or some other stimulant. The medication is fairly effective, but James is irritable and can't fall asleep. Clonidine is added for sleep and seems to help. Now James, who used to be a cheerful if hyperactive child, has become really irritable, even depressed. The psychiatrist makes a diagnosis of comorbid depression and starts an antidepressant like Zoloft or Prozac.

Now James is on three medications, and no one knows which medicine is doing what, or whether the first two medications are the cause of the depressive symptoms that are now being treated with an additional drug. If he's among the really unfortunate ones, James will start to act out behaviorally while under the influence of this medication cocktail — and, as a result, will end up on Risperdal (an "atypical antipsychotic") because he's been diagnosed with bipolar disorder. If you were to look at the prescribing information for atypicals such as Risperdal, you would find a very long list of highly undesirable side effects. In addition, these drugs have barely been researched at all for safety in children — even when it's the only drug being administered.

What a mess! Does James really have depression and bipolar disorder, or did these symptoms originate from a negative reaction to the initial stimulant and snowball from there? By this time, no one even knows!

You may think I'm making this up or exaggerating, **but it happens regularly and frequently.** It was such a problem in Arizona that administrators in the Medicaid system had to start a special monitoring program to discourage it. In the months before finishing this book, I saw a child who had been on Concerta and Buspar (an anti-anxiety drug) for five years. The mom had no idea why the Buspar had been started in the first place; it just kept being refilled through a number of different doctors. When we slowly tapered him off this medication, he felt much better and suffered no loss of function.

You might think that doctors would only prescribe combinations of psychotropic drugs in children if these practices had been thoroughly researched and proven safe and effective. Would you like to know how much research there is on combining psychotropic medications in children? *None! Zero! Zilch!*

There is *no* research examining the short- or long-term side effects of these combinations in children, and barely any in adults. It is one large, completely uncontrolled experiment on our children. In my experience, it isn't working very well at all. And, by the way, most child psychiatrists — the worst offenders — are, I am sorry to say, doing this kind of prescribing in the context of 15-minute visits once a month, if that often. It is impossible for a child who is on two to four psychotropic medications to be accurately evaluated under these circumstances.

Let me make clear that I have great respect for child psychiatry and the dedication of many practitioners in that field. I have collaborated successfully with many of them. But there are child psychiatrists as well as other doctors who are definitely over-prescribing such medication combinations without proof that it is safe to do so.

The Bottom Line. Any parent should be extremely reluctant to combine psychotropic medications for their child without very good reason. Even if that very good reason seems evident, seek a second opinion from someone who will spend the time necessary to be sure it is right for your child.

Combining Medication and Alternative Approaches

Even if you and your child's physician decide that your child will benefit from medication, keep up any integrative or alternative treatments that have been effective and stay open to new possibilities. Just because Lori is on Concerta for ADHD does not mean she should stop eating sensibly or should start ingesting artificial colors and preservatives or stop taking her omega-3 fatty acids. Continuing with these basic health measures may make a big difference in the long run. They might even mean that her ADHD symptoms can be controlled on a dose of 36 mg rather than 54 mg with correspondingly fewer side effects.

As already mentioned, some herbal products could augment the effectiveness of the medication — again leading to a lower required dose. Each product is different, and you need to check for drug-herb interactions whenever you start a new herb with your child, but few of the interventions recommended in this book, whether herbal or nutrition or neurofeedback, would be contraindicated while using psychostimulants. In fact, use of those supplemental or alternative therapies might just reduce or eliminate the child's need for the medication.

When to Stop ADHD Medications

Once parents determine that medications work well for their child's ADHD and don't have terrible side effects, they — and their child's doctor

— tend to be reluctant or unwilling to stop the medication for fear of some disastrous consequence. What might help ease this decision is a trial of stopping the medication once a year or even more often if the parents and doctor both agree. The benefit of these trials is that the effect can quickly be determined — particularly with psychostimulants, which wear off by the next day when stopped — and a conscious choice made about whether to begin them again.

Admittedly, for some kids with severe symptoms, it will take about an hour to see the results. When Jason forgets his medication for one day and becomes an uncontrollable whirlwind, you pretty much know what the result will be of stopping medication and a trial would be pointless. But with other children whose symptoms are less severe, it might take a while to see if they're able to cope without medication. Why not give it a try? As long as you are closely monitoring the situation, the worst that can happen is things won't go well and you will need to restart the medication.

Let's consider one of my patients, Alan, a young teenager who really didn't like being on a medication but who had major academic struggles without it. Every school year he would attempt to go without the medication and often succeeded for months at a time — until the effort became too much and the workload too great. Then he would tell us he was ready. His family did not have the resources to find a school more suited to his needs, so they elected to continue the medication. I am convinced that one day he will no longer need medication as he matures and finds his own way.

The Bottom Line

Medications do seem to be necessary and effective for a certain percentage of children with ADHD. What that percentage may be is a matter of opinion. Short-term side effects are common, and they range from severe to very mild. We do not really know the long-term side effects of these medications, so the decision to use them must be made with great care. If you do decide to go the medication route, remember the cardinal rule: *the key to successful medication treatment of ADHD is regular and thorough follow-ups.*

Summary

We have discussed many types of interventions that can help children who have Attention Deficit Hyperactivity Disorder. Perhaps you are wondering where to start or how to put it all together. Because every child is unique, I cannot give you a cookie-cutter approach that will work for everyone, but the following is a general summary that may help you to get started.

Although I've placed these steps in a sequence that will work, they do not have to be done in any particular order. Some parents may feel drawn to begin one of the later interventions right away.

1. Make sure the diagnosis is correct. If your child has already been diagnosed with ADHD, think about how this diagnosis was made and whether you feel confident about its accuracy. Make sure that other problems, like learning disabilities, have not been overlooked. It is often very helpful to get a fresh look at the issue from someone who has the time and expertise to do a good job — the type of diagnostician described in Chapter 3. If your child has not yet been diagnosed, this is your chance to do it right at the outset.

2. Take a look at your child's nutrition. Are you giving him or her foods needed for optimal function? Are you avoiding artificial colors and other additives that can negatively affect his or her nervous system? If food sensitivities seem possible, consider a two- or three-week trial elimination diet to assess the impact any food sensitivities might have on behavior and academic functioning.

   I know that changing a child's diet is not always easy, but if a drastic change seems too overwhelming, just begin with small changes and add to them regularly. You might be surprised at the positive results.

3. Find an omega-3 fatty acid supplement that your child will ingest. Begin giving it regularly.

4. Ask your doctor to check your child's blood levels of ferritin, zinc, and magnesium. If any of these are low, begin appropriate supplements.

5. Reassess how things are going in school. Is your child's school fulfilling his or her needs to a reasonable extent? Is a change of school or of teacher indicated? Are there adequate classroom modifications, with or without a formal 504 plan? It is almost always helpful to meet with the teacher to review progress if you have not done so recently.

6. Assess how you are managing your child's behavior at home. Look carefully at the principles outlined in Chapter 12. Make sure your child is getting a chance to participate in activities he or she is really good at, and that achievement in those activities is being appropriately rewarded. If you are not satisfied with the results you are getting, consider the Nurtured Heart Approach or any other consistent approach that appeals to you.

If you have instituted a number of the above changes, it might be worthwhile to pause, take a deep breath and give them some time to take effect before moving on to any of the following.

7. Next, consider whether some of the more "alternative" interventions we discussed may be a good fit for you and your child. Perhaps one of the herbal therapies may have a place. If you have the time and resources, neurofeedback or other mind-body therapies could be effective. Consider whether homeopathy or traditional Chinese medicine is of interest to you. I suggest picking one of these therapies and giving it a reasonable chance to work before starting another. Doing too many things at once may be counterproductive, or it could leave you confused about what's working and what isn't.

8. If your child takes medication for ADHD, ask yourself if it is really necessary. If it is, are you are satisfied with the impact of the particular medication that was chosen? Are the positive effects what you expected and are any side effects tolerable? If the answer is not a clear yes, then I would advise going back to the doctor who prescribed the medication and discussing your reservations. If that doctor is not willing to take the time to consider your reservations, look for another one. Special care is warranted in your exploration of this issue if your child is taking more than one psychotropic medication, given the almost complete lack of research on the effects of multiple medications.

I have tremendous respect for those parents of children with ADHD who have dedicated themselves to helping their children achieve their highest potential while maintaining the essence and spirit unique to each of them. I know it is not easy, but the rewards are great.

My hope is that this book has offered not only practical interventions to help you along this difficult road but also given you a sense of support and optimism: a feeling that you aren't alone; that what you are doing is worthwhile; and that you *can* help your child be both happy and successful without necessarily relying on medication.

Once again, I wish you great good fortune on your journey.

Footnote References

Chapter 1: What Is ADHD – and Why Is There So Much of It?

1. Environmental Working Group. (July 14, 2005) Body Burden: The Pollution in Newborns. Retrieved from http://www.ewg.org/reports/bodyburden2/execsumm.php.

2. Kaiser Family Foundation. (2005) Generation M: Media in the Lives of 8-18 Year Olds. Retrieved from http://www.kff.org/entmedia/entmedia030905pkg.cfm.

3. Soma Y, Nakamura K, Oyama M, Tsuchiya Y, Yamamoto M. (2009 Mar) Prevalence of attention-deficit/hyperactivity disorder (ADHD) symptoms in preschool children: discrepancy between parent and teacher evaluations. *Environmental Health & Preventive Medicine,* 14(2):150-4.

4. Antrop I, Roeyers H, Oosterlaan J, Van Oost P. (2002 Mar) Agreement between Parent and Teacher Ratings of Disruptive Behavior Disorders in Children with Clinically Diagnosed ADHD. *Journal of Psychopathology and Behavioral Assessment,* 24(1):67-73.

5. Polanczyk G, de Lima MS, Horta BL, Biederman J, Rohde LA. (2007 Jun) The worldwide prevalence of ADHD: a systematic review and metaregression analysis. *American Journal of Psychiatry,* 164(6):942-8.

6. Tavis Smiley (interviewer) and Paul Orfalea (interviewee). (October 6, 2005) Retrieved from http://www.pbs.org/kcet/tavissmiley/archive/200510/20051006_orfalea.html.

7. Hallowell, Edward, MD. Can you prevent your child from developing ADHD? *ADDITUDE –Living Well with ADHD and Learning Disabilities.* Retrieved from http://www.additudemag.com/adhd/article/695.html.

Chapter 2: The Neurobiology of ADHD

1. Spencer, TJ, Biederman J, Mick, E. (2007 June) Attention-Deficit/Hyperactivity Disorder: Diagnosis, Lifespan, Comorbidities, and Neurobiology. *Journal of Pediatric Psychology*, 32(6):631-642.

2. Gizer IR, Ficks C, Waldman ID. (2009 Jul) Candidate gene studies of ADHD: a meta-analytic review. *Human Genetics*, 126(1):51-90.

3. Executive Function. In *Encyclopedia of Mental Disorders*. Retrieved from http://www.minddisorders.com/Del-Fi/Executive function.html.

4. Shaw P, Eckstrand K, Sharp W, Blumenthal J, Lerch JP, Greenstein D, et al. (Dec 4, 2007) Attention-deficit/hyperactivity disorder is characterized by a delay in cortical maturation. *Proceedings of the National Academy of Sciences of the United States of America*, 104(49):19649-54.

5. Makris N, Biederman J, Valera EM, Bush G, Kaiser J, Kennedy DN, et al. (2007 Jun) Cortical thinning of the attention and executive function networks in adults with attention-deficit/hyperactivity disorder. *Cerebral Cortex*, 17(6):1364-75.

6. Castellanos FX, Lee PP, Sharp W, Jeffries NO, Greenstein DK, Clasen LS, et al. (2002) Developmental Trajectories of Brain Volume Abnormalities in Children and Adolescents with Attention-Deficit/Hyperactivity Disorder. *JAMA*, 288:1740-1748.

Figure 4 source: Neuron (2010, January 12) In *Wikipedia, The Free Encyclopedia*. From http://en.wikipedia.org/wiki/Neuron

Figure 5 source: Neurotransmitter (2009, December 31). In *Wikipedia, The Free Encyclopedia*. From http://en.wikipedia.org/wiki/Neurotransmitter

7. Pliszka SR. (2005). The neuropsychopharmacology of attention-deficit/hyperactivity disorder. *Biol Psychiatry*, 57(11):1385-90.

8. Curatolo P, Paloscia C, D'Agati E, Moavero R, Pasini A. (2009 Jul) The neurobiology of attention deficit/hyperactivity disorder. *European Journal of Paediatric Neurology*, 13(4):299-304.

Chapter 4: The Importance of Good Nutrition

1. Gantz W, Schwartz N, Angelini JR, Rideout V. (2007 Mar) Food For Thought: Television Food Advertising to Children in the United

States. A Kaiser Family Foundation Report. Retrieved from http://www.kff.org/entmedia/upload/7618.pdf.

2. Begley, Sharon. (Sep 21, 2009) "Born to be Big: Early exposure to common chemicals may be programming kids to be fat." *Newsweek*. Retrieved from http://www.newsweek.com/id/215179/page/3.

3. Keeley, Jennifer, and Fields, Michael. (2004 Nov) Case Study: Appleton Central Alternative Charter High School's Nutrition and Wellness Program in Better Food, Better Behavior. Retrieved from http://www.michaelfieldsaginst.org/work/urbanag/case_study.pdf.

4. Ibid.

5. Ibid.

6. Scholastic Parent & Child. (2007 Sep) Turn off the TV to fight fat and ADHD: television commercials can affect your child's diet, and in turn, his learning. Retrieved from http://www2.scholastic.com/browse/article.jsp?id=1441.

7. Benton D, Maconie A, Williams C. (Nov 23, 2007) The influence of the glycemic load of breakfast on the behaviour of children in school. *Physiology & Behavior*, 92(4):717-24.

8. Benton D, Ruffin MP, Lassel T, Nabb S, Messaoudi M, Vinoy S, et al. (2003 Feb) The delivery rate of dietary carbohydrates affects cognitive performance in both rats and humans. *Psychopharmacology*, 166(1):86-90.

9. USDA Agricultural Marketing Service. Program Overview: National Organic Program. (Jan 4, 2010) Retrieved from http://www.ams.usda.gov/nop/Consumers/brochure.html.

10. Environmental Working Group. (July 14, 2005) Body Burden: The Pollution in Newborns. Retrieved from http://www.ewg.org/reports/bodyburden2/execsumm.php.

11. Curl CL, Fenske RA, Elgethun K. Organophosphorus pesticide exposure of urban and suburban pre-school children with organic and conventional diets. *Environ Health Perspect* 111:377-382.

12. Lee DH, Jacobs DR, Porta M. (2007 Jul) Association of serum concentrations of persistent organic pollutants with the prevalence of learning disability and attention deficit disorder. *Journal of Epidemiology & Community Health*, 61(7):591-6.

Chapter 5: Practical Guildelines for Feeding Your Child

1. Satter, Ellyn. *Child of Mine: Feeding With Love and Good Sense.* Bull Publishing Company, Palo Alto, CA: 2000.

Chapter 6: ADHD and Food Sensitivities

1. Egger J, Carter CM, Graham PJ, et al. (1985) Controlled trial of oligoantigenic treatment in the hyperkinetic syndrome. *Lancet,* 1(8428):540-5.

2. Egger, Joseph, Stolla, Adelheid, McEwen, Leonard M. (May 9, 1992) Controlled trial of hyposensitisation in children with food-induced hyperkinetic syndrome. *Lancet,* 339:1150-53.

3. Carter CM. Urbanowicz M. Hemsley R. Mantilla L. Strobel S. Graham PJ. Taylor E. (1993 Nov) Effects of a few food diet in attention deficit disorder. *Archives of Disease in Childhood,* 69(5):564-8.

4. Boris M, Mandel FS. (1994) Foods and additives are common causes of the attention deficit hyperactive disorder in children. *Ann Allergy,* 72(5):462-8.

5. Bateman B, et al. (2004) The effects of a double blind, placebo controlled, artificial food colourings and benzoate preservative challenge on hyperactivity in a general population sample of preschool children. *Archives of Disease in Childhood,* 89:506-511.

6. McCann D, Barrett A, Cooper A, et al. (Nov 3, 2007) Food additives and hyperactive behaviour in 3-year-old and 8/9-year-old children in the community: a randomised, double-blinded, placebo controlled trial. *Lancet,* 370(9598):1560-7.

Chapter 7: Omega-3 Fatty Acids and ADHD

1. Colter AL, Cutler C, Meckling KA. (2008) Fatty acid status and behavioural symptoms of attention deficit hyperactivity disorder in adolescents: a case-control study. *Nutrition Journal,* 7:8.

2. Richardson, Alexandra J, Puri Basant K. (2002) A randomized, double-blind, placebo-controlled study of the effects of supplementation with highly unsaturated fatty acids on ADHD-related symptoms in children with specific learning difficulties. *Progress in Neuro-Psychopharmacology & Biological Psychiatry,* 26: 233-239.

3. Richardson AJ, Montgomery P. (2005) The Oxford-Durham study: a

randomized, controlled trial of dietary supplementation with fatty acids in children with developmental coordination disorder. *Pediatrics*, 115(5):1360-6.

4. Voigt RG, Llorente AM, Jensen CL, Fraley JK, Berretta MC, Heird WC. (2001) A randomised, double-blind, placebo-controlled trial of docosahexaenoic acid supplementation in children with attention-deficit/hyperactivity disorder. *J Pediatr*, 139:189-196.

5. Hirayama S, Hamazaki T, Terasawa K. (2004) Effect of docosa-hexaenoicacid-containing food administration on symptoms of attention-deficit/hyperactivity disorder: a placebo-controlled double-blind study. *Eur J Clin Nutr*, 58:467-473.

6. Dalton A, Wolmarans P, Witthuhn RC, van Stuijvenberg ME, Swan-evelder SA, Smuts CM. (2009 Feb-Mar) A randomised control trial in schoolchildren showed improvement in cognitive function after consuming a bread spread containing fish flour from a marine source. *Prostaglandins, Leukotrienes and Essential Fatty Acids*, 80 (2-3):143-9.

7. Nemets H, Nemets B, Apter A, Bracha Z, Belmaker RH. (2006 Jun) Omega-3 Treatment of Childhood Depression: A Controlled, Double-Blind Pilot Study. *Am J Psychiatry*, 163:1098-1100.

8. Colombo J, Kannass KN, Shaddy DJ, Kundurthi S, Maikranz JM, Anderson CJ, et al. (2004 Jul) Maternal DHA and the Development of Attention in Infancy and Toddlerhood. *Child Development*, 75(4):1254-1267.

9. Joshi K, Lad S., Kale M, Patwardhan B, Mahadik SP, Patni B, et al. (2006 Jan) Supplementation with flax oil and vitamin C improves the outcome of Attention Deficit Hyperactivity Disorder (ADHD). *Prostaglandins Leukotrienes & Essential Fatty Acids*, 74(1):17-21.

10. Sorgi P, Hallowell E, Hutchins HL, Sears B. (2007) Effects of an open-label pilot study with high-dose EPA/DHA concentrates on plasma phospholipids and behavior in children with attention deficit/hyperactivity disorder. *Nutrition Journal*, 6:16.

Chapter 8: The Minerals: Iron, Zinc, and Magnesium in ADHD

1. Lozoff B & Georgieff M. (2006) Iron deficiency and brain development. *Seminars in Pediatric Neurology*, 13(3):158-165.

2. Konofal E, Lecendreux M, Arnulf I, Mouren M.C. (2004) Iron

deficiency in children with attention-deficit/hyperactivity disorder. *Archives of Pediatrics & Adolescent Medicine*, 158(12): 1113-1115.

3. Konofal E, Lecendreux M, Deron J, Marchand M, Cortese S, Zaïm M, Mouren MC, Arnulf I. (2008) Effects of iron supplementation on attention deficit hyperactivity disorder in children. *Pediatr Neurol*, 38:20-26.

4. Toren P, Eldar S, Sela BA, Wolmer L, Weitz R, Inbar D, et al. (Dec 15, 1996) Zinc deficiency in attention-deficit hyperactivity disorder. *Biological Psychiatry*, 40(12):1308-10.

5. Bekaroglu M, Aslan Y, Gedik Y, Deger O, Mocan H, Erduran E, Karahan C. (1996 Feb) Relationships between serum free fatty acids and zinc, and attention deficit hyperactivity disorder: a research note. *Journal of Child Psychology & Psychiatry & Allied Disciplines*, 37(2):225-7.

6. Arnold LE, Bozzolo H, Hollway J, Cook A, DiSilvestro RA, Bozzolo DR, et al. (2005 Aug) Serum zinc correlates with parent-and teacher-rated inattention in children with attention-deficit/hyperactivity disorder. *J Child Adolesc Psychopharmacol*, 15(4):628-36.

7. Akhondzadeh S, Mohammadi MR, Khademi M. (2004) Zinc sulfate as an adjunct to methylphenidate for the treatment of attention deficit hyperactivity disorder in children: a double blind and randomized trial. *BMC Psychiatry*, 4(1):9.

8. Mousain-Bosc M, Roche M, Rapin J, Bali J-P. (2004) Magnesium/Vitamin B6 intake reduces central nervous system hyperexcitability in children. *J Am Coll Nutr*, 23(Suppl):S545-S548.

9. Starobrat-Hermelin B, Kozielec T. (1997) The effects of magnesium physiological supplementation on hyperactivity in children with attention deficit/hyperactivity disorder (ADHD). *Magnes Res*, 10:149-156.

Chapter 9: Herbs for ADHD

1. Heimann SW. (1999 Apr) Pycnogenol for ADHD? *Journal of the American Academy of Child & Adolescent Psychiatry*, 38(4):357-8.

2. Dvorakova M, Jezova D, Blazicek P, Trebaticka J, Skodacek I, Suba J, et al. Urinary catecholamines in children with attention deficit hyperactivity disorder (ADHD): modulation by a polyphenolic extract from pine bark (pycnogenol). *Nutritional Neuroscience*, 10(3-4):151-7.

3. Dvorakova M, Sivonova M, Trebaticka J, Skodacek I, Waczulikova I, Muchova J, et al. (2006) The effect of polyphenolic extract from pine bark, Pycnogenol, on the level of glutathione in children suffering from attention deficit hyperactivity disorder (ADHD). *Redox Report*, 11(4).

4. Trebaticka J, Kopasova S, Hradecna Z, et al. (2006) Treatment of ADHD with French maritime pine bark extract, Pycnogenol. *Eur Child Adolesc Psychiatry*, 15(6):329-35.

5. Tenenbaum S, Paull JC, Sparrow EP, Dodd DK, Green L. (2002) An experimental comparison of pycnogenol and methylphenidate in adults with attention-deficit hyperactivity disorder (ADHD). *J Atten Disord*, 6(49):49-60.

6. Muller SF. (June 12, 2006) A combination of valerian and lemon balm is effective in the treatment of restlessness and dyssomnia in children. *Phytomedicine*, 13(6)12:383-387.

7. Lyon MR, Cline JC, Totosy de Zepetnek J, et al. (2001) Effect of the herbal extract combination Panax quinquefolium and Ginkgo biloba on attention-deficit hyperactivity disorder: a pilot study. *J Psychiatry Neurosci*, 26(3):221-8.

8. Weber W, Vander Stoep A, McCarty RL, Weiss NS, Biederman J, McClellan J. (June 11, 2008) Hypericum perforatum (St John's wort) for attention-deficit/hyperactivity disorder in children and adolescents: a randomized controlled trial. *JAMA*, 299(22):2633-41.

Chapter 10: Neurofeedback and Other Mind-Body Therapies

1. Fuchs T, Birbaumer N, Lutzenberger W, et al. (2003) Neurofeedback treatment for attention-deficit/hyperactivity disorder in children: a comparison with methylphenidate. *Appl Psychophysiol Biofeedback*, 28(1):1-12.

2. Leins U, Goth G, Hinterberger T, Klinger C, Rumpf N, Strehl U. (2007 Jun) Neurofeedback for children with ADHD: a comparison of SCP and Theta/Beta protocols. *Applied Psychophysiology & Biofeedback*, 32(2):73-88.

3. Weydert JA, Shapiro DE, Acra SA, Monheim CJ, Chambers AS, Ball TM. (2006) Evaluation of guided imagery as treatment for recurrent abdominal pain in children: a randomized controlled trial. *BMC Pediatrics*, 6:29.

4. Goldin P, Saltzman A, Jha A. Mindfulness Meditation Training in Families. Abstract presented at the Association for Behavioral and Cognitive Therapies meeting, NY, Nov 19-22, 2009.

Chapter 11: The Alternative Therapies: Traditional Chinese Medicine, Homeopathy, and Energy Medicine

1. Linde K, Allais G, Brinkhaus B, Manheimer E, Vickers A, White AR. (2009) Acupuncture for tension-type headache: Review. *Cochrane Database of Systematic Reviews*, (1):CD007587.

2. World Health Organization Database. (2003) Acupuncture: Review and Analysis of Reports on Controlled Clinical Trials. Retrieved from http://apps.who.int/medicinedocs/en/d/Js4926e/.

3. Flaws B. Chinese Medicine update: recent Chinese medical research on the treatment of ADHD. *Townsend Letter for Doctors and Patients*, October 2003.

4. Ibid.

5. Linde K, Clausius N, Ramirez G, Melchart D, Eitel F, Hedges LV, Jonas WB. (1997) Are the clinical effects of homeopathy placebo effects? A meta-analysis of controlled trials. *Lancet*, 350: 834-843.

6. Kleijnen J, Knipschild P. (1991) Clinical trials of homeopathy. *B Med J*, 302: 316-323.

7. Strauss LC. (2000) The efficacy of a homeopathic preparation in the management of attention deficit hyperactivity disorder. *Journal of Biomedical Therapy*, 18(2):197.

8. Frei H, Everts R, von Ammon K, Kaufmann F, Walther D, Hsu-Schmitz SF, et al. (2005 Dec) Homeopathic treatment of children with attention deficit hyperactivity disorder: A randomized, double blind, placebo controlled crossover trial. *European Journal of Pediatrics*, 164(12):758-67.

9. Jacobs J, Williams AL, Girard C, Njike VY, Katz D. (2005) Homeopathy for attention deficit/hyperactivity disorder: A pilot randomized-controlled trial. *The Journal of Alternative and Complementary Medicine*, 11(5):799-806.

10. National Center for Complementary and Alternative Medicine: http://nccam.nih.gov/tools/map.htm.

Chapter 12: Behavioral Interventions: Supporting Your Child at Home

1. Glasser H, Easley J. *Transforming the Difficult Child – The Nurtured Heart Approach*. Center for the Difficult Child Publications, Tucson, AZ, 1998.

2. Glasser H, with Block, M. *All Children Flourishing – Igniting the Greatness of Our Children*. Nurtured Heart Publications, Tucson, AZ, 2007: 84.

Chapter 13: Working with Schools and Teachers

1. "Discover" September 2009. The Discover Interview: Roger Penrose, by Susan Kruglinski. 54-57.

Chapter 14: Medications for ADHD: When Are They Necessary and How Should They Be Used?

1. Wilens TE, Faraone SV, Biederman J, Gunawardene S. Does stimulant therapy of attention-deficit/hyperactivity disorder beget later substance abuse? A meta-analytic review of the literature. *Pediatrics*, 111(1): 179-85.

2. Lambert NM, Hartsough CS. Prospective study of tobacco smoking and substance dependencies among samples of ADHD and non-ADHD participants. *J Learn Disabil*, 1998, 31:533-544.

3. Harris, Gardener. Panel Advises Disclosure of Drugs' Psychotic Effects, The New York Times, March 23, 2006.

4. Nissen SE. ADHD drugs and cardiovascular risk. *N Engl J Med*, 2006, 354: 1445-8.

5. King S, Waschbusch DA, Pelham WE Jr, Frankland BW, Andrade BF, Jacques S, Corkum PV. (2009 May) Social information processing in elementary-school aged children with ADHD: medication effects and comparisons with typical children. *J Abnorm Child Psychol*, 37(4):579-89.

6. Navalta, Carrly P. (2004) Altering the course of neurodevelopment: a framework for understanding the enduring effects of psychotropic drugs. *International Journal of Developmental Neuroscience*, Vol 22, Issues 5-6, 423-440.

7. Jensen PS, Arnold LE, Swanson JM, Vitiello B, Abikoff HB, Greenhill LL, et al. (2007 Aug) 3-Year Follow-Up of the NIMH MTA

(National Institute of Mental Health Multimodal Treatment Study of Children With ADHD: clinical report). *Journal of the American Academy of Child and Adolescent Psychiatry*, 46(8): 989-14.

8. Biederman J, Monuteaux MC, Spencer T, Wilens TE, Faraone SV. (2009) Do stimulants protect against psychiatric disorders in youth with ADHD? A 10-year follow-up study. *Pediatrics*, 124(1):71-8.

9. Waschbusch DA, Pelham WE Jr, Waxmonsky J, Johnston C. (2009) Are there placebo effects in the medication treatment of children with attention-deficit hyperactivity disorder? *J Dev Behav Pediatr, 30:*158-168.

Appendix A

1. Braun JM, Kahn RS, Froehlich T, Auinger P, Lanphear BP. (2006 Dec) Exposures to environmental toxicants and attention deficit hyperactivity disorder in U.S. children. *Environmental Health Perspectives*, 114(12):1904-9.

2. Lee DH, Jacobs DR, Porta M. (2007 Jul) Association of serum concentrations of persistent organic pollutants with the prevalence of learning disability and attention deficit disorder. *Journal of Epidemiology & Community Health*, 61(7):591-6.

3. Schantz SL, Widholm JJ, Rice DC. (2003) Effects of PCB exposure on neuropsychological function in children. *Environ Health Perspect*, 111: 357-376.

4. Stein J, Schettler T, Wallinga D, Valenti M. (2002 Feb) In harm's way: toxic threats to child development. *Journal of Developmental & Behavioral Pediatrics*, 23(1 Suppl):S13-22.

5. Lederman SA, Jones RL, Caldwell KL, Rauh V, Sheets SE, Tang D, et al. (2008 Aug) Relation between cord blood mercury levels and early child development in a World Trade Center cohort. *Environmental Health Perspectives*, 116(8):1085-91.

Appendix A
Environmental Toxins

What is an environmental toxin? Broadly speaking, it is any substance present in our environment that can cause harm to our health. The media is often full of headlines about these toxins. Scary stories about mercury in fish or PCBs in our water make major headlines briefly and then disappear from sight.

After seeing so many (often divergent) stories like this come and go, it is tempting to just throw up your hands and stop thinking about the issue, hoping that any effects from these toxins will be minor or that they're very unlikely to affect you or your loved ones. This attitude is not surprising, given the reluctance of both industry and government to do anything about the problem unless their hands are forced by absolutely incontrovertible evidence.

The fact is that environmental toxins truly are a significant danger to our health. And unfortunately, they pose the greatest danger to children. Evidence supports a role for many of these toxins as contributing to the overall increase in ADHD and other developmental disabilities. Parents of children with ADHD are wise to be concerned.

In this brief Appendix, I will give an overview of the threat posed by environmental toxins, with a specific focus on those toxins known to be related to ADHD. I'll also make a few practical suggestions to help you reduce your child's exposure to these toxins without drastic changes in your lifestyle.

Naturally Occurring vs. Man-Made Environmental Toxins

Some environmental toxins are naturally occurring substances that are not harmful in normal concentrations but can cause great harm with increased exposure. A good example is mercury, which is naturally present in the earth's crust. Until the Industrial Revolution, mercury only made its way into our food and water in minute quantities. Since the advent of industry, mercury has been released in great quantities through the mining and refining of coal and other products. It then made its way into the food chain, where it became concentrated as toxic methylmercury in fish. Methylmercury is a potent *neurotoxin* (a substance that can cause damage to the brain and nervous system). It is especially damaging to the highly sensitive developing brains of fetuses, infants, and small children. Lead is another naturally occurring environmental toxin that has been introduced into the bodies of humans in high concentrations due to industrial processes.

Other environmental toxins of concern are new chemicals that have been created by industry. These substances, also known as industrial chemicals, do not exist in nature. Such chemicals are used to make pesticides, plasticizers, solvents, paints, building materials, and herbicides. A few you might have heard of: DDT, bisphenol-A, and PCBs.

Literally hundreds of thousands of man-made chemicals have been created in the last 100 years. A significant proportion of those that have been subjected to testing are proven to have, at some concentration, negative effects on human health. Cancer, neurological problems, hormonal issues, and immune problems are the better known of these potential adverse effects of man-made chemicals.

The vast majority of industrial chemicals have never been safety tested at all and probably never will be. Worse yet, we know that the effect of these chemicals increases when more than one is present. For example, if two or more endocrine disrupters are present, each at a harmless concentration, the effect of the chemicals together may be very significant. Given the thousands of chemicals out there, the magnitude of the problem becomes obvious.

Evidence in Favor of an Environmental Toxin-ADHD Link

Is there any evidence that environmental toxins may contribute to ADHD? Yes. Here are a few studies that point to the existence of such a link.

- Children who had a blood lead level between 2 and 5 were four times more likely to have ADHD than children with a level below 0.8.[1] This is especially remarkable because blood levels up to 10 are considered "normal" by the Centers for Disease Control (CDC). The article citing this study estimated that 290,000 excess cases of ADHD could be attributable to lead toxicity.

- This same article showed that a child born to a mother who smoked during pregnancy was 2½ times more likely to have ADHD than if the mother did not smoke.

- In one study, children with detectable levels of three *persistent organic pollutants* (POPs) were two to three times more likely to have ADHD — and twice as likely to have learning disabilities — than children with no detectable level of these chemicals.[2] POPs (in this context, "organic" means simply that they contain carbon atoms) are man-made chemicals that persist in the environment and tend to accumulate in the fatty

231

tissue of humans and animals. They are found in flame retardants, solvents, pharmaceuticals, and pesticides, and there are hundreds of them.

- A series of studies has shown that PCBs (polychlorinated biphenyls) negatively affect children's development, including producing reduced memory and attention, decreased verbal ability, impaired information processing, and behavioral problems.[3] The actual diagnosis of ADHD was not addressed in this particular series of studies.

Many other studies associate industrial chemicals with developmental problems and other disorders, including but not limited to ADHD.[4,5] Given that the vast majority of industrial chemicals have never been studied for any of their toxic effects, it is certainly likely that many would have an association with ADHD if studied.

What Can You Do?

Obviously, you can't keep your family in a protective bubble that would avoid all toxin exposure. However, there are some simple steps you can take to decrease the chance of harm from the most common toxins. Here are some suggestions:

Investigate the possibility of lead exposure. If you live in a house built before 1960 or if you are aware of potential lead sources in your home, test your child's blood lead level. It is easy and inexpensive.

Avoid pesticide exposure. Pesticides have been associated with a wide range of health problems, including developmental issues. As mentioned in Chapter 4 on nutrition, children are especially vulnerable to pesticides and most have detectable levels of them in their systems. The good news is that most of these pesticide levels disappear relatively quickly when exposure is eliminated. Avoid spraying pesticides and herbicides in and around your house, but if you must, then be sure to keep the children away during and after spraying.

Eat organic or locally grown food whenever possible. My recommendation is to eat organically whenever possible, especially avoiding the most highly contaminated foods.

Always choose *organic* or *pesticide-free* when buying the following fruits and vegetables since otherwise they tend to have the most pesticides:

Peaches	Cherries
Apples	Kale
Bell peppers	Lettuce
Celery	Imported grapes

| Nectarines | Carrots |
| Strawberries | Pears |

(Source: the Environmental Working Group's "Shopper's Guide to Pesticides" at www.foodnews.org. This is a great resource for up-to-date information on safe foods, plus you can subscribe to a free newsletter via the web site.)

Avoid mercury exposure. Unless you live where there is a heavy source of industrial exposure, high-mercury fish will be the most common source of exposure. For kids, tuna fish is the biggest culprit. Albacore tuna has three times the mercury content of light tuna. Use it sparingly.

Be aware that farmed salmon and other farmed fish have high levels of industrial toxins. When you purchase fish for family meals, opt for wild-caught varieties whenever possible.

Use safe cleaning products. Most cleaning products contain a wide range of possibly toxic industrial chemicals. Use "green" products. Chemicals used to create scents for room fresheners, detergents, and fabric softeners are potentially toxic. Avoid them.

Make sure your drinking water is safe. The laws that protect us from toxic chemicals in our water are seriously outdated, and many communities have levels of arsenic, uranium, and other substances in their water high enough to be associated with significant health risks. I recommend installing some type of water filter in your home to purify your drinking water.

Beware of plastic products. Toxic bisphenol-A easily leaches out of polycarbonate plastic bottles (the hard plastic bottles in which much bottled drinking water is packaged) and certain other containers. The research on this topic is ongoing, but for now avoid all plastics labeled with the numbers 3, 6 and 7. Phthalates, which are chemicals present in many types of plastics – including some infant products — have been implicated in reproductive problems and have been linked with ADHD.

Do not use plastic containers of any kind in a microwave. When heated, plastic more easily releases undesirable chemicals into your food.

The Bottom Line. Strike the best possible balance in the difficult task of avoiding environmental toxins. It is not possible to completely eliminate exposure, and it is not useful to obsess about the dangers that are out there. On the other hand, it is good to be aware of which risks are most serious and to do what is reasonable to avoid them.

Cast Your Vote for a Cleaner Future

It is also worth remembering that corporations are exquisitely sensitive to what you buy — if not to what environmentalists and scientists say. So every time you choose an organic vegetable or buy a green cleaning product, you are casting a vote for a cleaner and safer environment for ourselves and our children.

Appendix B
Resources

Books

Please Don't Label My Child by Scott Shannon (Rodale 2007). A wonderful book that deals with our society's tendency to immediately put a psychological label on any child who has any difficulties, often justifying pharmaceutical treatment. Dr. Shannon discusses with great insight a more careful, holistic, and effective approach.

Healing ADHD: The Breakthrough Program That Allows You to See and Heal the Six Types of ADD by Daniel G. Amen (Berkley 2001). This book outlines a very interesting approach to ADHD, dividing it into 6 types depending on other symptoms associated with the core problems. This can lead to a more individualized treatment approach.

The Last Normal Child: Essays on the Interaction of Kids, Culture and Psychiatric Drugs (Praeger 2006). Thought-provoking essays on our society's attitude toward mental health and illness in children.

Last Child in the Woods: Saving Our Children from Nature Deficit Disorder by Richard Louv (Algonquin 2006). A fresh and innovative perspective on how lack of contact with mother nature may be contributing to ADHD and other children's issues.

The Out-of-Sync-Child: Recognizing and Coping with Sensory Processing Disorder by Carol Stock Kranowitz (Skylight Press 2005). This is the classic book about Sensory Integration Disorder, well worth reading if your child has sensory issues.

The Omega-3 Connection: The Groundbreaking Antidepressant Diet and Brain Program by Andrew Stoll (Simon and Schuster 2001). This Harvard researcher's powerful case for the importance of omega-3s has been strongly supported by continuing research since its publication.

The Misunderstood Child: Understanding and Coping with Your Child's Learning Disabilities by Larry Silver (Crown 1998). This book is the classic in its field; a must for those parents whose children have learning disabilities.

Eating Well for Optimal Health by Andrew Weil (Alfred A. Knopf 2000). If I could have every parent read one book on nutrition, this would be it. Dr. Weil explains simply and clearly what we need to know about creating a healthful diet.

The Omnivore's Dilemma by Michael Pollan (Penguin Press 2006). An absolutely fascinating book about where our food comes from and why we have so much trouble figuring out what to eat. This is one of the most enjoyable books I have read in years.

The New Glucose Revolution: The Authoritative Guide to the Glycemic Index by Jennie Brand-Miller et al. (Marlowe & Co. 2006). Excellent book on the all-important glycemic index.

How to Get your Kids to Eat: But Not Too Much by Ellyn Satter (Bull Publishing Co. 1987). Ellyn Satter is a renowned expert on food issues for children, and this book is a classic.

Transforming the Difficult Child: The Nurtured Heart Approach by Howard Glasser & Jennifer Easley (Nurtured Heart Publications 1998). This ground-breaking book describing the Nurtured Heart Approach goes beyond diagnoses and labels and gives parents a tremendously effective system to bring out the best in their children.

The Sneaky Chef: Simple Strategies for Hiding Healthy Foods in Kids' Favorite Meals by Missy Chance Lapine (Running Press 2007). Great ways to get healthy foods into your children.

Is This Your Child by Doris Rapp (William Morrow and Co.1991). Although written 19 years ago, this was the first major work documenting the importance of food sensitivities in ADHD and other behavioral issues. It is still a powerful book and worth reading if you are interested in this subject.

The Highly Sensitive Child by Elaine Aron (Broadway Books 2002). Many children with ADHD are also highly sensitive. This book gives you another way to look at this sensitivity as well as suggesting useful parenting strategies.

Mental Health, Naturally: The Family Guide to Holistic Care for a Healthy Mind and Body by Kathi Kemper (American Academy of Pediatrics 2002). A great general overview of natural approaches to mental health by one of our leading pioneers in pediatric integrative medicine.

How Nutrition Deficit Disorder Affects Your Child's Learning, Behavior and Health, and What You Can Do about It — without Drugs by William Sears (Little, Brown & Co. 2009). A down-to-earth guide on how nutrition affects a child's development and mental health.

Web Sites

ewg.org – This web site of the Environmental Working Group has excellent and up-to-date information about every type of environmental toxin, and more importantly, what you can do to reduce exposure.

energyparenting.com/products/item34.cfm – At this site, preview or purchase Dr. Newmark's "ADHD: A Whole Child Approach," which is a 5-part teleseminar series (audio) covering many of the same topics as this book.

Drweil.com – Great information on many health issues, although not specifically related to ADHD.

bcm.edu/cnrc – Provides a great deal of nutritional information for and about children plus some great online nutrition games.

chadd.org – CHADD (Children and Adults with Attention Deficit Hyperactivity Disorder) is a national support group for ADHD and accomplishes much good work. There is a good deal of useful information as well as connections to CHADD's local support groups.

nccam.nih.gov – This web site of the National Center for Complementary and Alternative Medicine has good descriptions of alternative modalities such as acupuncture, homeopathy, energy medicine, and others. Although it is relatively conservative in its approach, it is a good source of basic information.

nih.gov – This is the web site of the National Institutes of Health where you can find a great deal of solid scientific information on nutrition and other issues such as the fact sheets on magnesium and zinc mentioned in Chapter 8. Be careful of some of the updates, however; the section on the multimodal research study was written in 2000.

difficultchild.com – This is the web site of Howard Glasser, whose Nurtured Heart Approach is discussed in Chapter 12. For those who prefer electronics to books, there are great CDs and DVDs on the approach, as well as much other useful information.